Post-Object Fandom

Post-Object Fandom

Television, Identity and Self-narrative

Rebecca Williams

Bloomsbury Academic
An imprint of Bloomsbury Publishing Inc

B L O O M S B U R Y
NEW YORK · LONDON · OXFORD · NEW DELHI · SYDNEY

Bloomsbury Academic

An imprint of Bloomsbury Publishing Inc.

1385 Broadway	50 Bedford Square
New York	London
NY 10018	WC1B 3DP
USA	UK

www.bloomsbury.com

BLOOMSBURY and the Diana logo are trademarks of Bloomsbury Publishing Plc

First published 2015
Paperback edition first published 2016

Library of Congress Cataloging-in-Publication Data
Williams, Rebecca.
Post-object fandom : television, identity and self-narrative / Rebecca Williams.
pages cm
Includes bibliographical references and index.
ISBN 978-1-62356-463-6 (hardback : alk. paper) 1. Television programs–Psychological aspects–United States. 2. Television viewers–United States–Psychology. I. Title.
PN1992.6.W58 2015
791.45'750973–dc23
2014033045

ISBN: HB: 978-1-6235-6463-6
PB: 978-1-5013-1998-3
ePUb: 978-1-6235-6210-6
ePDF: 978-1-6235-6140-6

Typeset by Fakenham Prepress Solutions, Fakenham, Norfolk NR21 8NN
Printed and bound in Great Britain

For my parents, my brother Gareth and my husband Ross

Contents

Acknowledgements

A big thank you to everyone at Bloomsbury for being supportive of the idea of this book, especially Katie Gallof, who was enthusiastic and encouraging about the proposal from the start. I'd also like to thank Mary Al-Sayed, who was fabulous with the design and production process and helped make the book look wonderful.

A huge thank you to my current and former colleagues at the University of South Wales, particularly Ruth McElroy, Caitriona Noonan, Steve Blandford, Stephen Lacey, Rob Campbell, Richard Hand, Ben Lamb and Huw Jones. Students on my modules on Digital Media & Society, Media Audiences & Fandom, and Media & Culture in Wales have consistently challenged and developed my ideas about contemporary media and I've enjoyed all of our debates and discussions. Outside of this project, I've been fortunate enough to work with other fantastic colleagues and editors in television and audience studies, including Kim Akass, Janet McCabe, Sarah Cardwell, Melissa Click, Mark Duffett, Stacey Abbott and Lorna Jowett. Thanks also to Matt Hills for the years of academic support, encouragement and friendship.

Huge thanks to the Fan Studies Network team of supportive colleagues and friends: Lucy Bennett, Bertha Chin, Bethan Jones, Richard McCulloch and Tom Phillips. To other wonderful friends made in academia and continued in the 'real world': Nash Jimenez, Inger-Lise Kalviknes Bore, Darren Kelsey, Choon Key Chekar, Janet Harris, Rachel Cohen and Emma Cooke. Outside of academia, a raft of support has come from Stacy Lynch, Rachel Pugh Alexander, Beth Setters, Claire Penny, Steph Wall, and Katie Hicks.

My family have been endlessly supportive of my academic career, so heartfelt thanks to Mum and Dad, and Gareth and Emma. Thanks, finally, to Ross. Despite all my thinking and writing about endings, I know that there's one I don't have to worry about.

Aspects of Chapters 2 and 5 have appeared in the following journals: *Popular Communication* and *Participations: International Journal of Audience Research*.

Introduction: The Beginning of the End

I am now officially, decidedly 100% OVER Angel: the Series! I feel like now I can finally let it go and move on with my life. Just remember it for the phenomenal show it once was, but with the serene peace of having accepted that it's over and done, never to return.

Questionnaire respondent, 2003

If texts no longer end, they still have endings that are enormously meaningful to both fans and creators.

Harrington 2013, 591

Among the countless memorable moments that television programmes have given us, it is perhaps the final scenes of many of these that stick most clearly in the mind. The contested and divisive spiritual focus of *Lost*'s (ABC 2004–10) finale; the seemingly premature conclusion of *Twin Peaks* (ABC 1990–1), which saw lead character Dale Cooper eerily possessed by his supernatural nemesis BOB; the sad postscript to science-fiction drama series *Quantum Leap* (NBC 1989–92) that informs the viewer that time-travelling hero Sam Beckett 'never went home'; the ambiguous conclusion of *Buffy the Vampire Slayer* (The WB 1997–2001; UPN 2001–3) spin-off *Angel* (The WB 1999–2004), with its final moments depicting the lead characters about to enter into a battle to avoid the apocalypse and their eventual fate left unresolved. As a viewer, and sometime fan of each of these shows, these are some of my own favourite examples. Each reader will surely have their own. However, while academic studies of fandom have examined the process of 'becoming a fan' (Hills 2002, 6), since this is often 'for most fans, a milestone in their lives in which "everything changed"' (Cavicchi 1998, 153), reactions to the cessation of fan objects have received comparatively less academic attention. However, a consequence of a commercially driven and ever-changing media landscape is that favoured bands split up, movie franchises come to an end, characters depart TV shows and television programmes draw to a close.

This book examines responses to the specific moment when a fan object moves from being ongoing to dormant, yielding no new instalments, and the period of 'post-object fandom' that follows. It focuses on television and also considers how new fans negotiate discovery of shows that have ended and how this is discussed. Accepting the importance of fandom in helping us negotiate our 'social, political and cultural realities and identities' (Gray, Sandvoss and Harrington 2007, 10), the book contributes to a number of key debates in contemporary audience and television studies. Acknowledging that fandom can, and often does, continue through watching DVDs and reruns, collecting merchandise, listening to podcasts or using other online media or conducting ongoing conversations with fellow fans, and that media texts offer a range of endings from character departures to the complete cessation of new episodes of a series, the book explores a range of examples of fandom, transitions and endings.

Fandom is now accepted as an integral part of everyday life which impacts upon 'how we form emotional bonds with ourselves and others in a modern, mediated world' (Gray et al. 2007, 10). What follows focuses on how fans form such bonds, drawing upon sociologist Anthony Giddens' (1990, 1992) work on 'pure relationships' to consider how endings may impact upon fans' self-identities and sense of ontological security when the cessation of 'a favorite program creates an emotional void and forced detachment from the program narrative' (Costello and Moore 2007, 135). The book provides empirical material to consider responses in the period immediately before the ending of shows, as their final episodes are aired and how fans continue to use and discuss the programmes in the following years. It also explores other moments of separation and detachment for TV fans, such as the departure of favoured characters, the replacing of actors or moments where the return of a show is uncertain. It argues that attention must be paid to fans' affective and interpretive responses to such TV events since 'observation of the way we react to the expiration of a television show offers us another chance to understand the complexities involved in the institution of television as a portion of our social fabric' (Anderson 2005, online). Consideration of various genres, such as reality television 'which eliminates characters on a regular basis' and would allow an interesting study of 'how viewers react when their favorite character is "voted off" the show' (Eyal and Cohen 2006, 519), or soap operas which routinely lose characters over their long-running histories, would offer an even broader range of fan responses. However, the book focuses on fans of television dramas and how they respond to the lack of new episodes of their fan objects but, in many cases, continue to engage with these objects. Many of the shows discussed here have been subject to prior academic study including *24* (FOX 2001–10), *The West Wing* (NBC 2000–6), *Lost, Doctor Who* (BBC 1963–89, 2005–), *Torchwood* (BBC Wales/Canadian Broadcasting Company 2006; BBC Worldwide/Starz Entertainment 2010–11), *The X-Files* (FOX 1993–2002), *Twin Peaks, Angel, Firefly* (FOX 2002) and *Sex and the City* (HBO 1998–2004). Discussing a range of drama series allows consideration of programmes that span different periods of longevity from those that continued for up to eight seasons and had a definite end point, to those that were cancelled prematurely and had much shorter television lifespans. The book takes a comparative approach by focusing specifically on fan audiences and considering these during the period of cancellation and beyond. The book thus contributes to debates around television fandom in three distinctive ways:

1. It argues for a rethink of how media scholars view old or 'dormant' texts despite the pressure on academics to focus on new media objects.
2. It urges a multi-site approach to studies of fandom, offering empirical work on how fans across different fandoms cope with the ending of shows and discuss these after networks cease airing new TV episodes.
3. It proposes the integration of approaches to fandom and identity with exploration of the concept of post-object fandom.

Revaluing dormant texts

The book focuses on older or 'dormant' television shows, whereas much current work within television studies has a tendency to privilege new programmes and has a 'preoccupation with examples that are themselves "current"' (Hastie 2007, 79). Amelie Hastie (2007) notes the commercial imperative for such a focus on liveness:

> Like its synchronous temporality with television, critical texts … are also born from the particularities of the medium and the texts themselves: after all,

television is first and foremost a consumerist medium, often with a proliferation of ancillary texts. In a sense, [academic collections of scholarship] take up the position of the ancillary text, or merchandise: the tie-in. (2007, 91)

Matt Hills takes this up to argue that this 'scholarly zone of liveness' (Hills 2010a, 101) means that older shows are often excluded from ongoing examination since they are deemed to be outdated and to have no more academic value to offer researchers: 'Publishing a study on *Buffy* or *The Sopranos* now, however interesting it may be, would tend to fall outside the zone of liveness, with these texts having become "old news", superseded by the next "event-made-present"' (Hills 2010a, 101). This book necessarily addresses the concerns of scholars such as Hills and Hastie, since its focus on fan responses to TV cancellations and their practices after this occurs means that older television shows must be revisited. In arguing that fan practices can still be usefully explored through re-examination of older media texts (especially given the appeal of box sets and reruns) the book also considers how fandom continues and attracts newcomers after the cessation of programmes. Thus, the book offers concrete examples of how older shows that may be seen to have exhausted their academic 'currency' (Hills 2010a, 97) can still offer new insights for both audience and television scholars.

Multi-site fan studies

Much fan studies work has been monolithic in approach, with research focusing on single fan communities such as *Star Trek* (Jenkins 1992), *Star Wars* (Brooker 2002), *Buffy* (Gatson and Zweerink 2004), *The X-Files* (Scodari and Felder 2000) or soap opera (Harrington and Bielby 1995; Baym 2000). Thus, 'Though we know that they can engage with various objects and phenomenon at the same time, fans' interests have often been understood singularly and their communities falsely bounded' (Duffett 2013, 29). Consideration of fandom that 'explores the parallels between fans of different texts or genres' (Sandvoss 2005, 8) remains atypical and immersion in ethnographic approaches to individual fandoms continues to be the norm. However, this neglects the possibilities of multi-fandom research which may uncover new similarities or disparities in the ways in which fans engage with their varying fan objects and with one another. One notable exception is Steve Bailey's (2005) work on identity and self-construction in fandom. He offers three diverse case studies of a local underground film network, fans of the rock group Kiss and online fans of the adult cartoon series *Futurama* (FOX 1999–2003; Comedy Central 2008–13). Bailey argues that, rather than forming disparate studies, these work together to highlight the 'practices of self-construction and self-reflection' (2005, 8) that occur within each fandom. He notes that:

> These empirical investigations might be characterised as a 'collective case study', to refer to the distinction made by Robert E. Stake, who differentiates such studies, that are designed as a group to 'provide insight into an issue or refinement of a theory', from 'intrinsic case studies' that are designed primarily for 'better understanding of this particular case' (Stake 1994, 237). (Bailey 2005, 8)

Drawing on Bailey's methods here, I follow the notion of the collective case study, as well as his use of 'Michael Buroway's "extended case method" in which empirical research serves a dialogical role, informing and reshaping theoretical work' (Bailey 2005, 8). This allows 'insight into an issue or refinement of a theory' (Bailey 2005, 8) surrounding fan identity and ontological security. Other examples of more comparative research include Bury's (2005) work on fans of *The X-Files* and *Due South* (CTV/CBS 1994–9), Whiteman's (2009) study of fans of *Angel* and *Silent Hill*, and Whiteman and Metivier's (2013) work on *Angel* and *Harry Potter* online fandoms. Despite this work, however, the use of 'collective case studies' to draw points of cohesion or conflict across apparently incongruent cultural sites remains rare. The research presented here aims to move beyond enquiry into singular fan communities and to embrace the comparative potential of multi-site case studies. It seeks to follow those scholars who, as Harrington and Bielby summarize, 'are moving away from studying specific fan communities – soap fans or *Doctor Who* fans or fans of China's *Super Girl* singing contest – to focusing on broader dimensions of fandom or fan affect' (2013, 99). In offering a way to understand a range of different television fans the book concurs with Matt Hills's contention that 'a general theory of media fandom is not only possible but also important; too many previous works have focused on single TV series, singular fan cultures, or singular media ("TV fans" versus "cinephiles")' (Hills 2002, 2).

Fandom, identity and post-object fandom

The book's most ambitious aim is its contribution to the existing and developing literature on television and audience research. The broader concerns of this monograph have been shared by other writers. For instance, whenever studies have examined fan campaigns to prevent the cancellation of television shows such as *Star Trek* (NBC 1966–9), *Angel*, *Veronica Mars* (UPN 2004–6; The CW 2006–7), *Chuck* (NBC 2007–12), *Roswell* (The WB 1999–2001; UPN 2001–2), *Jericho* (CBS 2006–8) or *Firefly* (FOX 2002) (see Abbott 2005; Scardaville 2005; Menon 2007; Whiteman 2009; Paproth 2013; Barton 2014b, 165–6) they have been implicitly concerned with reactions to the ending of fan objects. Furthermore, wider studies on aging in Goth fandom (Hodkinson 2011) or punks (Bennett 2006) and elderly fans of a Flemish singer (Van den Bulck and Van Gorp 2011), approaches using the notion of 'status passage' to understand fans' changes over time (Crawford 2003, 2004), and discussion of 'enduring fandom' (Kuhn 2002) and 'lifelong fandom' (Stevenson 2009) all speak to the importance of considering fandom as a continuing part of an individual's life, one that can have a profound impact on their sense of identity and self-narrative. For instance, Paul Hodkinson's study of Goths found that fans' 'intensity of involvement [with the Goth scene] would fluctuate to and fro at various points, often in relation to developments or ruptures in other elements of individual life trajectories' (2011, 272), while Harrington and Bielby's ongoing research into the 'life course of fandom' suggests that 'changes in the fan self over time, age norms within fandom, and changes in the fan object over time' mean that 'fans' identities, practices and interpretive capacities have more age-related structure than has previously been addressed in fan studies' (Harrington et al. 569–70). Clearly, fandom and self-identity are closely linked. As Mark Duffett summarizes:

> Fans tend to periodize their lives around autobiographic turning points where 'everything changed' and they became interested. Their initiation frequently becomes an important personal memory, recalled and discussed with others. Autobiographical first-person 'becoming a fan' stories are usually the first things fans talk about when they get to know others, whether in person or online. Such stories allow each individual to locate his or her fandom as a shift in personal history. (2013, 154)

In addition to contributing to studies of fandom and self-identity, the book also speaks to debates regarding the endings of television series, whether in reference to the finite episodes of a show or smaller endings such as the exit of particular characters. For instance, Elena Levine and Lisa Parks (2007) argue that examining the 'afterlife' of *Buffy the Vampire Slayer* has much to tell us about a dormant TV text. Similarly an emerging body of work has focused on the importance, both textually and for the audience, of the television finale, with specific cases focusing on *Seinfeld* (Morreale 2003), *Lost* and *The Prisoner* (Morreale 2010), and *The Sopranos* (Corrigan and Corrigan 2012), as well as Jason Mittell (2013) and C. Lee Harrington's (2013) attempts to theorize television finales more broadly. There is also emerging work on practices in specific fandoms after series end, including Chin's discussion of fan/producer relationships in *The X-Files* fandom, which suffers an apparent 'absence of new materials to be discussed, analysed and expanded on creatively' (2013, 88), Thompson's (2014) exploration of the ongoing fandom of *Dark Shadows* and Bore and Hickman's (2013) analysis of post-*The West Wing* fans' use of Twitter to portray the characters and continue the diegetic world of the series. Perhaps the most discussed television series, however, is *Friends*, which has attracted academic study of fan responses to the temporary loss of characters in the show during the 2007–8 writers' strike (Lather and Moyer-Guse 2011) as well as analysis of fan responses to the show's ending (Eyal and Cohen 2006; Todd 2011). The work of Eyal and Cohen and Lather and Moyer-Guse draws on Horton and Wohl's (1956) theory of parasocial interaction to examine fans' attachment to characters, arguing that both temporary and permanent loss of contact with those characters can lead to a form of 'parasocial breakup' (Cohen 2003). In both cases, links were found between the depth of parasocial relationship and the impact of the breakup. Amanda Todd's work, in contrast, emphasized the construction of the *Friends* finale by its US broadcasting network NBC and the companies that produced it, considering its positioning as 'a media event, one that exhibits an awareness of the end of an era' (2011, 858). Todd also notes how the episode's narrative deliberately referenced fans' emotional attachment, as: 'The self-referential plot framed the finale as part of life experience, fans were not just watching the end of a show, they were saying goodbye to *Friends* along with millions of other viewers, experiencing the sadness that the characters expressed' (Todd 2011, 859). Todd's work on *Friends*, as well as Harrington's (2013) work on TV finales more broadly, highlights the importance of the television industry in terms of understanding endings for texts and audiences. While NBC heavily promoted the end of *Friends*, labelling it 'the "end of an era"' and airing advertisements for the finale that asked viewers to 'join us' as 'we say goodbye to our best friends' (Todd 2011, 863), Harrington cautions that 'the good death of a TV series is meaningful only to creators and audiences as the industry itself aims for the profit potential of narrative immortality and/ or resurrection (in syndication, in another medium, etc.)' (2013, 584). Indeed, televisual endings can be hugely profitable media events, ensuring continued streams of revenue via reruns or licensing (e.g. continuation of a series in novels or comics; ongoing sales of merchandise) and attracting large audiences. Three examples will suffice here: the audience of 52.56 million in the United States for *Friends*, 11.9 million viewers for HBO cable series *The Sopranos*, which beat viewing figures for all network shows in the week it aired except *American Idol* (Associated Press 2007), and a respectable 6.5 million viewers in the UK for the series finale of *Ashes to Ashes* (French 2009). Thus, while industrial practices and the mechanisms of constructing the 'end of texts' are not my focus here, fans' position as 'part-time collaborators with official producers seeking to incite and retain dedicated fan audiences, and part-time co-opted word-of-mouth marketers for beloved brands' (Hills 2010b, 58) means that we must maintain an awareness of fans' relationship with this industrial context. As participants within the media industry, fan responses to the ending of programmes, and their practices afterwards or in the interim, are always in sway to the whims of creators and industry that produces their favourite shows.

Since I first wrote about 'post-object fandom' (Williams 2011a) it has been used to explore reactions to the end of the BBC series *Merlin* (Athkar 2013) and been developed by Whiteman and Metivier (2013) to explore the endings of online fan communities which they characterize as 'zombie communities … that have entered into a state of atrophy, decline or impending demise' (2013, 270). In focusing on 'how these decaying communities die or are killed off, and what fans' responses to these deaths can tell us about the formation of fan subjectivity online' (2013, 270), they argue 'for an understanding of ruptures/ endings as ongoing, constant and generative of subjectivity' (2013, 294). Indeed, the end points of texts (and whether these endings are defined by scholars, the TV industry or fans themselves) are subject to negotiation and are not always, in the era of transmediality and media convergence, clear-cut. However, as the quote that opens this chapter states, even 'if texts no longer *end*, they still have *endings* that are enormously meaningful to both fans and creators' (Harrington 2013, 591 italics in original). This book posits that these endings, and their meaning for fans, are worthy of our scrutiny and understanding.

Methods

In keeping with the multi-site approach outlined above, the case studies and data discussed here are drawn from a range of sources. Specific methodological detail appears in certain chapters but the overall approach was to gather data from a range of sites, including online message boards and forums and surveys conducted by the author. This approach was necessary to explore the different fandoms needed in a study that spans a broad period of time (from around 2004 until 2013) and different fan groups. Online forums have long been the focus of fan studies, from early work on fans of shows such as *The X-Files* (Clerc 1996), *Twin Peaks* (Jenkins 1995), *Buffy the Vampire Slayer* (Zweerink and Gatson 2002; Cantwell 2004; Williams 2004), *Quantum Leap* (MacDonald 1998) and soap opera (Baym 2000) through to more contemporary studies of shows including *Doctor Who* (Hadas 2013), *Prison Break* (Knaggs 2011), the soap opera *Neighbours* (Williams 2010) and non-television fandoms such as music (Bennett 2013) and film (Hills 2005b; Bore and Williams 2010). It is tempting to regard online message boards as potentially obsolete in the face of social media such as Facebook (which offers space for fan groupings, both official and unofficial) or Twitter (which allows instantaneous fan reactions and discussion). Indeed, fan studies have embraced social media and focused on practices including the maintenance of fictional 'character' accounts for shows such as *Veronica Mars* (Booth 2008), *Glee* (Wood and Baughman 2012) or *The West Wing* (Bore and Hickman 2013), discussing television shows while they air (Deller 2011) to capture the 'pseudo "group viewing" experience of television' (Wohn and Na 2011), and live-tweeting while attending events such as music gigs (Bennett 2012b) or conventions (Williams 2013c). However, the depth and range of fan responses that forums allow are not engendered by social media's focus on brevity and ' "presentism", the belief that only things that are happening now are what matters' (Gruzd, Wellman and Takhteyev 2011, 1303). Thus, forums continue to be useful sites for fan research, given the space they offer for lengthy conversations as well as their ability to archive and maintain older discussions for the future. When fan discussions from forums are drawn on in this research, they are from the established site Television Without Pity (TWoP), which hosted recaps of episodes of television series alongside forums for a variety of US-based television shows. Established in the 1990s and origi-nally called Dawson's Wrap (solely focused on the teen drama *Dawson's Creek*) then Mighty Big TV, TWoP was bought in 2007 by the American cable and satellite channel Bravo (owned by NBC Universal), which resulted in accusations of it becoming less independent and more commercial (Donaghy 2007). In March 2014 the closure of both the site and the forums was announced, ending Television Without Pity's crucial presence in online fandom. Clearly, as fan objects end, so too do the spaces where fans can discuss them.

Television Without Pity was the focus of online analysis given this research's interest in both positive and negative fan reactions, as well as in ongoing debate during the years after a series ends. TWoP is more likely to offer anti-fandom and criticism than official fansites or other more fan-specific online spaces because of its focus on a range of programmes, which attracts both avid fans and more casual television viewers who watch, and comment on, a range of different shows. It possesses parallels with the movie site Internet Movie Database, which is 'not wholly fan-centric, instead offering a more diffuse forum ... that encompasses fan responses and those of more "generalized" movie-goers [or TV viewers]' (Hills 2010c, 113). TWoP members pride themselves on their sense of 'snark', referring to their ability to be often scathing about the perceived failings of television shows. As a site that actively encourages 'snark' and modes of anti-fandom, it offers a chance to view the range of discourses that fans deploy to discuss programmes that they were once fans of. Thus while not all posters at TWoP are anti-fans (see Peters 2006; Williams 2011a), the site is 'renowned for its sarcastic and at times brutal honesty, encouraging play with and criticism of television ... TWoP simultaneously creates ample room for networking textual disappointment, dislike, disapproval, distaste, and disgust' (Gray 2005, 841). TWoP provides opportunities for considering more positive and approving fan commentary alongside 'clusters and even communities of antifandom' (Gray 2005, 841). As such, TWoP is a prolific site which has attracted prior academic attention and has been a source of valuable and detailed analysis of contemporary fandom (see Gray 2005; Peters 2006; Andrejevic 2008).

The online research drawn from TWoP concerns the case studies of *The West Wing* and *Lost*. In the case of *The West Wing* threads covering the final episodes of the series during 2006 were analysed. Once a show ceases airing, it is archived (or put on 'permanent hiatus') in the TWoP forum. While users can no longer post to *The West Wing* threads, they can still be accessed online (TWoP '*West Wing* thread archive'). I archived threads about each new episode of the final season, from the first episode on 25 September 2005 until the finale on 14 May 2006. There were twenty-two threads to examine, as well as a thread dedicated to the cancellation entitled 'It's Official—*West Wing* to Conclude Sunday, May 14' and a thread entitled 'The Reflecting Pool: A Look Back at the Show'. In July 2006, *The West Wing* discussions were moved into the general Drama forum, where it was merged into one thread (TWoP *The West Wing*). Across these threads, all comments directly related to the cancellation or ending of the show were archived and quotes included below were chosen to demonstrate commonalities in fan discussion or to highlight occasions where dissenting views are heard. In relation to *Lost*, comments were drawn from the thread about the final episode 'The End' only (TWoP 'The End'). As Gray notes, posters at TWoP are 'aware of speaking potentially to thousands and [are] already reasonably anonymous; and the performative nature of much TWoP commentary itself belies an awareness of (or even a desire for) a considerable audience' (2005, 847). Such performativity, size and openness renders privacy at TWoP impossible and, as such, all postings made at this site can be considered to be in the public domain. In their discussion of fan research ethics, Kristina Busse and Karen Hellekson specifically mention Television Without Pity as an example of a site where more relaxed ethical rules can apply. They question 'What about fans who post in public forums, such as Television Without Pity ... that have a much different sort of community, with different, more open expectations of privacy? In these cases, a requirement for obtaining permission may be waived' (Busse and Hellekson 2012, 52; see also Ess 2002). There are numerous ethical issues that are pertinent to fan studies research and all fan scholars must 'confront issues of citing, naming, and referencing pseudonymous fans and their writings ... Given the range of positions among and within different fan communities and different disciplines' diverse methodologies and conduct of research, there can be no hard-and-fast rule' (Busse and Hellekson 2012, 41). Instead, a policy is needed that 'remains open enough to accommodate different scenarios while protecting fannish spaces and individual fans – as well as a researchers' code of ethics and academic rigour' (Busse and Hellekson 2012, 41–2). Thus, the specificity of Television Without Pity has been considered in formulating the ethics approach for this research. The final main method of accessing fan views was an online survey that asked participants a range of questions regarding their 'post-object fandom', without using this particular term. The survey was launched in June 2013 and left online for a two-week period, during which it attracted sixty-six replies. The survey aimed to attract responses from those who may not normally discuss fan objects at forums and to gain a sense of the wide array of television shows that people had strong attachments to.

Fan responses, whether via survey, forum or social networking site, have been treated as texts that are both performative and discursive rather than expressions of the 'truth' about fandoms or individuals since the internet is not a 'transparent form of mediation' that holds the 'essence [of fandom] up to the academic gaze' (Hills 2002, 175). Online communication is mediated both by fans themselves and by the researcher since postings are 'representations of [social] experiences, constructed first by the participants themselves and then by the researcher in the analysis of the data and the presentation of the findings as a coherent text' (Bury 2005, 29). Furthermore, it is the researcher who ultimately 'includes, excludes, arranges and manipulates the "second-hand" memories in order to construct a coherent narrative in which she has material and symbolic investments' (Bury 2005, 30). There are also ethical issues that must be negotiated as the internet blurs 'categories such as public/private, audience/author, producer/consumer, and text/human subject' (Gajjala 2002, 184). Although personal emails and conversations (e.g. Blackberry Messenger, Facebook messages) constitute private communication, there is much debate over how to categorize postings made on message boards, forums and social networking sites. The 'technological point of view' (Frankel and Siang 1999, 13) suggests that accessibility means that such forums are public, while others posit that such communications are private (Waskul and Douglass 1996, 132). These debates are inextricably linked to whether online communication is written or spoken, for if postings can conceivably be studied as texts, 'our only responsibilities as researchers lie in issues of intellectual property rights' (Cavanagh 1999, online). Hine argues that delayed online interaction means that postings are textual and that research is a process of understanding 'the meanings which underlie and are enacted through these textual practices' (2000, 50). Online spaces can therefore be seen to resemble newspaper articles or other archival data and as 'analogous to letters published in magazines or newspapers, being accessible to anyone who can access the World Wide Web' (Allington 2007, 50). Study of postings is therefore ethically acceptable since it 'does not constitute an interaction with a human subject, and ... avails itself of existing records' (Walther 2002, 207). Thus, following such online researchers, this book asserts that, given their textual nature, once postings enter the public domain they can be studied without the explicit permission of each poster. Indeed, it has been argued in parallel that in many cases 'it is considered acceptable for researchers to utilize data from "real world" public spaces if the participants have the "reasonable expectation" of being overheard, among other considerations' (Freund and Fielding 2013, 332).

However, in taking measures to ensure the anonymity of those referenced in my work, harm to participants can be avoided. Informed consent was obtained from those who responded to online questionnaires by providing them with information about the research and asking them to complete a standard ethics form in an online format. However, permission for use of postings is difficult to attain owing to the transitory nature of online environments in which posters often leave communities. The notion of 'implied consent' has been used to analyse online material due to the public nature of internet postings (Walther 2002, 212) as 'the author could not reasonably expect to exclude any person from gaining access to his or her words, even if any particular individual were not specifically envisioned as part of the audience' (Reid 1996, 170). However, to maintain anonymity all postings in my research are identified by an assigned pseudonym along with the title and date or number of this posting. Furthermore, throughout the research none of the quotes drawn from online posts or questionnaires has been amended for spelling or grammar to try to 'preserve some of the feel of the original [online texts]' (Hine 2000, 82) and to avoid the presumption that fan commentary needs to be modified or 'improved' by the researcher. Finally, the maelstrom of data one can collate online risks becoming 'virtually unmanageable in terms of the sheer weight of communications traffic' (Hills 2002, 174). The information here offers a snapshot of the often messy, yet intriguing, online communications and practices of contemporary media fans.

What's next?

The research conducted in this book builds on a range of prior academic work to examine what happens at various points of 'ending' for fans of television programmes. In providing sustained analysis of responses to a range of different types of ending across different television texts, the book offers empirical research specifically examining television fandom at the period of shows' cancellation or directly afterwards. Responding to Levine and Parks' call for more work on the afterlife of (un)dead texts, it aims to offer some answers to their 'set of questions about television and endings, whether we imagine them in terms of cancellation, replacement or death' (2007, 4). The chapters that follow cover a range of different fan case studies to investigate how fans themselves conceive of endings since we 'need to recognize that the endings we examine are always a product of our analysis, and work in relation to the multiplicity of micro-level deaths/endings (both substantive and imagined) that are experienced from day to day in online fan communities' (Whiteman and Metivier 2013, 271).

Chapter 2 explains the concept of post-object fandom, arguing that although fans can re-watch DVDs or reruns and new audiences might find the show through these means, their fandom enters a period in which practices and interactions inevitably change. While many will continue to self-identify as fans of objects, watching DVDs, buying merchandise or discussing with fellow fans, new fans will also 'discover' older television shows and discuss their experiences with both existing fans and other newcomers. Rather than considering post-object fandom as indicating that fandom is 'over', the term is intended to allow consideration of the differences in fan practices between periods when objects are ongoing and dormant. Chapter 2 offers a comprehensive introduction to this concept, discussing its relation to ontological security and identity and setting up the theoretical framework that will inform what follows in the remaining chapters. It then sketches out the ways in which fan endings will be understood in the case studies that follow.

Chapter 3 explores examples of 'smaller endings in the context of fandom' which 'demonstrate the continuity of loss in fan cultures' (Whiteman and Metivier 2013, 292). Character departures are examined via three examples: a fairly typical character departure (Cordelia Chase's exit from *Angel*); the real-life and fictional death of two actors (John Spencer and his character Leo McGarry in *The West Wing* and Cory Monteith and his *Glee* character Finn Hudson); and the relatively unique case of *Doctor Who* where actors depart but the character of The Doctor endures via regeneration. This final example of *Doctor Who* allows consideration of a rare instance when fan relationships with a character/actor can often be disentangled to consider the differences between those whose fandom is reliant on attachment to a specific actor (such as Matt Smith or David Tennant) and those whose fandom is more closely aligned with the character and mythology of The Doctor.

The next three chapters set out the most common discourses fans used when negotiating their responses to the end of shows. These, broadly, consisted of fans rearticulating their reasons for their love of a show and bidding it a fond farewell, stating that they did not care about the ending of the show as it had already begun to lose its appeal for them or admitting that their fandom would need to be renegotiated in the face of the show's cessation. These responses, referred to as the reiteration, rejection and renegotiation discourses, enable us to examine fan responses to the demise of a range of television texts via their invocation of themes such as quality or 'good' television, authorship, grief and mourning and textual 'closure'. Chapters 4 and 5 draw on the same case studies in order to sketch out a more complete picture of how fans respond across a range of discourses. These examples are *Lost* and *The West Wing*, though reference is made to other programmes where necessary. By considering the common and disparate topics of fan discussion as both shows draw to a close, these two chapters offer a detailed insight into the positive and negative reactions of fans to the cessation of the programmes and consider how threats to fan self-identity, narrative and ontological security are negotiated within the reiteration and rejection discourses. The third chapter in this section, Chapter 6, examines the reactions of fans within the context of renegotiation when they take a more negotiated approach to responding to the endings of series. This chapter examines fans who seek to both reiterate their fandom *and* 'move on', and explores how fans move on to new objects of interest and how this is often linked to favoured actors, writers and producers.

The final section of the book offers two chapters more specifically focused on how fans respond in the years after a show's cancellation. The first, Chapter 7, examines the impact of new technologies and how existing fans can revisit texts via DVDs, downloads and reruns, while new fans can discover a series, leading to an ongoing cycle of fan performance and practice. Through examples including *24*, *Firefly* and *The X-Files* this chapter explores how fan objects can 'live on' after the text itself ceases to produce new instalments, suggesting that the specifics of how fans re-watch, encounter, and reinterpret programmes in this period can be a key element of their fandom, as can ongoing engagement with the surrounding and surviving elements of fan community. The final empirical chapter, Chapter 8, turns its attention to the 'afterlife' (Levine and Parks 2007) of shows, exploring how favoured narratives are kept alive through the creation of both official para-texts and fanfiction, videos and other user-generated texts. This chapter thus considers instances of textual regeneration or resurrection when a thought-dead programme returns to life as a series or in another media form. It examines fan comments on examples where dormant television shows have been made into films and had a second lease of life on the cinematic screen such as *Firefly*'s transition to *Serenity*, the second *X-Files* movie *I Want to Believe* and *Sex and the City* which spawned two movies. It also considers fan views on televisual resurrections and revivals, including *Arrested*

Development, Doctor Who, Dallas and *24*. The chapter finally examines the case of science-fiction series *Torchwood* which is, at the time of writing, in a state of liminality – neither officially cancelled nor assured of a return to the television screen. In considering fan reactions to such textual resurrections and uncertainties, the chapter introduces the concept of 'interim fandom' and explores what happens when texts are neither alive nor entirely dead. These two chapters draw on recent work that has questioned definitions of the concept of the 'text' (see Gray 2010) and argued that 'the bounded "text" may no longer exist for audiences navigating their way through dispersed yet organized networks of textuality' (Hills 2007b, 153). Clearly, in many cases both official and ancillary textual materials continue to be produced after a show's cancellation. Thus, while post-object fandom refers to fandom of any object which can no longer produce new texts, fan attachment will not necessarily end in the post-object period. Rather, post-object fandom can often offer new opportunities for reboots, reinventions and resurrections.

The final chapter of the book, Chapter 9, draws together conclusions regarding the importance of studying endings and revisiting fan investments in series that have long been off-air. It also outlines the scope for further work on post-object fandom, including other television genres such as soap opera, reality television or factual television, or on other media and cultural forms such as film, music or sport. It has been argued that the importance of fandom in contemporary society is due to 'the ways it can heighten our sense of excitement, prompt our self-reflexivity, encourage us to discuss shared values and ethics, and supply us with a significant source of meaning that extends into our daily lives' (Duffett 2013, 18). The analysis that follows treats fandom as such a 'source of meaning' and an avenue for 'self-reflexivity', demonstrating that fan reactions, debates and practices before, during and after periods of post-object fandom have much to tell us about contemporary audiences and their relationship with the televisual medium in all its current forms.

2

Ontological Security, Self-Identity and Post-Object Fandom

Henry Jenkins notes that fandom is widely perceived to be 'everywhere and all the time, a central part of the everyday lives of consumers operating within a networked society' (2007, 361). This has largely resulted from an increase in online fan activity since 'The digital space has clearly augmented the practices and methods of interpersonal connection amongst fans, even as many fans continue to adhere to offline practices ... Online fandom has made fandom as a whole more visible, and while this may have "mainstreamed" fan identity, it has also increased fan awareness of their own online representations' (Booth and Kelly 2013, 57).

There have been numerous studies of fandom and fan practices since the early 1990s when scholars were fighting against commonly held stereotypes of the fan as obsessive, lonely and unhinged (see Jenson 1992) and popular culture was still treated with derision and suspicion in many quarters. Although the media forms and case studies that have been explored are varied, previous approaches have tended to emphasize resistance and poaching, affective investments and psychoanalysis or forms of cultural, social and symbolic capital. For instance, many early fan studies scholars highlighted the meaning-making of audiences who were resistive and could actively 'poach' from texts to creatively appropriate chosen elements for their own ends. Drawing on Michel de Certeau's (1984) work Henry Jenkins conceptualized fans as such poachers who 'transform the experience of watching television into a rich and complex participatory culture' (1992, 23) and engage in acts of re-appropriation and textual productivity via the creation of fanfiction, artwork, videos and other fan texts. However, such approaches – which Gray et al. (2007, 1) refer to as the 'fandom is beautiful' wave of fan studies – fail to account for the fragmentation of the audience and it has become increasingly difficult to define what is being resisted or what an oppositional reading constitutes. Fandom is also far from the stigmatized pastime that it once was and fans often specifically align themselves with the dominant values of mainstream culture, perhaps most notably in their attempts to ally their fan objects with the discourses of 'quality television' perpetuated by producers and academics (Williamson 2005, 100). Fandom is also often actively encouraged as it provides a lucrative market with fans acting as 'media consumers *par excellence*' (Gwenllian-Jones 2003, 167) whose spending contributes to the economic and symbolic power of producers. Furthermore, recent studies have suggested that activities such as producing fanfiction or 'shipping' (the act of actively supporting an onscreen romantic relationship) are not always resistant as they are often implicitly encouraged by a show's creators via deliberately polysemic subtext (Williamson and Amy-Chinn 2005).

The 'second wave of fan studies' (Gray et al. 2007, 6) instead drew on the work of Pierre Bourdieu (1984) to understand how hierarchies and value judgements were made and continued within fan and other subcultures. Rather than focusing on the more utopian and collective aspects of fandom favoured by theorists such as Jenkins, Bourdieuian approaches emphasized how 'the interpretive communities of fandom (as well as individual acts of fan consumption) are embedded in the existing economic, social and cultural status quo' (Gray et al. 2007, 6). Thus, subcultures such as horror fans (Jancovich 2000), comic book collectors (Brown 1997) and vampire fans (Williamson 2005) were explored in terms of how fans form distinctions regarding their fan objects, fellow fans and non-fans. Other fan studies drew on the concept of affect, most notably in the work of Lawrence Grossberg (1992), who considers affect as a non-emotional and non-libidinal force which explains how we form attachments to certain cultural objects (Puoskari 2004). Grossberg argues that cultural practices can be conceptualized as 'affective investments' and he posits the existence of 'mattering maps', which order our affective ties: 'for fans, popular culture becomes a crucial ground on which he or she can construct mattering maps. They may construct relatively stable moments of identity ... Fans let them organize their emotional and narrative lives and identities' (1992, 59). Thus, fans can use popular culture to construct self-identity, and since what people may 'invest' in via their mattering maps necessarily differs from person to person, affect is 'integral to the notion of individuality, to the sense of what makes each of us "distinct"' (Harding and Pribam 2004, 875).

Fan studies have also drawn on psychoanalytic thought to understand fandom as a site of powerful emotional investment. Psychoanalysis has been used by theorists who have, for example, drawn on Melanie Klein's (1952) work on object relations to consider fan reactions to horror films such as *The Exorcist* (Hoxter 2000). Others have theorized fans via the work of object relations theorist Donald Woods Winnicott which suggests that infants need to negotiate their inability to distinguish between object and subject through the use of a 'transitional object', for example a toy. This object offers a third realm between the inner and external worlds, an 'intermediate area of experiencing' (Winnicott 2005, 2), a space that is 'neither inside nor outside but in between [the self and the outside world]' (Bateman and Holmes 1995, 42). Such objects continue to be important to the infant but eventually they lose meaning 'because the transitional phenomena have become diffused, have become spread out over the whole intermediate territory between "inner psychic reality" and "the external world as perceived by two persons in common", that is to say, over the whole cultural field' (Winnicott 2005, 7). Such work has been utilized to consider fan–object relationships via the notion of transitional objects (Lembo and Tucker 1990; Silverstone 1994; Turkle 2004) or fandom as a transitional realm (Harrington and Bielby 1995; Hills 2002; Sandvoss 2005). Furthermore, Matt Hills distinguishes between the '*proper transitional object (pto)*' of childhood (Hills 2002, 107) and a 'secondary transitional object', which is '*a transitional object which has not altogether surrendered its affective charge and private significance for the subject* ... [or] enters a *cultural repertoire which "holds" the interest of the fan and constitutes the subject's symbolic project of self* (2002, 109, his emphasis). Thus, the secondary transitional object may be one that was used in childhood and remains personally important to the individual (e.g. a television programme from one's early years) or a new object that contributes towards his/her construction of self-identity (e.g. emerging fandom of a rock band in one's teens). It is these later transitional objects that theorists are usually discussing when they consider fan objects as transitional phenomena. Like Hills, Sandvoss develops the idea of transitional objects within fandom, arguing for the existence of a 'second order transitional object' (2005, 90). This refers to material objects such as posters and records that 'constitute transitional objects that create a common realm between the fan and the star, while the star remains the primary object of fandom' (Sandvoss 2005, 90). Prior work on transitional objects and fan cultures has usefully enabled consideration of links between fan emotional involvement and cultural value (Hills 2002, 109). For example, a teenager may distance himself from an object perceived as 'childish' and this may also be dependent upon whether fan objects are 'culturally designated highbrow or lowbrow' (Harrington and Bielby 1995, 136). Furthermore, such work accounts for fans' displeasure and anger at fan objects that violate their expectations as the transitional object is subject to both 'good' and 'bad' emotion (Winnicott 2005, 7). Therefore, the notion of fandom as a transitional realm or object can account for instances when fans become dissatisfied with their chosen fan objects, often expressing anger towards those in charge of a favourite show (see Chapter 5).

Fandom and 'pure relationships'

There is great potential for continuing to draw on the notion of transitional objects or a transitional realm via the work of Anthony Giddens in under-standing fandom. Such approaches allow consideration of the '(psychical as well as social) uses that can be made of television and its texts; and of how a medium such as television ... can be embedded into the "ontological security" or object-constancy of trusted, ritualized daily life and its everyday creativity' (Hills 2013a, 80). Giddens' theory of 'structuration' (1984) attempts to bridge the divide between the 'macro level' of society as a whole and the 'micro level' of what life means to the individuals who are experiencing it. Giddens views people as 'knowledgeable agents' (1984, 281) who, in the current state of late modernity, have increased reflexivity that enables development of a self-narrative. Late modernity is, according to Giddens (1991, 20), characterized by a separation of time and space which he calls 'time–space distanciation'. Such ' "emptying out" of time and space allows for the stretching of social relations' (Stevenson 2002, 134) but it also carries a greater sense of risk since individuals are now required to place their trust in 'abstract systems', including 'symbolic tokens' such as money and 'expert systems' (Giddens 1991, 18) such as medicine, transport and so on. For example, when we fly we place ourselves in the hands of the techni-cians, mechanics and pilots, and trust that the transport we are using is safe. According to Giddens, modernity increases reflexivity due to these conditions so, for example, the time–space distantiation means that 'our past, present, and future become visible and are held up in front of us like a mirror ... Thought and action are constantly refracted back upon each other' (Kaspersen 2000, 88). Giddens argues that self-reflexivity enables development of a self-narrative that 'continually integrate[s] events which occur in the external world, and sort[s] them into the ongoing "story" about the self' (1991, 54). He also proposes that in late modernity sexuality has become severed from its associations with childrearing, reproduction and kinship and is a self-identity that individuals develop (1992, 15). Related to this is the 'pure relationship', 'a social relation [that] is entered into for its own sake, for what can be derived by each person from a sustained association with another; and which is continued only in so far as it is thought by both parties to deliver enough satisfactions for each individual to stay within it' (Giddens 1992, 58). It is my argument that we can view fan–object interactions as 'fan pure relationships'. Indeed, 'a pure relationship is one in which external criteria have become dissolved: the relationship exists solely for whatever rewards that relationship can deliver' (Giddens 1991, 6) and these rewards are: (1) the reflection of a desirable and appropriate self-identity and self-narrative; (2) a sense of ontological security or 'trust'.

Extrapolating from this, particularly Giddens' admission that pure relationships need not be reciprocal or inter-subjective (1992, 58), I propose that at the core of fandom lie two types of 'fan pure relationship': fan/object pure relationships (fan attachment to fan objects) and fan–fan pure relationships (fan attachment to fellow fans). Given the importance of fans' use of fandom to negotiate self-identity, this book considers how the television fans examined in the various case studies draw on the texts to perform identity work through points of identification including fans' attachments to individual characters or onscreen romantic relationships (often called 'ships'). In addition, given that the other reward gained from pure relationships is the provision of a sense of ontological security or trust in the surrounding world, I also examine how fans may gain such trust from engagement with fan objects since 'the routinisation of day-to-day life … is the single most important source of ontological security' (Giddens 1981, 37). However, as ontological security is not constant and can be threatened by external factors (Giddens 1992, 40), the focus is on considering how fans respond to threats that may occur as a result of the loss of favourite aspects of their fandom, or the loss of the object entirely.

Although the concept of the pure relationship has been used to examine online interactions (Clark 1998; Henderson and Gilding 2004) and to consider the 'quality' of television texts (Hills 2004), it has not yet been utilized in studies of fandom. Giddens' himself acknowledges that pure relationships 'are not limited to two-person settings [such as romantic pairings or friendships]. A given individual is likely to be involved in several forms of social relation which tend towards the pure type' (1991, 97). Furthermore, such relationships do not need to be reciprocal. For example, Clark argues that online dating among teenagers is often non-reciprocal and that the greatest importance comes from the way that the relationship can encourage 'affirmation of self, its gratifications resting in its ability to provide opportunities for self-reflexivity and even self-consciously imagined (or constructed) intimacy' (1998, 179). The emphasis here is on one person self-reflexively deciding to end a relationship that offers them no 'reward'. If the emotions of the other individual within that relationship are rendered almost irrelevant, then the pure relationship can surely be applied to those instances when there is only one person within a 'relationship'. The 'pure relationship' can, therefore, be used to consider fan attachments precisely because requited emotion is not a requirement for their existence. If fans are attached to their fan objects despite the fact that inanimate objects, distant personalities or fictional characters cannot love them back, then there must surely be some reward reaped by these fans. To clarify here: it is a central idea of this book that, provided that fans continue to enjoy that which can be 'derived ... from a sustained association with another' (Giddens 1992, 58), they will continue in their fan/object attachments. It is only when there are no such rewards that they may cease to be a fan, often despite considerable readjustments to their identity and self-narrative.

Self-identity, self-narrative and fandom

It has been argued that individuals 'draw on mediated experience to inform and refashion the project of the self' (Thompson 1995, 233) and that use of media texts is crucial to the development of reflexive self-narratives. This is often related to the experience of becoming-a-fan since this is 'typically experienced as a major turning point that profoundly reshapes one's identity, daily activities and life trajectory. Indeed, becoming-a-fan narratives are central to fan studies – fans' stories of encountering media texts that resonate with them in such deeply personal ways that a fundamental transformation of the self occurs' (Harrington and Bielby 2010b, 437). Mediated texts may become a source of comfort and pleasure for fans, working alongside their memories of their own histories and past selves. There are numerous examples of this but two will suffice here. The first is Lyn Thomas's work on fans of the radio series *The Archers* and the importance of the show for memory and a connection to the past, allowing it to function as 'a kind of marker in a life history and prevising a sense of continuity'

(Thomas 2009, 52). For many adults who listened to the show at home with families and loved ones, there is an intimate connection to *The Archers* and 'the familiar voices … and theme tune have a comforting effect' (Thomas 2009, 52). These radio listeners are not deluded and have not confused their own real childhoods or homes with that of the series; rather their 'imaginative work allows the real inhabited spaces and the images generated by broadcast sound to merge, flow into each other and overlap … the programme has 'seeped' into the respondent's memory of home' (Thomas 2009, 52). Second, Nick Stevenson's work on lifelong male fans of musician David Bowie found that 'an interest in Bowie helped them to construct a sense of themselves across time … many of the men suggested that they turned to Bowie in times of trouble and personal uncertainty' (2009, 85). Many of these fans returned to Bowie's music over time, sometimes with lessened interest in the artist but always certain of the ability to draw on him as a symbolic resource when needed (2009, 85–6).

Fan self-narratives may also change over time and be reshaped and reworked as fandoms change, or across the 'life course' and due to developments related to life stage or age since, for example, 'changes in emotional investment may reflect crucial self-transformation over the life course as fans negotiate developmental challenges associated with middle and late adulthood' (Harrington et al. 2011, 577). In television fandom this is often demonstrated by fans who link themselves with characters and use programmes to make sense of their own experiences. Cornel Sandvoss argues that our chosen fan objects are 'intrinsically interwoven with our sense of self, with who we are, would like to be, and think we are' (2005, 96). However, while 'objects of fandom … gain the ability to profoundly shape the fan' (Sandvoss 2005, 112), this appears to suggest that fandom may lead fans to accept and adjust to 'changing external textual characteristics of their object of fandom, even when they are understood to be in opposition to the fan's world view and self-image' (2005, 112). Thus, fans may adapt to changes in texts even if they appear to contradict their own ideological views of issues such as gender, nationality and so on. It is clear that television shows can become indelibly interwoven with fans' lives and histories, carrying deep meaning for them which transcends identification with characters. Fans often use their fan objects to understand their own life trajectories by 'bring[ing] the drama into their own lives, making sense of the story in terms of the norms by which they make sense of their own experiences' (Baym 2000, 71). Such notions of 'lifelong' (Stevenson 2009) or 'enduring' (Kuhn 2002) fandom allow examination of the ways in which 'media fans' life narratives might thus be said to comprise complex interactions between our "real" life (our biography), our autobiography (our storying of our life), and the media texts which help construct, give meaning to and guide the relationship between the two' (Harrington and Bielby 2010b, 444).

Ontological security and television viewers

As noted, 'pure relationships' continue for as long as they provide two necessary rewards: the reflection of a desirable self-narrative and ontological security. The two are closely intertwined since 'self-identity is one dimension of ontological security, and for Giddens this is narratively based' (Hills 2012a, 113). Giddens argues that ontological security offers an 'emotional inoculation against existential anxieties – a protection against future threats and dangers which allows the individual to sustain hope and courage in the face of whatever debilitating circumstances she or he might later confront' (1991, 40). Ontological security is a key reward gained from pure relationships and is closely linked to the basic trust established in early childhood. Ontological security presupposes a 'shared – but unproven and unprovable – framework of reality' (Giddens 1991, 36), and when events such as the 9/11 terrorist attacks suggest that this 'framework of reality' is not universal, our ontological security is undermined (Zaretsky 2002, 101). Simply put, ontological security 'means the psychical attainment of basic trust in self-continuity and environmental continuity' (Hills 2012a, 113). Giddens' work on ontological security draws on the concept of Winnicott's transitional object, as discussed above, since he argues that transitional objects establish ontological security and 'are both defenses against anxiety and simultaneously links with an emerging experience of a stabilized world of objects and persons' (Giddens 1991, 39). These links between the transitional realm and ontological security enable consideration of the ways in which fandom allows fans to 'understand the fluctuating and contradictory experience of daily life and to make connections with other people around them' (Cavicchi 1998, 185).

The concept of ontological security has been drawn on to understand the media, in particular television (see Silverstone 1994). This is linked to Giddens' assertion that 'the routinisation of day-to-day life ... is the single most important source of ontological security' (Giddens 1981, 37). Thus, 'routine – the placing of the world in time–space sequences of practical consciousness' – can ward off ontological insecurity and anxiety (Tulloch 1990, 280) and this predictability may come, in part, from the media. For example, Roger Silverstone notes that 'routines and rituals of television "disturb but also regulate everyday life" and thus manage crises and insecurities. Ontological security is sustained through the familiar and the predictable. Our common sense attitudes and beliefs express and sustain our practical understandings of the world, without which life would quickly become intolerable' (1994, 19). Similarly, Moores notes that 'fixed [television] schedules, in which the same programme is put on at the same time of the day … mean that audiences can come to find the overall shape of output to be ordered and predictable' (2005, 20), while Georgiou argues that transnational television 'supports links between individuals' realization of the self through being part of the world and it has the ability to reproduce the familiar and ordinary at times of intense global risks' (2013, 312) for global or diasporic viewers. More specific to fan studies, Matt Hills's (2007a) work on DVD box sets and ontological security, his later study of spoilers and security (2012a) and Ross P. Garner's work on fans of *Doctor Who* and *Sarah Jane Adventures* actress Elisabeth Sladen have begun to draw on the concept to explore fan culture (2013).

This book argues that fandom of specific objects may provide individuals with a sense of ontological security that derives from the fan's devotion to his/her fan object and also from the resultant fan community. Ontological security may develop from the constancy of a fan object, for example television programmes that are screened regularly and that return with each new 'season' of television. As Subramanian notes, 'Saying goodbye to a television show is an odd feeling, particularly because you are saying goodbye to a habit, to a time slot, or, in recent years, to part of a "list" of DVR recordings' (2011). There is also a 'communal context of a significant proportion of fan consumption' (Sandvoss 2005, 100) and fan–fan relationships may provide security if they remain unchanging and constant (e.g. an online forum being permanently accessible). Even when fans have no explicit involvement in fandom, they may still visualize themselves as part of an 'imagined community', which they find reassuring. Such fan community often provides validation of a fan's established self-identity by virtue of the fact that others share their interests, reinforcing the 'appropriateness' of these choices. Furthermore, relationships may develop into friendships that transcend commonality of interest, offering emotional support and superseding the existence of the fan object itself (see Gatson and Zweerink 2004).

Self-identity, ontological security and threat

Threats to self-identity and ontological security are often deeply felt because a fan object's or community's sudden inability to provide ontological security impacts upon fans' established self-identities. Giddens argues that the second 'reward' gained from pure relationships is the provision of a 'facilitating social environment for the reflexive project of self' (1992, 139). Since people 'increasingly draw on mediated experience to inform and refashion the project of the self' (Thompson 1995, 233) fans may actively seek out the most appropriate objects to enable them to construct their identities. Fans can intertwine aspects of their fan objects with themselves, 'bring[ing] the drama into their own lives, making sense of the story in terms of the norms by which they make sense of their own experiences' (Baym 2000, 71). Blurring the lines between narrative and 'real-life' events and drawing upon personal expertise to inform fan discussion is common (McKinley 1997, 115). However, fans also often demarcate their identity against non-fans or what Jonathan Gray calls 'anti-fans' (2003; 2005), establishing fan hierarchies since 'incorporating the identities of viewer and fan into one's self-concept distinguishes the self from nonviewers and nonfans in meaningful ways' (Harrington and Bielby 1995, 97). However, identity work is not a simple process of 'reflecting' back an imagined identity but is 'negotiated through linked processes of self-exploration and the development of intimacy with the other' (Giddens 1991, 97). Self-identity is never stable and can be undermined as self-narratives have 'continually to be reworked, and life-style practices brought in line with [them], if the individual is to combine personal autonomy with a sense of ontological security' (Giddens 1992, 75). Fandom may also impact significantly upon an individual's sense of self-identity, causing them to confront hitherto unchallenged opinions or actively make changes to their life, such as changing career.

However, individuals may experience threats to their ontological security through the demise of, or loss of interest in, a fan object or through the failure of fan community (for example, if a favourite message board shuts down). Thus, a fan pure relationship may only be sustained while it offers ontological security and a sense of trust in the other party. For example, if a favourite character is killed off in circumstances that the fan finds implausible or unwelcome, trust in the text can be destabilized and the fan's self-narrative must be reworked in order to cope with this disruption. The development of ontological security is crucial in the advancement of self-identity, offering 'protection against future threats and dangers which allows the individual to sustain hope and courage in the face of whatever debilitating circumstances she or he might later confront' (Giddens 1991, 40). However, pure relationships often end, resulting in 'loveshock' which refers to the emotional trauma of falling out of love. This leads to a period of mourning and 'of letting go of habits which otherwise translate themselves into affective habits in the present' (Giddens 1992, 103). Thus, for both the rejector and the rejected party, the feelings of loss and mourning need to be negotiated as 'loveshock has a "psychological traveling time", which may take a period of many months to work through' (Giddens 1992, 103). Accordingly, when one is engaged in a fan pure relationship with an object that ends (e.g. the cancellation of a show or the break-up of a band), the fan is always cast in the role of the rejected party. Although the fan object clearly does not make the explicit choice to reject the fan (as it is a text or a distant figure), the fan *does* fall into the position of the person who is abandoned by the object and must necessarily cope with any associated feelings. When fans' relationships with objects end they may suffer loveshock and need to cope with this period of mourning before refashioning their self-identity to deal with this rupture. If a fan pure relationship offers ontological security as one of its rewards, how do fans cope with the loss of a fan object that may provide such a sense of security? For although fans may gain comfort from the routine of their fandom, ontological security is not solely dependent upon such repetitions and expectations. Rather than providing the 'emotional inoculation' that Giddens imagines (1990, 94), ontological security can never fully protect against the possibility of disruption to one's sense of self (Giddens 1991, 40; 1992, 40). However, it does enable individuals to cope with change and the basic ontological security gained in early childhood should allow fans' emotional pain at the end of programmes to be 're-internalised as bearable, manageable feelings' (Craib 1997, 357).

However, despite ontological security enabling fans to cope with the end of shows (or other unwanted developments), loveshock takes time to experience and an individual's self-narrative needs 'continually to be reworked, and lifestyle practices brought in line with it, if the individual is to combine personal autonomy with a sense of ontological security' (Giddens 1992, 75). Maintenance of ontological security depends upon constant renegotiation of identity and self-narrative and fans must undertake this when their fan objects become 'dormant'. Indeed, self-identity is found 'in the capacity to keep a particular narrative going … The individual's biography … must continually integrate events which occur

in the external world, and sort them into the ongoing "story" about the self'
(Giddens 1992, 54). Furthermore, when one suffers loveshock as a result of the
ending of a pure relationship, there must be a 'cognitive and emotional coming
to terms with the psychological past, and a rewriting of the narrative of the self'
(Giddens 1992, 103). It is essential for individuals to deal with the loss of the
beloved object (whether a person, a text, etc.) and to incorporate this demise
into their self-narratives in order to avoid damaging 'repetition[s] of similar
patterns of behaviour' (Giddens 1992, 103).

Thus, although fans may gain comfort from the routine of their fandom
(for example, anticipating the regular scheduling of drama shows such as *Lost*,
Firefly or *The West Wing*), ontological security is not solely dependent upon
such repetitions. It cannot provide 'an emotional inoculation which protects
against ... ontological anxieties' (Giddens 1990, 94) but rather ensures that
one can deal with the unexpected and adjust to changes in routine. Giddens
himself notes that 'a sense of self-identity is often securely enough held to
weather major tensions or transitions in the social environments' (1992, 55)
and he does acknowledge that the 'protective cocoon' or 'protective barrier
[ontological security] offers may be pierced, temporarily or more permanently'
(Giddens 1992, 40). Thus, ontological security can never fully protect against
disruption to one's sense of self and traumatic events such as bereavement
(Mellor and Shilling 1993, 413) may interrupt an established self-narrative,
causing self-identity to be renegotiated from, for example, a wife to a widow.
However, ontological security equips us to deal with such happenings without a
potential breakdown of our sense of self. Most people do not entirely lose their
sense of self-identity when faced with a disruptive life event and are able to deal
with what has happened and accept it into the ongoing narrative of the self.
However, how are events related to fandom negotiated and accepted by fans?
While life events such as bereavement or divorce have been theorized, how have
fan-related transitions and endings been discussed?

Transitions and endings in fandom

This section offers an overview of prior approaches to transitions and endings
within fandom, considering how this necessitates a period of adjustment and
re-narration of the self. It argues that we view television shows that have ended

(and other fan objects such as bands that have split up) as 'dormant fan objects' and define fandom that continues after the cessation of the fan object itself as 'post-object fandom'. However, while some may continue to self-identify as fans of those objects, persisting in watching DVDs and talking about their fan objects in online forums, not all fandoms continue once programmes end production or bands split up. For example, in the absence of live gigs to attend or a lack of new material to enjoy, a fan of a rock group may still occasionally listen to CDs or wear a T-shirt but consider themselves to have a lessened investment in this group. Those who react to the cessation of fan objects in this way devolve their once powerful passions into 'peripheral fandoms' which have had an impact upon the formation of a fan's self-identity but which, owing to their dormant status, can no longer provide an avenue for ongoing or transformative identity work or ontological security.

A fan object's movement from active to dormant may necessitate a period of identity transition for the fan, as 'the altered self has to be explored and constructed as part of a reflexive process of connecting personal and social change' (Giddens 1991, 33). Transitions 'have always demanded psychic reorganization' (Giddens 1991, 32), which was commonly seen in *rites of passage* in which events such as birth, marriage and death were marked by special acts or rituals (van Gennep 1960, 3). However, such rites of passage may 'also concern entry into a new achieved status, [such as] … membership of an exclusive club or society' (Turner 1967, 95). Such ideas have been taken up to examine the media by writers such as Will Brooker (2007), Nick Couldry (2000a; 2002) and Matt Hills (2002), while Armstrong and Hognestad (2003) explored football and Mark Jancovich (2000) examined horror fandom as offering 'rites of passage' where identity can be negotiated. Similarly, Garry Crawford (2003) draws on the work of van Gennep (1960) and Glaser and Strauss (1971) to use the concept of 'status passage', which is defined as 'the passage of an individual through various stages in a life course (such as shifting from being unmarried to married' (2003, 224). Crawford uses this to argue for a model of fandom that accounts for varying levels of fandom over time and moves away from rigid categorization of fan 'types' (2003, 225). However, this model fails to account for what may happen when a fan object ceases to provide any new episodes, albums or sports matches.

Tania Zittoun has also examined how young people deal with 'transitions in the life course – periods that follow ruptures, and during which people define new identities, new skills, and confer meanings to their trajectory and their world' (2006, xviii). She argues that they utilize 'movies, books, songs and so forth to help them work through transitions and thus organize psychological development' (2006, xviii), referring to these as 'symbolic resources'. Young people use these resources to negotiate ruptures in their lives such as leaving home or the death of family members. Zittoun's work is persuasive and can account for why fans draw on chosen objects to help them through times of personal crisis. However, it cannot explain how individuals respond when their fan objects change from being active to dormant. If it is the cessation of an object *itself* that causes a rupture and necessitates a period of transition, this object's use as a symbolic resource is inevitably reduced. When faced with a television series' cessation, fans will inevitably react in different ways in order to negotiate the rupture and change in self-identity caused by the cancellation of the show. Thus, Whiteman and Metivier have cautioned that 'official endings, such as final broadcast date, are also significant to fandom, but may not be experienced by all communities in the same way' (2013, 292), and that 'the "post-ness" we attach to particular objects defines endings in terms that are important to us as researchers and to others within the same field' (2013, 292). It is crucial, therefore, to listen to fans themselves to understand the range of modes of defining and dealing with endings. In the discussions that follow, a range of fan responses to the ending of television shows will be explored, as will different types of ending beyond cancellation.

Television finales, endings and fandom

Fans may respond quite differently when faced with the ending of a fan object that they know is coming to a close, such as *Lost*, rather than when they are surprised by the sudden cancellation of a show that is pulled from the air without foreknowledge (e.g. Joss Whedon's sci-fi/Western *Firefly*). Jason Mittell has usefully defined a range of different televisual endings from the stoppage through to the finale, as well as discussing resurrections. For Mittell, stoppages are 'an abrupt, unplanned end to a series when the network pulls the plug midseason (usually in its first season)' (2013, paragraph 3), which usually driven by an economic rationale concerning low ratings (e.g. *Firefly*). In contrast, 'the wrap-up, a series ending that is neither fully arbitrary nor completely planned. Typically, this is at the end of a season, where producers have come to a natural stopping point but without planned series finality' (2013, paragraph 4), while 'the conclusion, [is] where a program's producers are able to craft a final episode knowing that it will be the end' (2013, paragraph 5). Examples of the conclusion include *Angel* and *Twin Peaks*, where the shows' endings were known only a short time in advance, allowing some conclusions to be made but without the opportunity to fully end the series as it would ideally have been concluded. For Mittell, a finale is relatively rare since this is often more related to the 'surrounding discourse and hype than any inherent properties of the narrative itself, with conclusions that are widely anticipated and framed as endings to a beloved (or at least high-rated) series' (2013, paragraph 8). This would include shows such as *Lost, Breaking Bad* or *The Sopranos*, where 'finales are not thrust upon creators, but emerge out of the planning process of crafting an on-going serial, and thus the resulting discourses center around authorial presence and the challenges of successfully ending a series' (2013, paragraph 8).

The different ways in which television shows end necessarily impact upon how fan audiences respond to them. What may be forgiven in a final episode that was unplanned or forced upon the creators may not be tolerated when fans are aware of a longer term plan for the closure of a narrative. As Mittell notes, 'Such discursive prominence of finales raises the narrative stakes of anticipation and expectation for viewers, and thus frequently produce disappointment and backlash when they inevitably fail to please everyone' (2013, paragraph 8). Thus, 'a good serial death requires creative foresight, "knowing when to fold 'em" and industry support for doing so, careful planning, and a Conclusion or Finale that is internally coherent, satisfies fans and stands the test of time' (Harrington 2013, 586). The remainder of this chapter explores what some fans consider to be a 'good serial death', discussing their expectations for what a television series *should do* when it draws to a close. Drawing on online postings and online survey data, it questions whether the notion of a 'good ending' is dependent on expectations and norms from within specific fan communities, or on individuals themselves. It considers also whether examples where such fan-created criteria are met have a stronger post-object fandom that has endured beyond the final episodes. In pondering these questions and others, and in exploring the specificities of different online fan spaces, consideration of different types of ending and how they are experienced in various ways is possible in the chapters that follow.

The majority of the shows discussed in this volume are American and, as such, are designed to run for, on average, thirteen episodes per season for cable shows and around twenty-two episodes per season for network drama. In contrast, the majority of television programmes produced in the UK context have much shorter runs of episodes and it is not uncommon for programmes to have as few as three episodes per series (e.g. *Sherlock, Wallander* and the first two series of *Whitechapel*) and a maximum of thirteen (*Doctor Who* and *Torchwood* are relatively unusual in this regard). Thus, in addition to considering how the different ways in which shows end (i.e. the difference between a planned finale and an abrupt cancellation) it is necessary to examine the variations in how fans may respond to the cessation of programmes that have shorter or longer runs of episodes. The next section explores how some fans discuss this, paying particular attention to how they articulate their reactions and their responses to endings. As noted in Chapter 4, television finales are often heavily promoted by the television industry and fans are acutely aware of the prospect of a series drawing to a close. Here, then, I examine fan discussions of endings more broadly, considering how this might help these fans to respond with renegotiation due to their wider acceptance of endings as an aspect of television culture.

Many fans surveyed or who posted on online message boards operated forms of distinction based on hierarchies of 'good' and 'bad' endings. For example, in a post on the Television Without Pity forum for *Lost*, one poster notes, 'I guess that's as good as it could be, considering the web of complexity Darlton [a fan nickname for producers Damon Lindelof and Carlton Cuse] and Co., spun the last six years … To me, this was closer to *SIX FEET UNDER* than *ST. ELSEWHERE* in the mindfuck territory' (Post #154, 'The End'). The impossibility of the task that *Lost*'s creators faced in terms of drawing together their complicated narrative aside, the fan refers to the potential for 'mindfucking' the audience with a final episode and offering inexplicable or disappointing finales. Here, however, other series are drawn on to qualify the success of *Lost*'s ending; while not perfect, it is seen as preferable to the ending of *St. Elsewhere* (which strongly implies that the series' events had taken place in the imagination of autistic character Tommy Westphall) and similar to *Six Feet Under*'s finale which showed flashforwards to the deaths of all the major characters in its last few scenes. More broadly, in the course of discussing Matt Smith's departure from *Doctor Who*, fans of the show on the *Doctor Who* Forum debated their wider views on the endings of television series. As with the debates about UK and US TV contexts that emerged in relation to Smith's exit, here the comparison between the two television systems was drawn on. In a thread entitled 'Matt

Smith and practical reasons for leaving' fans note their enjoyment of endings and the importance of knowing when a series will end:

> Yep. I like shows with defined endings. Massive fan of British tv, because of that, and also miniseries. It's a big reason I loved *Babylon 5*, and one reason I enjoy shows like *Breaking Bad* and *Mad Men*, because they have a rough, if not outright, idea of when they will end. If you want to talk about milking, I can think of several shows, starting with *ER* and *NYPD Blue*, which went on about 8 or 9 years longer than they should have. Then there are shows like *The Wire*, which could have gone on forever and yet finishing after 60 episodes seemed absolutely correct. I think *Who* is unique in how adaptable it is. I embrace the changes that are sure to come every few years. (Post #53, 3 June 2013)

> Thank you! I always have such a hard time explaining this to, for instance, fans of the American *Office*. American networks are looking for a sustainable formula to keep us tuning in, and happily do so at the expense of story, and will happily run a show into the ground at which it ceases to be a cash cow. *Seinfeld* was smart to end when he did, and probably should have ended a season or two sooner. Of course, I say this as a fan of a 50-year-old drama speaking to a fan of the same. ;) (Post #55, 3 June 2013)

Here there is a clear sense that endings are to be desired and that, for this poster at least, they offer a form of pleasure in the narrative since the end point is assured. This echoes the views of *Lost*'s creators and their declaration that an ending would be satisfying for audiences; Executive Producers Carlton Cuse and Damon Lindelof 'promised that *Lost* would have closure. Yet, as Cuse warned, "you have to watch because you're enjoying the journey, not because you are waiting for the endgame"' (cited in Morreale 2010, 184). However, it also shares overlaps with Matt Hills's work on television box sets and ontological security. Hills argues that the knowledge of a finite end point for a television series can offer a sense of ontological security for viewers since they are reassured that the programme won't be suddenly cancelled or taken away from them. He notes:

> Contra downloads, which viewers may watch while a show is actively in production, DVD releases tend to offer a 'completeness' which makes them worth of fan attention per se (Dobson 2006): viewers can begin watching a series knowing that they will be able to follow it through to its conclusion (or perhaps knowing in advance that it will end at a particular point), rather than being subjected to the disruption of a broadcast show's sudden cancellation.

DVD, in a sense, therefore offers a more 'trustable' or 'ontologically secure' re-versioning of broadcast TV. (Hills 2007a, 57–8)

The importance of DVDs will be discussed more specifically in Chapter 7, but these ideas can be used to understand the desires of these posters on the *Doctor Who* fan board for closure and clear points of ending. As DVDs can offer a sense of 'trust' for viewers, so too can the promise of an ending; ontological security can be maintained by the knowledge that a series will continue until a certain point and that its conclusion will be planned and satisfactory for the fan. A television series that overstays its welcome, however, poses the danger of falling out of favour with the fan and thus threatens their sense of self-narrative and their fan identities. There are other distinctions at work here – the UK/US distinction is clear but this is also mapped onto other binaries. The American system is perceived by these two posters as being more focused on economics than quality – turning shows into 'cash cows' that can be 'milked' for money for as long as possible.

Another poster in the *Doctor Who* 'Matt Smith and practical reasons for leaving' thread makes judgements about American television shows being unable to deliver good endings, a point that is quickly countered by a fellow fan:

> The reason most American shows don't last is because you guys are right, they over pay and bribe. But they also under deliver. I mean I can't remember the last show in america where I sat there with my jaw open for a couple minutes trying to absorb the ending … The season ender of *Who* has done that to me successively every year. (Post #132, 7 June 2013)

> I guess you don't watch *Game of Thrones*. I can't remember anything that made my jaw drop more than last week's episode! :eek: (Post #135, 8 June 2013)

Fans are thus clearly aware of the variation in endings. These posters, for example, discuss issues of national difference and commerce and art, as well as operating clear criteria for what 'good' and 'bad' endings are. Shows that are perceived to overstay their televisual welcome (such as *ER* and *NYPD Blue*) are seen to have decreased in quality, while others (such as *Mad Men* and *Breaking Bad*) offer a more bounded and discrete sense of their own narrative and their end point. In addition, a programme's ability to 'end' well (albeit temporarily at the end of an episode or series) is also valued; both *Doctor Who* and *Game of Thrones* here are deemed to cause jaws 'to drop' and to surprise their viewers. These fans are acutely aware of the range of endings that fan objects are subject to, indicating that 'ruptures/endings [are] on-going, constant and generative of subjectivity' (Whiteman and Metivier 2013, 294). This is further indicated by the following poster, who notes the importance of both endings and beginnings to television producers:

> *Doctor Who* is one of the only shows that not only thrives on the main cast change, it wants it. The producers of this show love beginnings and endings. The starts of every season are events as are the ends and the Christmas specials. They usually get the highest ratings. That is why we are getting a split season every year now – there are two starts and two endings. This is all good for the producers because now the next two Matt Smith stories are going to be huge events and the 8th season is also going to be a brand new start. (Post #139, 9 June 2013)

Again, this post demonstrates loyal viewers' awareness of the almost constant renegotiation of the fan object that must be undertaken in order to respond to changes and endings.

Fans who responded to my survey demonstrated clear ideas about what they felt that the ending of a show should provide. Overwhelmingly, the sense that it should be 'true to the series' was expressed, with fifty-six of the sixty-six respondents indicating that this was important. Similarly key was the ability of a show's finale to 'provoke an emotional response', which forty-nine respondents indicated was an important trait. These criteria suggest the importance of fidelity to the narrative and characters in a final episode but the focus on being 'true' to a show indicates also an element of respect paid to the mood and 'essence' of what a series has been about. Second, the focus on the importance of an emotional response indicates that fans expect to be moved when television shows draw to a close, although this emotional response could also be negative and include feelings of disappointment or even anger. Closely related to these responses is the importance of being given the 'opportunity to say goodbye to the characters' and 'offering closure to the narrative' (with forty-one respondents indicating that both of these were important). The high levels of importance given to closure and the chance to 'say goodbye' are, of course, linked to the other important aspects such as the provocation of an emotional response and being 'true' to a series. These four aspects of a show appear to work in conjunction; while what being 'true' to a series means is unclear for these respondents, the emphasis placed on closure and a sense of finality regarding the characters indicates that narrative resolution is part of this. A series that fails to wrap up its core narrative enigmas or fails to present an appropriate chance to bid farewell to characters appears to violate the core 'meaning' of what a show stands for. This is highlighted in Corrigan and Corrigan's discussion of reactions to the end of the comedy series *Seinfeld*:

> The *Seinfeld* finale suggests that television programming, while offering the never-ending flow of televisual delights, is an open process, incapable of providing closure, unlike the beloved finale of *M*A*S*H*, 'Goodbye, Farewell and Amen,' that draws the characters' stories to a tear-jerking close as, one by one, they take their leave of South Korea to return to their homes. In 'The Finale,' there is no such finality; the characters are simply transposed from Manhattan into a new arena of amusement (in this case, jail)—and *Seinfeld*'s mass audience had to adjust its expectations and allegiances to newer productions and products, largely designed not to satisfy a thirst for content but to perpetuate this desire endlessly. (Corrigan and Corrigan 2012, 96)

Fans in the survey also indicated the importance of the lasting legacy of a series, with forty-three respondents indicating they felt that a good finale should 'be remembered in the future'. As Harrington points out, 'Serial endings today are ideally anticipated in advance and written to be celebrated and remembered in textual death. Model endings are those that live on in the public (and industry) imagination' (2013, 584). Many series finales fall into this category and some, such as *Lost* and *Twin Peaks*, will be discussed in future chapters. These and other final episodes have already become almost canonical in discussion of series finales. Corrigan and Corrigan, for example, analyse the often-discussed final scenes of *The Sopranos* and its subversion of viewer expectation:

> Right at the moment that the words of the final chorus [of Journey's song 'Don't Stop Believing'], 'don't stop,' blast out, the shot cuts suddenly to black. The 'never-ending' televisual flow, which 'goes on and on and on and on' has been disrupted, the viewers' expectations not simply thwarted, but attacked, even ridiculed as part of a consumer mentality that requires sustenance. Here, the 'don't stop' refrain ironically leads to total blackout; some viewers even initially thought that their television sets were broken. (Corrigan and Corrigan 2012, 100)

The final episode of *The Sopranos* is just one instance of a finale that is already being 'remembered' as an important piece of television. Ongoing analysis of the finale of *Lost* (which is still being defended by the creators ten years after the show's debut (Harris 2014)) and the 2013 conclusion of *Breaking Bad* suggests that these too will be considered key examples of series finales in years to come. Thus, there is much to suggest that 'a good serial death … [is one that] stands the test of time' (Harrington 2013, 586)

The fans surveyed also indicated that series finales should be aimed more towards a loyal audience, rather than the casual viewer. Although only seven of the sixty-six respondents indicated directly that it was important that a final episode 'appealed to fans more than casual viewers', thirty-nine out of sixty-six respondents agreed that it should 'reward the viewer'. Furthermore, very few (six out of sixty-six) indicated that a good finale must 'appeal to a wide audience'. Such results indicate the common sentiment that fans deserve to be rewarded for their devotion and that a finale should privilege the needs of long-term viewers over the less dedicated audience. This can be seen in Chapter 4's discussion of the finale of *The West Wing*, where fans discuss elements of the final episode as appearing to be 'gifts' to fans by referencing earlier storylines and relationships, as well as offering the chance to say goodbye to their favourite characters. The tension between satisfying fans and/or the wider audience has also been discussed by academics: for example C. Lee Harrington notes that 'a good [textual] death is one that satisfies the fan community and this serves as a final gift from the writers/creators' (2013, 590), while Joanne Morreale concludes that *Lost*'s final episode was a success since it 'managed to resolve its narrative dilemma in a way that could satisfy mass and cult audiences' (2010, 184). Such fan service may be possible in cult series with smaller audiences, but the comments of fans who responded to my survey belie the broader economic imperatives for successful series finales. However, in the case of a widely viewed series fan demands must be balanced with resolution for the more casual audience. For instance, Deborah Jermyn discusses the fanfare that accompanied the final episode of *Sex and the City*:

> … [the finale] was met on both sides of the Atlantic with the kind of widespread public and media attention that had come to characterize its run over the previous six years. Public screenings of the final episode, evidence of an "event television" status usually reserved in the United Kingdom for royal weddings and World Cup games, were held in venues such as The Grand nightclub in South West London. (2009, 91)

However, once the wider viewer is drawn to the heavily promoted series finale (see Todd 2011 on *Friends*) and their audienceship (and viewing share) is assured, the producers and writers are still creatively free to present whatever ending they see fit, whether it satisfies fans, casual viewers or, in some cases, nobody at all.

Fan respondents also indicated a, perhaps unsurprising, preference for well-planned endings; over half of the survey responses suggested that this was a key characteristic of a good finale. Again, this connects with wider academic debate over endings where a well-planned and thought-out finale is considered to offer a greater chance of satisfactory resolution. This would appear to be more likely for programmes such as *Lost*, *Breaking Bad* or *Mad Men*, whose endings were known in advance and planned for. However, some series with more sudden endings – such as Mittell's 'stoppages' where 'an abrupt, unplanned end to a series' occurs after a 'network pulls the plug midseason' (2013, paragraph 3) – have managed to offer episodes that, while not anticipated to be the last time the series aired, are well received by fans and considered to be somewhat fitting final glimpses of a show. The most famous example is the hastily rewritten final episode of *Twin Peaks*' second season, which suddenly became the finale to the series as a whole. Despite the relatively well-known story of how director David Lynch rewrote the final episode – offering an 'emergency transfusion' to the script (Nochimson 1997, 94) and offering a 're-establishment of the centrality of the mind–body connection' that had been so central to the series (Nochimson 1995, 156) – the episode has become a testament to the overall success of the series, seeming to encapsulate its strangeness, its frustrations and its ultimate lack of closure. While not the ultimate intended end point for the show, the final episode nonetheless offered a 'painful impact' (Nochimson 1995, 156) for viewers and has become one of the most widely discussed and analysed finales in television. Thus, while fans indicate a preference for endings that are planned out and intended, endings that are contingent or, sometimes, not intended to be endings at all can still offer pleasures of analysis and discussion, and prompt affective and emotional responses.

Other aspects of what constitutes a successful finale were less coherent across the respondents. Few were concerned with whether or not a show had a 'happy' ending (ten out of sixty-six), while only twenty-three suggested that a 'realistic' ending was important. This, along with the preference for premeditated and designed endings, suggests that finales that respect the history of the programme and appear to 'do it justice' are more important than offering neat or contented resolutions for characters. The lack of interest in a 'happy' ending indicates a broad inclination towards narrative resolutions that fit with a programme's style and mood, even if this results in onscreen events that could be considered to be 'sad' or 'negative'. Indeed, while some final episodes such as *Friends* or *The West Wing* do offer happy endings for the majority of characters and offer a sense of a 'throw-forward' about what their lives will be like, many other programmes do not. For example, both *Six Feet Under* and *Lost* depict the deaths, or afterlives, of most of the key characters, and shows such as *Angel* and *Buffy the Vampire Slayer* kill off at least one of the lead characters in their final instalments. Similarly, both the previously discussed *Twin Peaks* and *The Sopranos* offer instability and a lack of conclusion for the characters and neither could be categorized as shows with 'happy endings'. Fan preference here for 'authentic' endings that reflect the core values or ideas of a programme supersede their desires for characters to be represented as having a happy ending, suggesting a complex relationship and tension between fan attachment to characters and their broader connections to, and appreciation of, television series themselves. In terms of beginning to understand fan reactions to the endings of series, this suggests that finales that reinforce fans' views about the programme are valued, possibly because they work to highlight and reiterate what fans' enjoyed about the show in the first place. Again, Harrington discusses 'the necessity of coherence and closure for a good demise of both persons and texts', arguing that 'from a thanatological perspective a good death is understood most simply as the culmination of a good life: "People should die as they lived ... Why try to reshape a person's life at the last moment?" (Kastenbaum 2004, 131–5)' (Harrington 2013, 582). As with people, programmes that attempt to 'reshape' their meaning or their textual lives during their final moments can be seen as inconsistent and thus less able to provide the closure necessary for mourning and moving on. These fan responses are discussed in more depth in Chapter 4 but it appears from the survey responses that finales that remain 'true' to the programme are less likely to pose a threat to fans' sense of identity and to the sense of fan ontological security that they may derive from their fandom. A finale that suddenly works to contradict previously held ideas about a show can rupture fans' understandings and connection to a fan object, undermining their former knowledge and investment in a show. A classic example of this would be a story that concludes with the lead protagonist waking up and finding that it was all a dream. In the context of television series, this may explain the contested reactions to the end of the series *St. Elsewhere*, which is briefly discussed above and which suggested that the narrative events had taken place only in someone's imagination. This is an extreme and relatively unusual example. However, disappointment in series that appear to abandon their usual worldviews, or in other cases violate generic expectation, indicates the potential threat of such narrative manoeuvres. For example, the Showtime series *Dexter* portrayed a grey moral universe, offering a serial killer as the central 'hero' and protagonist and offering complex representations regarding crime, loyalty and murder, across its eight series. However, when the show aired its final episode in September 2013 it was critiqued in reviews for apparently lacking the confidence to either kill off or incarcerate its lead character, bemoaning the fact that 'Dexter survives eight seasons of hacking and stabbing, leaving a trail of blood and body parts, and yet we don't get to see him caught or killed' (Day-Preston 2013). Instead, Dexter was allowed to escape the consequences of his prior crimes, fake his own death and live under an assumed identity. Here, the lack of consistency with the programme's previously established worldview was seen to be evidence of a lack of courage in killing off or punishing the lead character. While one could counter that allowing Dexter to live without punishment for his murders is actually entirely in keeping with this moral ambivalence (see Green 2011), the finale was widely considered to have 'failed' to live up to expectation.

How much finality was deemed necessary was also complex – eighteen of the sixty-six respondents suggested that it was important a final episode should 'leave the audience wanting more', while one-third suggested that a good finale should 'offer the option for a series to return'. The return of programmes in a variety of forms is discussed in Chapter 8, but the apparent contradiction here between fans wanting an ending while the series is on a high (as *Breaking Bad* creator Vince Gilligan puts it, 'knowing when to fold 'em' (Gilligan, cited in Harrington 2013, 585)) and leaving the door open for possible returns suggests fan anxieties about the resolution of their favourite programmes. While wanting a final episode to be 'good' and to 'end on a high', the relatively high percentage of fans who desired the possibility of a series return suggests a possible nervousness about the finite ending of a programme. Indeed, 'A textual death that leaves open the possibility of an afterlife or re-boot can be "good" from a fan perspective insofar as that possibility is realized and well-handled' (Harrington 2013, 591). While, as this book discusses, texts can be returned to and revisited in a variety of ways after a show itself ceases to produce new episodes, the sense of total and absolute conclusion to a fan object's narrative universe can be a source of potential anxiety and threat to fans' sense of ontological security. In hedging one's bets a little, in desiring a more open narrative resolution that provides an opportunity for return rather than entirely killing off characters or destroying a programme world, such threats can be appeased. Even if a show ultimately does not return, whether on television or in another form of media, the potential for such resurrection at the point of a show's cessation appears to be important for some fans as they negotiate the move from fandom of an active to a dormant fan object. Alternatively, as will be discussed in Chapter 8, this potential for continuation and return may, rather than offering a sense of security and safety, offer its own potential threats and problems. Rather than being an appeasing and appealing proposition, the potential return of a fan object may cause anxiety for some fans who may fear the inferiority of the reappearance or reinvention of a beloved object of fandom and its potential 'corpse defilement' (Harrington 2013, 590–1).

The end of the fandom?

For many fans, engagement is shared with others and when exploring endings in fandom attention must also be paid to the consequences for fan–fan relation-ships or community when an object of fandom changes or ends. Whiteman and Metivier (2013) have analysed the endings or 'deaths' of online fan commu-nities, arguing that in the case of *Angel* forum City of *Angel*, fan responses were complex and intense. They outline how:

> This response to the end was intertwined with a concern to protect the memory of the site; a sense that the memories of what had passed should not be allowed to be corrupted (had the forums perhaps gone on for longer than was good for them?). In such posts we find the idea that the COA forums as they were — as they had been — no longer existed, that the golden age of the site was past, and that the end had already been experienced (even if it had not been formally marked by a closure, or by those in authority at the time). (2013, 282)

The closure of City of *Angel* discussed by Whiteman and Metivier occurred in 2012, eight years after *Angel*'s final episodes in 2004, indicating that fan communities can be maintained far beyond the original transmission of a television series. Similarly, Gatson and Zweerink work on the *Buffy the Vampire Slayer* board The Bronze found that, despite the end of *Buffy* and the closure of the forum, group members maintained a sense of community although this became necessarily more dispersed through new websites and blogs (2004, 237). Bertha Chin (2013) has also focused on the continuation of online fandom surrounding *The X-Files* in a post-series landscape, noting how:

A new type of website has become popular among certain groups of X-Philes in recent years, which highlights fan–producer collaborations. Sites like 'XFilesNews.com' ('X Files News'] offer exclusive and original interviews with the cast and crew as those involved with the show move on to new projects. The site also acts as a grassroots promotional vehicle for them as fans are kept updated with the latest news, including the ongoing campaign for a third *X-Files* film, which the producers support. (Chin 2013, 88)

Survey results collected from fans during the summer of 2013 indicated a similarly strong sense of continuation since, for those who responded, the lack of new episodes of a favourite series had not ended their fandom. While their engagement had clearly changed, 38 per cent of those surveyed indicated that their fandom had increased since the ending of the show, with 36 per cent stating that it had stayed the same. Only 18.18 per cent of respondents declared that their fandom had decreased, suggesting that post-object fandom must be understood as a period of change and transition rather than as a state that indicates the total ending of attachments to objects or fellow fans. Respondents indicated a range of ways in which their fandom had continued, with the majority of these being centred around rewatching and engaging with the series. For example, fifty-three of the sixty-six fans re-watched specific episodes, forty-seven of the fans also engaged in viewing of the entire series and forty-seven had purchased box sets of the series (this will be discussed in more detail in Chapter 7). One respondent made the importance of continued engagement with the episodes explicit, noting 'I like the show. However, im more keen on reliving the show through watching it again than some of the more overt fan activites. As a whole im not too keen on fanfiction of TV shows – reading a story doesn't feel the same as watching it for me'. This fan indicates a preference for the 'original' text of the series over fan-created narratives, while another respondent articulates a broader enjoyment with the rhythms and patterns of re-watching favourite shows: '[I continue to rewatch] Because these are very well told stories worth telling. I also re-read novels I love, why wouldn't I do the same with TV series? At the same time, I like this kind of repetition'.

While the show itself was of key importance, continued engagement with fellow fans was important for many respondents, with 60 per cent continuing to discuss their fandom via social media sites such as Twitter, Facebook and Tumblr, and 27 per cent discussing online on message boards and fan forums. Off-line contact with other fans had remained important for many fans, 32 per cent of whom had attended events such as conventions or signings related to their fandom. Such findings offer further evidence to support the view that television fandom often continues in a range of ways beyond the final episodes of a series and that continued contact with other fans is important. As this book demonstrates, online fan spaces can offer places for remembrance and nostalgia as a series draws to a close, echoing Todd's description of how fans used message boards after the finale of *Friends* to 'reminisce and talk about buying DVDs as a way to preserve their "dear 'funny' memories" of the characters, who one fan proclaims "will always be in my heart for all time!" (*Friends* Fan)' (Todd 2011, 866). This was reflected in survey respondents who stated that they had continued to discuss favourite programmes with other fans long after the ending of new episodes of that show for a variety of reasons:

> If a show ran for a long time (like *House MD*), its because the show was such a part of my life for some long, and I learned to love those characters so much, they are a part of my life now, and I cant just give up on them and move on.

> Most obviously, I continue to engage in these practices because the shows were important to me and watching and discussing them has a sense of nostalgia and is enjoyable.

> I continue these fan practices because just because a show has ceased airing new episodes does not mean that the impact it had on people is forever lost.

While these fan responses share commonalities in terms of the level of attachment fans have and the impact that programmes had on them, there are also differences in how such impact is articulated. For the first respondent, the intertwining of the show *House MD* and its characters with her own life is clearly stated; as a long-standing fandom that was a part of her life it is difficult for this fan to 'give up on them and move on' to something else. For the second fan there is a sense of nostalgia and remembrance involved in engaging in post-object fandom and re-watching and discussing the show, while the third fan makes explicit that the ending of a show's run of original episodes does not necessarily equate with the end of a fandom. Across these three responses, terms such as impact and importance, as well as the clear sense of attachment that these fans possess, suggest that the various fan objects have been important in maintaining a sense of fan identity and self-narrative. This sense of self cannot simply be replaced or 'lost' when the series ends, rather it can instead be reworked, renegotiated and maintained, albeit in a different form, in the post-object era of fandom. Such intertwining of self and fan object and relationship between 'our "real" life (our biography), our autobiography (our storying of our life), and the media texts which help construct, give meaning to and guide the relationship between the two' (Harrington and Bielby 2010b, 444) is further suggested in another fan response which states, 'I would like to not just keep the good memories of the show alive, but also the memories of myself during that period alive.' Here, memories of the fan object and the self are inextricable and ongoing fan engagement helps to maintain connection to both the fan object and to the 'self' who was the fan at that time. This response is complex, suggesting numerous versions of the self and a complex sense of the current fan self and the self during the ongoing period of fandom. Maintaining such links offers a way to preserve that sense of established self-identity, not just as a fan, but as the broader cultural self who was embodied across the period of fandom. Finally, one respondent points out that they continue with their fandom 'because I want to. I enjoyed [*Lost*] so just because its ended doesn't mean you forget about it. My nanna died years ago & we still have to talk about her and she wasn't as great as "LOST".' While their reference to the loss of their grandmother must be read as performative and, most likely, taken as humorous in intent, the comparison does suggest the overlap between the death of fan objects and other instances of bereavement. These fans reject the suggestion that fandom ends simply because a show is no longer in production, positing instead that ongoing re-watching, discussion and analysis offer important ways to sustain identity, self-narratives and ontological security, related to both their fandom and beyond.

For others, the face-to-face meetings engendered by fandom were a way to maintain the connection to a favourite show and to fellow fans. One respondent notes:

> For conventions, to be able to meet those involved in the series and to enjoy their point of view about the series as well as to find out about other work that they do. It is also more to meet other fans in person that you might only know on line and getting a chance to deepen friendships over time. I've been involved in fandom and on line message boards for over 20 years and it is through the love of the genre that I have met wonderful people over those years who are still great friends today, even though we are geographically separated.

Here, as in the comments above about ongoing online connections, it is the fan–fan relationships and encounters that form a crucial aspect of the ongoing post-object fandom. For fans who maintain close ties with fan communities after a series ends, such connection forms a useful avenue for adjusting to the loss of the fan object and re-narrating and re-evaluating fan identity in the post-object era. Connection to others allows remembrance and discussion of favourite episodes, characters and actors as well as facilitating links with other fandoms that may share commonalities. As discussed in Chapter 6, following actors or producers across different fan objects can allow a wealth of overlaps and an often complex web of fan attachments to be created and maintained. Here, however, connection with fellow fans both within and across fan objects and communities is a key way in which threats to fan identity and self-narrative or security can be negotiated and managed. The relationships established between fans enable not only discussions and a flow of information but also an 'affective flow … [which] mirrors the fan's attachment back to him or her, validating this affective experience itself' (Hills 2002, 181).

Finally, in addition to maintaining membership of fan communities, some survey respondents also continued their fandom by engaging with official and fan-created paratexts: 54 per cent had read official novels or comics related to a series and 44 per cent had read fanfiction based on a show. Purchasing of other memorabilia was also a key way for fans to continue their attachments: 31 per cent had bought items such as clothing or posters. Fewer fans had watched fan-created videos (41 per cent) or created these (4.55 per cent), while only 10 per cent had created fanworks such as fanart. This will be discussed in more depth in Chapter 8, but such statistics suggest that, for many fans, the cessation of new episodes of a series does not equate with a loss of fandom. For some, however, fandom clearly did not continue after the ending of a show: while 54 per cent of respondents had read official continuations, this means that 46 per cent (almost half) had not, while fewer than half had continued their involvement by reading fanfiction. Thus, while it cannot be assumed that fandom ends for everyone once the television credits roll for the final time, we must also be cautious that we do not underestimate the number of fans for whom this is, ultimately, the end of the road for their involvement and interest.

Conclusion

The endings of television series, and fan reactions to them, have begun to attract academic attention. The discussions of the textual attributes of final episodes for series such as *Seinfeld*, *Lost* and *The Sopranos* indicate an emerging aesthetics of finales, while work on the promotion of the event status of the *Friends* finale offers understanding of their value for television producers and networks. Furthermore, fan discussions of endings including hierarchies of what constitutes 'good' or 'bad' finales, the imagined audience for such final episodes and the range of practices fans engage in after these episodes air, offer compelling starting points for understanding the range and variety of endings that fans are faced with and must negotiate. Indeed, studying fandom reveals that 'different endings emerge as more or less important to different groups. For some, the end of a ship [onscreen romantic relationship] may be significant, for others the death of a character. This experience of loss is everyday and on-going' (Whiteman and Metivier 2013, 292).

The next chapter begins to examine this range of endings by focusing upon the departure of characters from television shows. It considers a departing actress in the fantasy series *Angel*, the real-life deaths of actors and the onscreen demise of their characters in *The West Wing* and *Glee*, and the more unusual case of *Doctor Who* when specific actors leave a role but are replaced because the central character of The Doctor endures. Considering these forms of character- and actor-based ending allows understanding of how fan ontological security and self-narrative are impacted by these changes and how fans discuss such developments in a range of ways.

3

Departures, Deaths and Replacements: When Characters Leave

This chapter begins to explore endings by considering fan responses when specific elements of beloved shows end. The most common example of this is the departure of a favourite character or, in some rarer cases, the replacement of one actor with another. Prior academic work has examined the impact of departing characters and the intention here is to build on such studies by examining this work through the ideas of ontological security and identity. Much work on television programmes has considered the importance of affective connections between fans, characters and the actors who play them (Bird 2003; Gwenllian-Jones 2003; Hills and Williams 2005), since the bond between viewers and characters is one of the main ways in which audiences become attached to specific shows. One need only look, for example, at the response when HBO series *Game of Thrones* aired an episode entitled 'Red Wedding', where several popular main characters were violently killed off, for evidence of the strong bonds viewers may have with characters and the often powerful reactions they demonstrate when those characters are taken away (Smithsonian 2013). However, given their awareness of production conditions, fans are acutely aware that characters may leave programmes, whether this is a result of production decisions to write them out or the actor's own choice to leave a series. There are clearly differences between genres; soap operas, for example, have longer narrative arcs and can run for several decades. The expectation here for viewers is that characters will inevitably depart the narrative even though this may cause some disruption to their viewing and need to be dealt with. In cult or drama series, however, the reduced number of episodes in such genres means that character departures are not always as expected as in long-running soaps and that the loss of specific points of identification may be more shocking or surprising.

Similarly, there are different ways in which characters can exit narratives and this, too, can influence how fans respond. This may depend upon whether the actor in question chose to leave or was sacked and written out against their will; fans may be more willing to accept the former and support the actor's choice. There are also differences regarding the narrative resolution to a character's storyline and whether the character is killed off or simply leaves the narrative (e.g. moving to another location within the narrative world). The latter allows some room for hope for a potential return of a beloved character, while being killed off usually suggests a total end to a character (although some characters have returned from the dead in soap operas such as *Dallas* or in cult/fantasy shows where the boundaries between life and death are often more permeable). Fan reactions are often especially pronounced with characters who are killed off within the narrative, as the fan campaigns and protests regarding the narrative death of Tara Maclay (Amber Benson) in *Buffy the Vampire Slayer* (Tabron 2004) or Ianto Jones (played by Gareth David-Lloyd) in *Torchwood* (Cubbison 2012) demonstrate. When necessitated by real-life deaths, characters can also be killed off within narratives in cases including *The West Wing* star John Spencer (as discussed below), *Dallas* star Larry Hagman and his iconic character J. R. Ewing or the *Glee* character Finn Hudson who died off-screen following the untimely death of Cory Monteith, the young actor who played him. Similarly, the real-life death of actress Elisabeth Sladen, who played the character of Sarah Jane Smith in *Doctor Who* and its child-friendly spin-off *The Sarah Jane Adventures*, led to a process of grieving and shock for its fans, both young and old (see Garner 2013). In these cases, fans are often left to deal with grief for both the character and the actor who portrayed him/her, adding another level of complexity to how audiences respond to departing characters.

This chapter explores such fan responses, examining how they discuss their emotional attachments and their sense of disruption when favourite figures leave television shows. First, it considers fan reactions to the departure of the character of Cordelia Chase in the fantasy series *Angel*. Her final departure occurred in a stand-alone episode entitled 'You're Welcome' after being previously written out of the show at the end of the prior season. Second, it examines fan reactions to one of the examples noted above in relation to *The West Wing* – the narrative and real-life death of Leo McGarry – and also outlines the case of *Glee* character Finn Hudson, following the death of actor Cory Monteith. In investigating how fans respond to the deaths of actors and characters, the chapter explores the intertwining of threats to fan ontological security via the occurrence of both textual and real-life deaths, considering how such events can cause ruptures in fans' sense of self-identity and trust. Finally, the chapter explores a more unusual example of when one actor leaves a show and is replaced by another – the British science-fiction series *Doctor Who*. This explores the reactions of fans after the departure of David Tennant from the title role in 2009 and his replacement by Matt Smith, as well as immediate responses to the news of Smith's exodus from the show which was announced in June 2013. In this unique case, both actors are playing the same character. All three of these examples draw on fan comments from message boards, forums or qualitative surveys. While social media has undoubtedly had a transformative impact upon fandom through sites such as Twitter, Facebook and Tumblr (see Bury et al. 2013), it was felt that such platforms fail to allow the space necessary for fans' detailed discussions of character and actor deaths. As Goh and Lee point out in their study of Twitter reactions to the death of pop star Michael Jackson, 'users viewed Twitter as more of a platform for disseminating (mis)information … rather than as one for grieving' (Goh and Lee 2011, 441). They argue that this is likely because 'unlike platforms such as social networking services, discussion forums and blogs, the restrictive character limit of tweets prevents elaboration of information being shared, which would be needed for the provision of assistance such as tangible aid and network support' (Lee and Goh 2013, 475). The chapter thus draws on material from surveys and 'threaded discussions where rich conversations over a particular topic may occur' (Goh and Lee 2011, 441) to explore how fans responded to character or actor deaths and actor replacements and how this led to shifts in ontological security, explorations of self-identity and value judgements.

'I just hope they do her justice': The contested departure of *Angel*'s Cordelia Chase

The character of Cordelia Chase (played by Charisma Carpenter) appeared in the series *Angel*, which ran on the WB network in the US between 5 October 1999 and 19 May 2004. Cordelia was written out of the show at the end of the fourth season after falling into a mystically-induced coma but returned for one final appearance in the show's one hundredth episode during the fifth and final series. This section examines the responses of twelve fans, gathered from surveys conducted in February 2004, which asked a range of questions both before and after the airing of the hundredth episode in order to gauge their views on the departure of the character. Although a small sample, the depth of information available from their detailed qualitative responses offers an interesting opportunity to explore fan reactions to a pre-ordained character departure (that is, one they 'knew was coming'), since Carpenter's return for the hundredth episode was widely publicized and known to be her final appearance.

Several of the fans who replied to the survey highlighted the importance of a 'fitting exit' and not violating the character or being unrealistic. For example, before the episode aired one fan noted, 'As far as Cordelia is concerned, I just hope they do her justice and don't give her a storyline that is strange and out of character. If they did that is would just negate the whole point of having her back' (Sarah). Similarly, after the show was screened, fans who enjoyed it as well as those who were more critical commented on the way that the character was represented:

> I thought they did a great job. They managed to capture her honesty and sharpness without making her too bitchy. Yet, I believe there wasn't enough follow up on season 4 events. As in Expecting and the Pylea arch, when bad things happen to Cordelia, they just don't/didn't deal with the consequences. (Elizabeth)

> The point of the 'Cordelia character' was watch a metamorphises ... watching the changes unfold, I would think any true Cordelia fan would be happy with the way her story ended. She died happy. She died safe in the knowledge that she had known love in whatever form it was. She died content to have known love. And she died believing that the work that she dedicated herslf to would go on. (Kelly)

For such fans, it is important that a character's departure befits their established character and is seen to 'do them justice'. Jenkins refers to this as the 'fannish ideal of "emotional realism"' since 'transgressions of "common sense" assumptions about social reality will be harshly criticized not simply as ideologically motivated but as violating the integrity of the represented world' (Jenkins 1992, 116). In the case of *Angel*, however, many fans felt that Cordelia's character was not well served by this episode, indicating fan displeasure with the mode of departure. Fan disappointment here was primarily linked to two main issues: first, the perception that the actress Charisma Carpenter had been badly treated by the show's creator Joss Whedon and the show's other producers and that this was the main cause of her being written out of the show, and second, conflicting feelings over the fact that the character had been killed off.

In terms of the first of these issues, many fans who identified chiefly as fans of Charisma Carpenter herself or who viewed the character as their main point of interest in the series were often vitriolic in their views about the character's return. When it was first announced, they commented:

> Tuff question, what do I expect from the hands of [*Angel* production company] ME [Mutant Enemy]? Honestly, I expect closure in such a way that ME/JW can put the whole debacle behind him, and I expect that the closure is going to piss me off royally. (Jean)

> I want it to have everything and do justice to both CC and the character she has played for over 7 years. I know Charisma will shine. She continuously takes what lame-ass script she has and shines so you don't care that there are plot holes, you're just glad that she's there to make it better. She takes the lemons and makes lemonade. When she left, the whole show was left thirsty. That's what effect she has on the show. She is the lifeblood. (Mrs O)

> Regarding the character, i'm afraid i'm sceptical … with all the press recently over Joss and Charisma's differences, I feel he may mangle and distort the character even more. But if he's got his business head on, he'll hopefully redeem her character and leave it open for her to return. That way he won't alienate all her fans. (Alex)

In terms of the fact that Cordelia was killed off, many fans anticipated this conclusion to her storyline, noting for example that 'I knew it was the end. When I saw she was coming back for one episode and the interviews that had Joss saying "We want to have closure" etc. It's the end for Cordelia and it makes me sad' (Mrs O) and:

> After I really thought about it I grew more and more apprehensive. I started to realize that this probably won't be good news. I mean, one little episode spells 'kiss-off' in TV land. I am really glad to see the character back, but I feel upset on her behalf because I am skittish of what will happen to her. This character has already been through so much hell and I hate thinking that something else is gonna happen. (Celestia)

However, after the 100th episode aired, fan respondents to the survey expressed less grief and sadness at the character's death than one might have expected. For many, this resulted from their broader dissatisfaction with the show and their expectation that such a limited one-episode return would make the character's death the easiest way to offer 'closure' to her storyline. One respondent noted that 'I feel like Cordelia should have gotten more than one measly episode. She definitely deserved an arc at the very least. I don't think one ep was enough to really provide closure to such a major character and they could have fleshed it out a lot more' (Celestia). Thus, respondents to this survey did not express the same levels of sadness that one might have expected to see at the loss of a favourite character. Rather, they articulated a sense of disappointment and anger that was directed at the way in which both the character and the actress who played her had been treated. Along with a sense of mourning here, fans also displayed 'frustration and antagonism' (Jenkins 1992, 23) with those responsible for writing Cordelia out of the series. Furthermore, several fans responded positively to how the character had been portrayed in the episode. One noted that they were 'pleased [with the episode]. Lots of folks were surprised they killed off Cordy, but frankly, I expected it to happen … [Charisma Carpenter] really doesn't need to be back on *Angel*, I thought it was fantastic' (Elizabeth), while another commented, 'Even though I knew she would die, I loved the episode. Like LOADS. It's now probably my favourite episode of *Angel* AND *Buffy*. I really loved it and I like the way they wrote her and how it did end. Even if she was dead' (Mrs O). Another fan, who in the first survey had expressed a concern that the character would be killed off, noted '[In the first survey] i said that Cordelia dying would be the worst case scenario, and while it is bad, they handled it well and let her be a hero, so i'm all right with it' (Alex). It may be that these fans' desire to see both Cordelia and the actress Charisma Carpenter back onscreen outweighed the potential devastation of her narrative death. Given the contested status of Carpenter's departure from *Angel*, for these fans, any return for the character appears to have been welcomed, especially since it was able to offer some form of closure. As one fan noted before the episode aired, 'Leaving her in a coma left us fans with many loose ends and questions. Hopefully they will bring her out of the coma and resolve some of those issues' (Sarah).

Another fan was more negative about the death, stating in response to a question about whether they were pleased with the episode, 'No – but for the ending. I understand that this is Whedonverse, which means no one has to stay dead, but I feel slapped in the face' (Jean). Again, Cordelia's death was not a surprise to many of these fans: 'I saw it coming a mile away. It obviously wasn't real, though I admit I thought it was a dream and didn't really put it together until about one minute before they said it. But I knew it had to be an illusion of some sort and that she'd be dead by the end of the hour' (Celestia). This may go some way to accounting for the lack of grief and sadness expressed by these fans since there was a broad expectation that narrative death was the only way to offer any form of closure in only one episode. In this case, ontological security was not as threatened as it might otherwise have been since fans had some time to prepare themselves for fact that Cordelia was likely to be killed off. In contrast to the surprise of unexpected character deaths such as in *Game of Thrones'* infamous 'Red Wedding' scene or the killing off of major characters in shows including *Breaking Bad, Boardwalk Empire* or *The Good Wife*, Cordelia's demise was anticipated and therefore presented less of a shock to fans who identified with the character. In his discussion of television spoilers Matt Hills argues that a 'fan's very identity could be called into question by unwanted developments or characters in their show, meaning that forthcoming episodes will be freighted with both desire and anxiety' (Hills 2012a, 115). In the case of Cordelia such anxiety has been, in part, warded off by fans' assumption that the character would be killed off, even if this had not been overtly confirmed via spoilers.

However, in addition to this, many of the fans who responded to the survey drew on their broader issues with the series and Carpenter's perceived negative treatment by producers. For example, Mrs O noted before seeing the episode, 'I just hope [writer] Joss doesn't make a sham of it. I hope he gives her a decent storyline. But it's Joss. He'll screw it up anyway. If it sucks, I hope the show is cancelled. By God, I hope it crashes and burns and there is no more hope for the show'. Such expressions of 'anti-fandom' (Gray 2003) towards Joss Whedon and the series as a whole are fairly widespread and there is a clear sense among Cordelia fans that their enjoyment of the show and their respect for its writers and producers had diminished as a result of her character's treatment. As discussed in Chapter 5, fans often articulate this disappointment through a rejection discourse that often takes the creative personnel behind a series as a point of particular critique. In the case of *Angel*, it is creator Joss Whedon who bears the brunt of fan anger, even though his role on the show had been substantially reduced by the time of the hundredth episode. Before the airing, one respondent articulated this at length:

> But as far as the character goes I'm not happy at all. I simply don't believe it will be possible for [Mutant Enemy] to address the heavy themes of incest, rape and loss of self in a single episode—or how a family feels when they lose their 'heart' … Hopefully I'm wrong, but I just have the suspicion that the character will be

there for a cheap heave ho (with the ME-obligatory 'gotcha'.) Of course, I'm so cynical at this point that I don't believe ME and the WB care what viewers like me think or watch. They seem to have forgotten the percentage of the audience that didn't watch *Buffy*. (Elizabeth)

Another fan noted that 'I used to have every confidence in ME to pull some amazing stuff. But after *Buffy* 6–7 and this year's disappointing season on *Angel*, I am not expecting anything good to happen' (Delyth), while another commented that 'unfortunately, I don't expect much. I am so disillusioned with the entire show at this point, that really I don't put anything past JW and ME. I really don't think it will be anything that we (the fans) will really want to see. Whatever occurs, I don't think CC and Cordy fans will be happy with it' (Celestia). For the unhappy fans, a sense of loss or disappointment is palpable. Fans often react intensely to such events, feeling a sense of grief which they then need to work through 'because supposedly shared desires [about the show] had been foreclosed by narrative developments, [fans] perceived a failure in ontological security, in the somehow truer hyperdiegetic "heart" of the series in which he or she had become invested' (Johnson 2007a, 289). Indeed, some of these more disillusioned fans treated the hundredth episode as a series finale of sorts, since many stated that they would not watch any further instalments of the show. The sense of closure was stated by one fan who argued that the episode offered some closure for Cordelia, 'but more I felt it gave closure to the show … And quite frankly, I felt like the show was saying good by to viewers like me as much as it was Cordelia last-night.' (Elizabeth). Another fan discussed their feeling of bidding farewell to the series after their viewing of the episode:

Before this ep, there was always that nagging feeling that I might possibly be missing something by not watching *Angel*. It was such a huge part of my life for so long and it felt weird to let it go … I kept thinking maybe something would be said or something C/A related would happen and it would all turn out to have been just a bad dream and the show would somehow get her back and magically go back to the way it was before. As long as she was still sleeping somewhere, it was like I just couldn't let go of it, couldn't get that wondering feeling out of my head. But now, after this episode that feeling is totally gone. I am now officially, decidedly 100 per cent OVER *Angel* the Series! I feel like now I can finally let it go and move on with my life. Just remember it for the phenomenal show it once was, but with the serene peace of having accepted that it's over and done, never to return. As far as I'm concerned, it may as well be off the air already. NO MORE wondering!! (Celestia)

These responses to Cordelia's departure indicate that, for many fans, trust in a text is linked to particular characters or actors and that their connection to this figure is stronger than the sense of ontological security generated by broader fandom of the series. For such fans, a pure relationship can only be sustained while it offers ontological security and a sense of trust in the other party. In this case, when Cordelia is killed off in circumstances that the fan finds implausible or unwelcome, their trust in *Angel* is destabilized and the fan's self-narrative is reworked in order to cope with this disruption. They declare themselves as being 'over' the series and ready to bid it farewell and move on.

A less common, but potentially even more disruptive, case of characters leaving a narrative occurs when the actor who plays that role passes away in 'real life'. There is much work on audience reactions to the deaths of the famous (see Rodman 1996; Turnock 2000; Jones and Jensen 2005; Wang 2007; Garner 2013). For example, in their study of online reactions to the death of American racing car driver Dale Earnhardt Sr, who was killed in February 2001 during the Daytona 500 race, Radford and Bloch (2012) draw on the concept of parasocial relationships to suggest that the break-up of such relationships can have profound effects upon fans: 'If the end of the relationship is final due to the death of the individual, such feelings may be more intense ... the loss is expected to be greater for celebrities with whom the individual feels a greater identification' (Radford and Bloch 2012, 139–40). My analysis here builds on Rob Turnock's (2000) and Ross P. Garner's (2013) work to use the notion of ontological security to explore the reactions to the deaths of two actors. This discussion complicates prior uses of ontological security to understand death to examine first the case of *The West Wing* star John Spencer (who died on 16 December 2005) and the narrative death of his character Leo McGarry and, second, the actor Cory Monteith who died on 13 July 2013 and whose *Glee* character Finn Hudson subsequently died in the fictional narrative. Anthony Giddens notes the disruptive potential of death to ontological security since death 'is the ultimate abject, the "great extrinsic factor of human existence", the "fateful moment" (of dis-order) which is ultimately resistant to human containment and control' (Ritchie 2003, 2). Death can threaten our sense of ontological security whether it is a close relative or friend who passes away or a mediated figure. For example, Rob Turnock discusses the impact of the death in 1997 of Diana, Princess of Wales, suggesting that 'Diana's death may have been socially and psychologically shattering because the experience of death can upset a stable sense of ontological security' (Turnock 2000, 52) since 'death calls into question that meaning ... It shatters ontological security; it calls everything into question' (Turnock 2000, 52). Meanwhile, Ross P. Garner has analysed fan reactions to the death of Elisabeth Sladen, who played the character of Sarah Jane in *Doctor Who*, arguing that 'fans negotiated the anxiety caused by Sladen's passing by nostalgically recalling memories of her from their individual pasts' (Garner 2013, 192). Arguing that Sladen's death presented a potential threat to ontological security, Garner focuses on the impact of Sladen's 'embodied presence' (2013, 192) as a cause of particular displays of grief and mourning, since 'embodied presence generates ontological security by providing television audiences with "a sense of co-temporality"' (2013, 203), growing older as characters and actors along with the viewers. Garner argues that, for some fans, recourse to the type of 'reiteration discourse' discussed in Chapter 4 offered a chance to negotiate the anxiety 'arising from Sladen's embodied absence ... by configuring their self-narratives via re-appropriating memories of Sladen' (Garner 2013, 204). However, Turnock's work focuses on a non-fictional mediated figure in Diana, and while Garner's analysis is persuasive, the character of Sarah Jane did not die in the narrative of her television series.

The section that follows thus poses two key questions: how do fans respond when both actor and character die? How does the ability to mourn the character impact upon their feelings about the death of the actor, if at all? There are also specificities to both cases. Given that Spencer/McGarry's death occurred in close proximity to *The West Wing*'s final episodes, I explore how this impacted upon fans' reactions and responses, while I am interested in the potential impact on *Glee* fans of the death of an actor who was of a similar age group and whose demise may have worked to 'remind [fans] of [their] own mortality' (Garde-Hansen 2011, 131). The analysis in the next section contributes to literature on fan reactions to both character departures and the deaths of celebrities more broadly.

'I can't believe he has died': John Spencer and *The West Wing*'s Leo McGarry

While characters frequently leave narratives and are often killed off onscreen, the dual death of an actor and his/her character is less common. The relatively few cases where this has happened include *Dallas* actor Larry Hagman and his character J. R. Ewing and John Ritter's character, father Paul Hennessy, in the sitcom *8 Simple Rules For Dating My Daughter*, whose death was incorporated into the narrative. The example discussed here is the character of Leo McGarry, who was a central character in *The West Wing*, functioning as best friend and Chief of Staff to the fictional President Jed Bartlet (played by Martin Sheen). In later seasons, he became a Vice-Presidential candidate, running alongside Presidential candidate Matt Santos (Jimmy Smits), and was engaged in storylines about the election campaign when John Spencer died. The discussions here occurred on the Television Without Pity message boards in the threads dedicated to the series' individual episodes (all quotes are referenced here by thread title and the number of the online posting).

Fan reactions to Spencer's death were largely ones of shock and surprise. After the first episode to air after his death – 'Running Mates' – was screened, fans online discussed their reactions to seeing the episode, as well as a short tribute by Martin Sheen before the episode:

> Of course, John Spencer gave a great performance and watching him was so bittersweet, but I'm just echoing the other posters. But man, why did this happen??? Ugh, to think of all the more great work he could have done. Its just so sad … I'm getting off topic. (Post #138, 'Running Mates')

> I really liked it. Reaffirmed why I am going to miss John Spencer. (Post #23, 'Running Mates')

> Oh my God, I am *so* going to miss John Spencer. I have to say that the only time I teared-up was when Leo was talking about the fact that when he had his heart-attack, he had gotten the best health care, and it had saved his life. Cried like a baby. Again. Dammit. (Post #28, 'Running Mates')

> I enjoyed this episode more than I thought I would; I feel that it was worth the wait. I thought Martin did a great job in remembering Spencer, and I found it very hard to watch the scene with Leo and Annabeth working on the 'smirk.' That just about broke my heart and I was almost in tears at that point. (Post #80, 'Running Mates')

Expressions of sadness and grief are not unusual after the death of a celebrity or public figure. For example, Margaret Gibson has discussed the public mourning that followed the death of Australian celebrity Steve Irwin in 2006 (Gibson 2007), while Yiman Wang has analysed the posthumous fandom of Chinese star Leslie Cheung. Wang outlines how fans mourned the star, noting that one fan commented '[his suicide] feels odd. I've never shed tears for a stranger. Yet the thought of him brought tears to my eyes' (2007, 335) and how 'Taiwan fans described Cheung's death as bereavement as part of oneself. Kathy T. wrote, "His departure took away the memories of our generation"' (2007, 335). Similarly, in an example of sport fandom, Radford and Bloch discuss 'fan grieving in the days following [race car driver Dale Eckhart Jr.'s] death and the consumption behaviours associated with the mourning process for members of online fan communities' (2012, 142). Such expressions of mourning also occurred online after John Spencer's death and many fans chose to praise Spencer's performance in the first episode that aired after his death. They often discussed the fact that his presence had allowed them to forget the death of the actor since the character was still 'alive':

> I was worried that the next few *West Wing* episodes wouldn't be able to escape the pall that John Spencer's death cast over the show's future. It is a testament to Spencer's ability, however, that ten seconds into the show I stopped thinking 'it's too bad about John' and just thought 'Hey, there's Leo' like usual. It didn't hit me again until Josh's line about the next VP debate in four years. (Post #114, 'Running Mates')

Lisa Bode has discussed how posthumous performances can be digitally (re)created through the case of Livia Soprano, a character in the television series *The Sopranos*, played by actress Nancy Marchand. When Marchand died between the second and third seasons of the show, 'rather than simply referring to an offscreen car accident or an equally sudden demise, they produced an entire scene in which Livia has one final fraught interaction with her son before her death offscreen' (Bode 2010, 54). By digitally melding the actress's face with the actions of a body double, the effect of the scene was largely to disconcert and, in some cases, offend, with the decision to digitally resurrect the actress, albeit briefly, deemed to be a '"ghastly" … bizarre Frankenstein experiment' (Kantor, cited in Bode 2010, 54). The overall effect of this is described by Bode as being uncanny, since posthumous performance 'challenges or disorientates familiar, taken-for-granted ideas about screen acting as an effect produced by an intentional, present human being' and 'raises questions about the nature of personhood' (Bode 2010, 60). In addition to threatening our own sense of subjectivity and identity, there are also clear taboos about 'symbolic uses of the dead' (Bode 2010, 60) and the unease surrounding the posthumous re-cutting or violation of a deceased person's image. While the appearance of John Spencer as Leo in the two episodes he filmed before his death do not contain instances of posthumous performance as Bode discusses them, there are overlapping issues surrounding the concept of Spencer's appearance onscreen as uncanny. As the fans here discuss, there is an odd tension in seeing Spencer alive onscreen as Leo while knowing that the actor himself is deceased. The almost ghostly appearance of the actor onscreen provokes sadness in some fans and potentially prompts, as with the case of digitally created posthumous performances, reflection on notions of mortality, selfhood and identity.

Fans did speculate as to how the narrative would deal with the death and many suggested that watching the onscreen passing of Leo would be more difficult for them than their feelings about John Spencer's own death:

> I was surprised that I was able to maintain my composure during MS's tribute to Spencer at the beginning of the show, but I know I'll lose it completely when the show deals with later. (Post #147, 'Running Mates')

> I thought this episode was good, but it seemed very slowly paced. In fact, this whole season I've been thinking of how slowly the episodes seem to go, especially if you compare them to the first 4 seasons of *TWW*. It was still good, though. All of John Spencer's scenes just made me so sad. The Leo Death episode, should they choose to do that, will be so heartwrenching. (Post #85, 'Running Mates')

> I really enjoyed this ep. I don't think the loss of John Spencer will fully hit me until I see it played out on the show, so the many eerie moments flew right over my head until pointed out here. I loved every Leo/Annabeth moment and that is one of the many stories I will be sad not to see continued. (Post #120, 'Running Mates')

There were also some discussions over what type of onscreen death would be most appropriate and respectful, given that the character of Leo had suffered with heart problems in the narrative. For some fans, his onscreen demise had to be realistic, while others felt that replicating Spencer's own death would be insensitive:

> It was gut-wrenching to watch Leo defend his health for obvious reasons. But how this has led people to want him to die in some sort of accident (plane, train, or automobile) I don't get. I think that given the circumstances, the cause of death should be kept in the background. The Leo episode really should deal with the life of Leo (and through that the life of Spencer). I think using what happened as the vehicle to some sort of *ER* helicopter-like plot device would

be unfortunate. I hope he dies quietly in his sleep and the rest of the episode is reflections upon the body of work he left (Leo and Spencer). (Post #148, 'Running Mates')

I don't think the American public is going to say they were lying [about the character's health]. Someone can honestly be in perfect health and die the next day of a heart attack. I definitely don't think they'd be accused of being dishonest. I just think something spectacular like a plane crash or shooting would be an insult to Spencer. No? (Post #230, 'Running Mates')

No. Why would it? Of a necessity, Leo's death (should they choose to handle Spencer's death that way) will have to be sudden. A heart attack? Uncomfortably close to home. Rule out plane/car crashes and shootings? What's left? Stroke? Hit by a bus? Don't have the answer, but I don't [know] why you think those things would be disrespectful. (Post #233, 'Running Mates')

At this point, fans were unaware of how Spencer would be written out and the show's finale dates had not been confirmed, even though many fans suspected that the seventh series would be the last. Spencer had filmed the episodes 'Running Mates' and 'The Cold' by the time of his death and it was decided by the producers and writers that the most appropriate way to explain Leo's departure from the narrative would be via his off-screen death, which occurred in the two-parter 'Election Day'. Leo's subsequent onscreen funeral was featured in an episode fittingly entitled 'Requiem'. This allowed fans to witness the responses of other characters and the actors who play them and to re-experience their loss and, in some cases, negotiate the threat to their sense of ontological security. In this case the 'traumatic loss and … subsequent collective mourning' (Wang 2007, 335) associated with the death of a celebrity were played out visually through the narrative events, providing fans with one way to come to terms with the potential ontological disruption they may have been facing. In the thread devoted to the episode fans discussed their reactions:

I was expecting more focus on the funeral, but I'm not at all sad at how it turned out. The episode took my breath away. It was the most real, honest thing I've seen in a while. Plus, it had a wonderful balance of humor and weight almost reminicent of '17 People'. Seriously, this is the best I've seen since S2. Wow. (Post #8, 'Requiem')

I loved it! I don't think I've ever cried so much at the BEGINNING of a show. Truly a great tribute to Leo and John. I was great seeing everyone, but where was Sam. I couldn't believe that he wasn't there. I like the way they are tying everything up, but I wish it didn't have to be so. (Post #16, 'Requiem')

What could be a better tribute to John Spencer and Leo McGarry than the camera panning across over a dozen familiar faces, all of whome were crying real honest-to-god tears. Nothing. That was excellent. (Post #40, 'Requiem')

However, not all fans were pleased with the episode, echoing the range of discourses that fans employ when series themselves come to an end. For some, this rejection discourse was used to dismiss the episode for lacking focus on Leo and for the writing, critiques that fans also drew on as the show itself drew to a close:

I'm so disappointed I can barely type. The first half completely sucked. A 'look, everyone's at the funeral' teaser, but no eulogy from anyone but a priest who looks a little too much like Peter Cook in [the film] *The Princess Bride?* ... The second half got a little better ... but the whole time, I'm waiting for them to get back to Leo, to a goodbye worthy of both the character and the actor, so the scenes didn't play as well as they might have otherwise. And finally — FINALLY — the Leo story session, good stuff, but too little, too late. Maybe even Sorkin would have found Leo's requiem a daunting task, but this was appallingly off the mark. Leo, and John, deserved better. (Post #7, 'Requiem')

That was wildly disapointing. I thought John deserved better. (Post #9, 'Requiem')

I have been a fan and a viewer since the beginning and I can honestly say that this episode was the biggest letdown of my *West Wing* viewing experience. This episode was ... sadly hollow and lacking. What a crime. (Post #6, 'Requiem')

This sense of 'deserving better' was a common fan complaint, suggesting that while there are expectations surrounding a good death or '*ars moriandi*' (Harrington 2013), for textual deaths of television series this can also be extended to the 'good deaths' of characters. This can also be seen in the fan discussions of Cordelia's exit from *Angel*, but it appears to be even more crucial when the actor has also passed away since this necessitates a dual honouring of both character and actor. Here, work on the deaths of celebrities is instructive, since the fans of *The West Wing* here suggest that John Spencer deserves an appropriate send-off via the character of Leo. For these fans, Leo's final episodes fail to offer the opportunity for 'collective mourning' often undertaken by fans, instead leaving little option for mutual grieving or the chance to celebrate the character and the actor. In this case, the possibility of such episodes offering a space for the negotiation of threats to ontological security (from both the threat to the fan text itself but also to the potential threat from sudden death more broadly) is reduced.

John Spencer's real-life death is clearly important for many fans, with this factor being discussed at length. One poster noted:

> I too am a viewer from the beginning and I was very disappointed that this episode wasn't more of a tribute to John Spencer. If John Spencer were still alive and had simply left the show for some reason then I probably would have liked this episode. I enjoyed the way 'Leo' was present throughout the whole episode without any soap opera theatrics. I liked the stories and the little asides. But the truth is John Spencer isn't alive and all those guest stars probably wouldn't have come back if he was. This episode should have been greater than simply serving the storyline. That's what made it such a let down. (Post #20, 'Requiem')

While this fan felt that the episode honoured the character, the dimension of Spencer's own death complicates this response. Although acknowledging that the episode was, in some ways, only possible because his demise prompted actors who had left the series to briefly return, this fan demonstrates the tension felt when fictional and 'real' death collide and the range of complex responses that fans must negotiate. Again, in failing to satisfy this fan's desire for resolution to both the Leo storyline and the actuality of John Spencer's death, trust in the fan object is destabilized and critique is deployed to evaluate the episode from a more disappointed standpoint.

Even after 'Requiem' Leo's character resonated across the final episodes of the series, most prominently in the final episode which ends with former President Bartlet flying away on Air Force One to enjoy his post-political life. As he does so he opens a present given to him by Leo's daughter Mallory, finding a framed restaurant napkin with the words 'Bartlet For America' written on it. Loyal audience members know that this was given to Bartlet when Leo was convincing him to run for President, an event that viewers witnessed in flashback in the third season episode 'Bartlet for America'. This narrative event both brings the story of Bartlet's Presidential journey to a close but also serves to remind viewers of Leo's legacy across the series, as well as further honouring John Spencer in the closing moments of the show. This moment was discussed at length online in the thread dedicated to the last episode 'Tomorrow':

> Of course, everyone knew what was in Mallory's package, but I still cried when I saw Leo's handwriting again. Seeing Leo cry in that episode always made me cry.

What an actor JS was, that one of his performances, merely *alluded* to, makes the audience weep! (Post #19, 'Tomorrow')

I loved it. At this point there was very little left to be said in the series. All the notes that needed to be hit were hit. It ended exactly as I always though the series would end. No complaints, and even though nothing shocking happened (like Jed and Abby skydiving out of the plane at the end while chugging Mountain Dew), nothing shocking should have happened. We all knew it was the napkin. That doesn't matter. It was the perfect way to close shop. (Post #34, 'Tomorrow')

Can I just say that I totally predicted the return of the Bartlet For America napkin from Leo's possessions? An absolutely perfect choice. I knew what it was the second Mallory showed up. So, thank you to all the actors, to the directors, writers, prop people, etc.; a special mention to John Wells, who took a lot of abuse, but kept me interested, and delivered an excellent final two seasons. (Post #22, 'Tomorrow')

For others, the episode was seen as a broader tribute to John Spencer and the character of Leo. One poster commented, 'I loved how Leo was there even though he wasn't. Er, that makes sense in my head, I promise. I don't know if it was intentional or not, but I thought the third, empty chair on the plane was a nice touch, and what a wonderful scene to end the show on' (Post #60, 'Tomorrow'). In further chapters, we will see the range of responses of *West Wing* fans around the series' ending, as well as how fandom has continued since the final episodes. Here, however, the death of Spencer/McGarry offers an opportunity to see how fans react to one form of ending (the death of an actor) and how this is played out onscreen (via the narrative demise of the character they play), as well as how this is negotiated alongside the larger ending of a series as a whole.

More recently another example of the real-life death of an actor being replicated via the demise of their character occurred through the case of *Glee* actor Cory Monteith and his character Finn Hudson. Monteith died on 13 July 2013 of a heroin and alcohol overdose at the age of thirty-one. As the lead male actor in the Fox teen musical-drama series *Glee*, Monteith was hugely popular with the show's fanbase and his unexpected death was met with shock and disbelief. The decision to have his character Finn Hudson die off-screen in the third episode of the show's fifth series before taking the show on an extended hiatus was described by series creator Ryan Murphy as being undertaken with the blessing of the cast and crew (Daniels 2013). Finn's death was not explained onscreen – a voiceover from the character Kurt simply stated: 'Everyone wants to talk about how he died, but who cares? It's one moment in his whole life'.

Thus, unlike the Leo/John Spencer case, the character and actor's deaths in *Glee* are not conflated, allowing the character to remain 'untarnished' by any overlap with the death of the actor who played him. As Ryan Murphy noted, 'At one point, we were going to have his character die after an accidental drug overdose – that was something we had considered. But we have decided that we're not going to have him pass from that' (Murphy, in Takeda 2013). The real-life and fictional death of Monteith/Hudson was further inflected by his off-screen relationship with the actress Lea Michele who played his onscreen girlfriend Rachel Berry. As a popular 'ship' for *Glee* fans, the fact/fiction blurring of the possibility of asking someone to grieve onscreen for their deceased partner offered a further dimension of complexity in terms of fans' grief and reactions to the situation. While John Spencer was an older actor whose death, although upsetting, was not entirely unexpected, Monteith's younger age offers a more shocking potential intrusion into ontological security for *Glee* fans. At the age of thirty-one, Monteith was older than many *Glee* fans, yet the sense of co-presence engendered by his playing of a much younger school and college-age character contributed to strong bonds for many fans. This has been described as 'co-temporality – events take place at the same time, in real-life time' (Turnock 2000, 48), which is often engendered by the 'embodied presence of TV actors' (Garner 2013, 203). Thus, this loss of a shared life trajectory can lead to ruptures in self-identity and ontological security for fans. Identification both with Finn himself or the onscreen relationship between Finn and Rachel Berry may cause fans to consider their own mortality and the intrusion of death and grief into their own life courses. If actors and characters perceived as 'like them' or of the same generational grouping can die, then their own reactions to death may need to be renegotiated. As Turnock points out, 'Ordinarily, with people living longer and death sequestrated into special institutions … death is something that is not normally encountered among young or middle-aged people', but when 'a known person of the same or a similar age' passes away this is viewed as 'unusual – yet it could have been us' (Turnock 2000, 51). While the death of an older actor such as John Spencer is undoubtedly sad, the loss of a character and actor from within a fan's own age bracket can be even more threatening to a sense of self and ontological security since 'the loss of embodied presence temporarily ruptures ontological security and fans' self-continuity' (Garner 2013, 203). Indeed, Monteith/Hudson's death caused some fans to rethink their fan narratives and self-identities, having a profound impact on how they responded to the show and how they identified within the fandom. In his work on Princess Diana, Turnock notes that 'death is discontinuous. It not only threatens the way the world is perceived, but it also has implications for the way individuals perceive themselves. In the constant re-creation and re-negotiation of self-identity (not in circumstances of one's own making), identity is always subject to change' (Turnock 2000, 52). While this applies to the death of someone who is personally known to you (e.g. the change from wife to widow, or to being an orphan), it can also be seen in the instance of fan bereavement discussed here. While the question of why fans 'feel compelled to memorialize a person they have never met and share their personal grief in a very public manner' (Radford and Bloch 2012, 138) remains complex, studying examples of such grief and memorialization go some way towards understanding how the layers of narrative, character, actor/actress and relationship are understood by fans in periods of mourning and remembrance.

'I don't want to go': *Doctor Who*, character and regeneration

You'll always love your first Doctor but eventually you'll need to move on ...
Post #85, 'Have you moved on from David Tennant yet?', *Doctor Who* Forum

This final section takes another approach to the departure of actors by examining the unusual case of *Doctor Who*, where actors leave and are replaced by another actor playing the same role, that of the titular Doctor. For example, at the moment of his regeneration – his change from one physical incarnation into other – the Tenth Doctor, played by David Tennant, tearfully declares that 'I don't want to go' before bursting into a ball of fiery energy and emerging the other side as actor Matt Smith, the Eleventh Doctor. This final case study explores the reactions of fans after Tennant's departure from the title role in 2009 and his replacement by Matt Smith, and the fan response to the announcement of Smith's departure from the show in June 2013. This allows us to consider fan responses at the point of narrative regeneration and extra-textual 'replacement'. For example, what does it mean for fans of David Tennant or Matt Smith when that actor leaves the series? Does fandom end for these viewers? If not, how do they continue to engage with the series? By linking such fan discussions to issues of ontological security, fan self-narrative and identity, this section explores reactions to the replacement of favoured actors who may have been the primary means of entry into the series for some fans, adding understanding to work on fan endings and transitions and on the concept, and limits, of 'post-object fandom'.

Much has been written on fans of *Doctor Who* (see for example Tulloch and Jenkins 1995; Hills 2006, 2010b, 2012a; Williams 2011c, 2013c; Cherry 2013; Hadas 2013) but my interest here is in the moments surrounding the Doctor's regeneration – the point where he ceases to be played by one actor and the role is taken over by another. In such cases, as Cherry notes, 'some fans might not like a particular Doctor or "era" of the programme and be waiting in anticipation of the next cycle of change. How, then, do audiences, fans and more casual viewers respond to change in a text they love but which is in a constant state of flux?' (2013, 205). Regeneration of The Doctor has become big news – the story of Matt Smith's departure was announced on the front pages of many UK Sunday newspapers on 1 June 2013 after an embargoed press release and speculation about his replacement featured on the main BBC news bulletins across the day. Fans cannot fail to be aware of the prospect of the lead actor departing the role and a certain level of expectation regarding this is always present. The analysis undertaken here offers a broader view of issues surrounding regeneration and how this is articulated in two distinct instances in order to identify both commonalities and differences in response. The data relating to Tennant and Smith's departures is collected from the online forum Gallifrey Base which is considered one of the largest and most popular *Doctor Who* forums on the internet, with over 70,000 members as of August 2013. Although the site requires registration with a username and password, there is academic precedent for using fan posts from the site and its predecessors Outpost Gallifrey and the *Doctor Who* Forum (see Hills 2006; Williams 2011c), since it is a hub for fans of the show and offers a range of opinions from the highly supportive to the more critical. Owing to the site's size, the material collected was limited using the message board's own 'search' function. The search terms used were 'David Tennant leaving' and 'Matt Smith leaving' and thread titles including these phrases were returned in the search with twelve forum threads for Smith and four for Tennant. To broaden this search, the terms 'David Tennant' (returning 237 threads) and 'Matt Smith' (accruing 300 threads) were also used. Each of these threads was then read and comments relating to the actors' departures were archived. Since the site is password protected, no usernames have been used in order to make identification of individual posters more difficult. Instead, as with the other chapters, quotes are labelled only with the thread title, the number of the posting and the date.

Since the site was only created in June 2009, immediate reaction to Tennant's decision to leave the show cannot be found in the archives. However, much discussion continues to relate to the actor and to his decision to move on from the show, especially around the period of Smith's departure announcement and the news in Spring 2013 that David Tennant, and Billie Piper playing Rose Tyler, would be appearing in the fiftieth anniversary episode of the series. Fan reaction to this news was generally of excitement and speculation about how a Doctor who had regenerated could return to the show's narrative. Such situations had been previously explored in classic episodes including 1972's 'The Three Doctors', 1983's 'The Five Doctors' and a 2007 short film *Timecrash* for the BBC charity telethon 'Children in Need' which saw Tennant's Tenth Doctor come face-to-face with the Fifth Doctor, played by Peter Davison. Fan reactions cannot thus be easily demarcated along topic lines and there are often overlaps between discussions of both the Tenth and Eleventh Doctors.

There are some commonalities between how fans of departing characters such as Cordelia Chase or Leo McGarry respond to the exits of their version of The Doctor. While the character himself continues, each actor inflects the role differently, giving rise to the argument that there is often very little continuity between the different incarnations. For fans attached to one specific version of The Doctor, this loss can lead to a range of responses. In the thread 'David Tennant's leaving the show! Matt Smith announced as Eleven!' (started in April 2011), fans recalled their opinions about the news of the Tennant/Smith regeneration:

> Ah, new Doctor day! Sitting down, watching the special Confidential and seeing the new actor they'd cast ... and thinking who the hell is he?! Glad he's proved us all wrong. I wasn't particularly fussed about David Tennant leaving – besides, they'd announced a year of specials, he'd gone off to do Hamlet, so it seemed likely – it was more the anxiety on how the next man would do it! (Post #7, 'David Tennant's leaving the show...')

> I loved Tennant's Doctor, but I was tiring of Mr. Shouty. *Live too long*. I was ready for change. (Post #26, 'David Tennant's leaving the show...')

Some fans also recalled in specific detail where they had been when they heard about Tennant's departure which he announced via satellite when receiving an award at the annual National Television Awards:

> Specifically, October 29, 2008! I remember this quite well, as I was in the audience for Tennant's *Hamlet* in Stratford that night, and when we got back to our hotel

after the show, we saw on the news that he had made the announcement from backstage at the theatre! (Post #12, 'David Tennant's leaving the show…')

Tennant announced he was leaving on October 29th 2008. It was the night I was at the *Quantum of Solace* premiere. Smith was announced around March time I think. (Post #14, 'David Tennant's leaving the show…')

The next chapter discusses the 'reiteration discourse' that fans often draw upon at periods of change or rupture in their fandom. In many of these instances fans are 'keen to reassert their fan identities, offering stories of how the show had impacted upon their lives and often revealing large amounts of personal detail. These often took the form of lengthy postings of 'goodbyes' to the show' (Williams 2011a, 273). While this level of detail was not always present in the 'Matt Smith and practical reasons for leaving' thread and the 'Are you over David Tennant yet?' discussions, some fans posted about their gratitude to Smith for his role in the series or about their emotional responses:

Will I be sad to see him [Smith] go? Absolutely, is he still my doctor, with his special place in my heart? Yes. But would I ever ask the BEEB to keep him on beyond his will? No. That is how you kill a show. That attitude can poison a healthy show. Give him a good send off, let him go out being the doctor. (Post #132, 'Matt Smith and practical reasons for leaving')

All I can say is, thank you Matt Smith for the enjoyment you have given me in your performances as The Doctor and all the best in your future. (Post #71, 'Matt Smith and practical reasons for leaving')

I wish Matt all the luck in the world ! He is young, unattached … why should he not give Hollywood a try, if that's what he wants … He has been a great doctor, and if DW lasts 1000 more years, I will think of the years with Eleven/River/ Amy/Rory as my most very favorite time of all. And may the future bring us all many Doctors and companions to love and root for. Thanks Matt, and good luck! (Post #133, 'Matt Smith and practical reasons for leaving')

Thus, while fans often give more detailed stories about their life courses and histories in relation to a specific TV show or celebrity, the *Doctor Who* fans here offer briefer goodbyes and declarations of support and good luck. However, in the refrain of having 'your doctor' or 'your first doctor' there is still striking evidence of fans intertwining their identity with the show, since 'by relaying their self-narratives, these fans rearticulate their identities and form their experiences with the show into a coherent story' (Williams 2011a, 273). By identifying strongly with a specific incarnation of The Doctor, many posters use the established fan discourse and shorthand of knowing what this means and the associated emotional ties that fans feel to particular actors.

In the same thread some fans also expressed more negative emotional responses, operating under the rejection discourse where elements of a fan object are evaluated or judged. One poster notes, 'It's sad to see him go. Unlike when David left I feel like we are just getting to know his Doctor. Too bad most his time was spent in bad unfinished timey whimey story arcs' (Post #76, 'Matt Smith and practical reasons for leaving'); while another summarizes their reaction to the news via apportioning some blame on the BBC for not allowing Smith to have a full run of four series of the show:

> I think that Matt probably had his own reasons for leaving. I very much doubt that the BBC would have wanted him to leave, simply because although the regeneration is a key part of *Doctor Who* it is also the time when the Series is at its most vulnerable. The BBC wasted Matt's four years with faffing around with just three seasons. That was absolutely stupid, and could come back to haunt them. If they do this again with Twelve, after his first full season, then I imagine that fans will get really fed up. If they were clever (and they ain't) they would have had full thirteen episodes of Season 7 in 2013, and taken up 2012 with 'Specials'. It is all very sad because I think it is generally seen that Matt's Doctor had at least one more season in him. *It is going to ruin Christmas for me, I know that.* (Post #96, 'Matt Smith and practical reasons for leaving')

This poster demonstrates an awareness of the production conditions of *Doctor Who* and suggests that while regeneration is necessary, it can also pose a threat to the series since it offers a vulnerability where the replacement actor may not be successful.

Some audience members may also decide to stop watching the series after a regeneration, especially if they are non-fans or more casual viewers. In his study of ontological security and *Doctor Who* spoilers, Matt Hills notes the potential threat of moments of change since this is when uncertainty is most likely. He notes that in these instances 'the idealized fan object is potentially threatened (in a way in which tie-ins, spin-offs, and unofficial material cannot pose a threat) – what if the new episodes are no good? What if unwanted story developments occur? Or much loved-characters leave?' (2012a, 117). Such threat is an issue for fans; for example, while the claim above that 'It's going to ruin Christmas for me' must be read performatively, the linkage between discussion of practical production information and this more personal claim suggests a complex range of responses from this poster from the personal and affective through to a wider critique of the show's writers and producers. For others, though, the changing of the actor is an accepted part of being a fan of this series – part of 'the bargain' of being a *Who* fan – and this is often dealt with via a process of renegotiation (see Chapter 6). In the 'Are you over David Tennant yet?' discussion, fans commented:

> It was 2 series ago. I'm hardly still pining for Tennant; I moved on during 'The Eleventh Hour', just as I move on every time a new Doctor is introduced. (Post #5, 'Are you over David Tennant yet?')

> Tennant was great, but I moved on from him about five minutes into 'The Eleventh Hour'. (Post #54, 'Are you over David Tennant yet?')

> I had moved on from Tennant by the moment he started glowing in 'The End of Time, Part Two'. Maybe he didn't want to go, but it was time … it was time. (Post #127, 'Are you over David Tennant yet?')

Similar comments can be found in the 'Matt Smith and practical reasons for leaving' discussion, where fans posted:

> If i were in charge of the universe, he'd stick around to do a special for the spring of 2014, and regenerate in that. But really, it's his decision, and there is no point worrying over might have beens. (Post #170, 'Matt Smith and practical reasons for leaving')

> I'm a big fan of three years for a Doctor, it's enough to establish the actor, give them a good spread of episodes and hopefully at least two sets of companions. After that I'm usually itching to see someone new in the role. (Post #22, 'Matt Smith and practical reasons for leaving')

> As an American fan, I absorbed regeneration as part of the logic of the show, and when 10 regenerated I was remorseful but excited at seeing what comes next. I'm a fan of 11 too, but when I read the news I actually felt eager for the change. It somehow seems due. (Post #47, 'Matt Smith and practical reasons for leaving')

The renegotiation discourse of acceptance and 'moving on' is discussed by a range of different posters. This process of renegotiation – coming to terms with the end of the fan object and discussing how their interactions and relationships with the text would change – is seen in reactions to a range of different forms of endings for fans. The very use of the term 'moving on', first used here by the original poster in the thread, evokes notions of closure, of coming to terms with a form of loss and accepting it before continuing onwards:

> I see 'moving on' from one Doctor to the next being quite a quite different thing from preferring one or other of the Doctors. I loved Christopher Eccleston and thought he did a great job bringing the Doctor back to TV. However, when David Tennant took over, I quickly moved on to seeing him as the present Doctor and quickly found I like him even more than Eccleston. (Post #73, 'Are you over David Tennant yet?')

> I wouldn't call where I'm at in my opinion of Matt as the Doctor as having 'moved on' from David—more like I've grown to see Matt as the Doctor as much as I saw/see David as him ... I'll always love Ten, as I consider him 'my' Doctor, but I like Eleven a lot, too, and am in no hurry to see him go. Nor have I, at any moment since Matt took over the role, wished I were watching David instead. (Post #88, 'Are you over David Tennant yet?')

There is a clear distinction made here between the natural progression in *Doctor Who* fandom of accepting the character's regeneration and the actor's replacement and having a personal favourite incarnation of The Doctor. As an established part of *Doctor Who*'s mythology, the fans here understand that to continue with their fandom of the series, they need to adjust to a new Doctor, even if they retain affective ties to previous versions. Indeed, the presence of the entire series (with the exception of deleted and lost episodes) on DVD means that fans can 'have their cake and eat it'; they can move on and accept a new Doctor while also being able to revisit the stories of their previous favourites through re-watching old episodes. The archive of the series provides one possible avenue for warding off threats to fan identity here since one can maintain their status both as a David Tennant/ Christopher Eccleston/Matt Smith fan while simultaneously renegotiating their ongoing fandom of the series itself. This is made clear in other posts which discuss the balance between a favourite Doctor and enjoying the series as a whole:

> I don't think you really ever move on from your favorite doctor ... but you embrace the new doctor and enjoy what new attributes the new guy brings to the character ... As long as no actor copies another actors doctor i'll be happy..keep some of the same personality traits ... yet still bring a whole new dimension.. to me that's the best doctor ... (Post #123, 'Are you over David Tennant yet?')

> I really don't need to move on, cos there isn't much that needs moving. I started watching *Doctor Who* when David Tennant was the Doctor, so he will always be

my Doctor. But it doesn't mean I cannot enjoy the other Doctors ... Like David
before him, and Christopher, Paul, Sylvester, Colin, Peter, Tom, Jon, Patrick and
William, Matt is the Doctor. And that, I think, is all that matters. (Post #163,
'Are you over David Tennant yet?')

However, for those who disliked David Tennant's incarnation, regeneration
offers a chance to re-engage with the beloved fan object and to re-evaluate their
feelings toward it. One poster comments that, 'I wasn't much of a Tenth Doctor
fan to begin with, and "The End of Time" only made me hate him more. I had
moved on before he even left. The Eleventh Doctor stands with the Fourth and
the Seventh as one of my all-time favorites. He's as good as it possibly gets' (Post
#11, 'Are you over David Tennant yet?').

The issue of gender was a key discourse at the site across discussions about
Tennant and Smith, with many posters disparaging those fans they perceived
to be solely interested in either actor's appearance. As I have argued elsewhere,
such dismissal of 'fangirls', especially in relation to David Tennant, is indicative
of how this is used to 'feminize and infantilize those who perform their fandom
in this way' (Williams 2011c, 174). However, this is also suggestive of the
importance of maintaining appropriate fan behaviours during periods of change
and potential rupture. In the 'David Tennant's leaving the show! Matt Smith
announced as Eleven!' thread, this was explicit:

> I am now prepared to read several posts that personally insult me and suggest
> I get psychological help because thinking that David Tennant is a bad actor
> is not considered a valid, sane opinion by his minions of fan girls and people
> who 'know better.' (Post #37, 'David Tennant's leaving the show! Matt Smith
> announced as Eleven!')

> I couldn't wait for Tennant to leave. I was seriously fed up with him in the role.
> The least Doctorish Doctor ever in my opinion. When they announced Matt,
> I admit, I thought he was too young but still had high hopes. These hopes
> would not only be met but totally smashed. Matt just simply shines as the most
> brilliant, mad, energetic Doctor since Tom. I believe that, by the end of series 6,
> the only doubters will be tennant fangirls. (Post #39, 'David Tennant's leaving
> the show! Matt Smith announced as Eleven!')

Here, fan preference for specific Doctors is clearly mapped onto hierarchies
of gender and generational tastes (see Williams 2011c; Busse 2013). Tennant
fans are viewed as 'fangirls', who are irrational and obsessive about an actor/
Doctor to whom they are attracted. They are, as the first quote attests, unable

to 'consider a valid, sane opinion' about Tennant, suggesting that their own opinions are the very opposite of this: invalid, crazy and misguided. In many cases, such 'problematic gendered responses reflect the differences that might exist between classic series (male) fans and the more active female fandoms around the new series' (Cherry 2013, 218).

However, not all fans were happy with these distinctions and the Othering of fans who disagreed with them:

> Or, you know, people who might genuinely prefer the Tenth Doctor to the Eleventh? I know it's such a stretch, but let's pretend for a moment that people can have different tastes without a shallow underlying reason for them, shall we? (Post #43, 'Have you moved on from David Tennant yet?')

> So once more the thread boils down to one group of fans belittling another group for amusement and patting themselves on the back for it. Thanks for reminding me why I don't post much round here anymore … cool. (Post #369, 'Have you moved on from David Tennant yet?')

> I really loved David as the Doctor, but you're going way off calling everyone who likes Tennant a fangirl … I also love Smith at the moment and it's possible I'll get to like him even more than Tennant (depending on the next season, this is for now mixed feelings, liked him in S5 but didn't like him in S6 …), but for now I prefer Tennant and the style of Doctor he was … it's just a mater of taste for God's sake … (Post #79, 'Have you moved on from David Tennant yet?')

Such debates indicate that periods of potential rupture or threat to a fan object and to fans' sense of identity and ontological security can be dealt with through recourse to established hierarchies surrounding gender, age and appropriate fan behaviours. Such manoeuvres are common across fan cultures; for example, when threatened with an influx of *Twilight* fans, online fans of the rock band Muse drew on similar discourses of infantilization, hysteria and sexualization to ward off these 'interloping fans' (Williams 2013a). What the discussions around David Tennant fans suggest, however, is that when a fan object faces periods of threat or vulnerability, such discourses can be employed with even more vitriol in order to allow certain groups of fans to protect themselves against the anxiety incurred by changes to their object of fandom.

While gendered responses and dismissal of Tennant 'fangirls' was common when discussing the Tenth Doctor's departure, this was far less pronounced in threads devoted to Matt Smith. Instead, some of these discussions tended to draw on distinctions along national lines with divisions between British and American television often highlighted. Like the gender debates, such nationalistic divisions have precedent among *Doctor Who* fans; as Matt Hills notes, the website Outpost Gallifrey (a predecessor of Gallifrey Base and the *Doctor Who* Forum) operated as both a community and 'a hierarchy in which claims over national(istic) identity, and claimed relationships to place, work to sustain versions of more-or-less authentic fandom' (2006, 66). In many cases, being a 'British' fan was esteemed, while their American counterparts were devalued. This distinction continues in discussions over Smith's departure from the series. In one thread entitled 'Matt Smith and practical reasons for leaving', one poster suggests that the BBC is at fault for allowing the actor to leave and not following the American model of television production and securing actors for longer employment contracts:

> Why is Matt Smith suddenly leaving after reportedly agreeing to do series 8? Change is good but too much change is simply rediculous. What's with the BBC? If you have a popular Doctor there is no need to replace him. The series is the biggest single money maker BBC has. Why take a risk on a new actor? I know its a *Doctor Who* tradition, but its a new age and a new series. The show and the character are global. Its a real cash cow for the network now. As such, three years is too short of a stay for a popular Doctor. Obviously, at some point change is good but I don't think this is that point. Not yet. So what is the rumored practical reason for Smith to leave? Not enough money being offered? New show? Doesn't make sense from an American prespective. On US TV these popular guys would be paid to stay. (Post #1, 'Matt Smith and practical reasons for leaving')

The division between American production systems and the British approach is debated throughout this thread, both in terms of the practicalities of 'forcing' or 'bribing' actors into staying with higher salaries and of subsequent broader debates over *Doctor Who* as 'British'. There is little consensus reached on the former point, with heated debate over perceived misconceptions about the American TV industry:

> You know America is not this dystopia, where actors are not allowed to leave their jobs. Even with contracts, most producers allow them to leave. (Post #32, 'Matt Smith and practical reasons for leaving')

> I bet you can't even name one instance where American actors aren't 'allowed' to leave a role if they're not under contract. Even when they are they often can if they forfeit part of their salary ... Good grief that's inflammatory! You must have a very blinkered and naive view of both UK and US people. (Post #37, 'Matt Smith and practical reasons for leaving')

This debate is summarized in a sarcastic post by one forum member:

Isn't [it] wonderful that so many forum users here have a such a comprehensive understanding of how television contracts work in various markets around the world. Thank God for that. Let me recap the comments so far to make sure I grasp what's being said, 1. In the UK, specifically the BBC, the contracts that actors enter in when they sign for a part are completely meaningless because the BBC, as a charitable organization, rarely holds any performers to the contracts that they negotiated and signed. Apparently, the entire process of contracting performers is nothing more than a formality and window dressing for a system that actually just lets performers come and go as they please with no concerns about what they may or may not have agreed to when signing the contract. 2. In the States, the Evil Empire forces actors into extensive, long term contracts where a performer and his/her agent are coerced into signing outrageously long and unfair deals. If and when an actor threatens or begins discussing a desire to leave a program prior to the contract being up, the relentless, evil machine that is the entertainment industry forces performers to do unspeakable, horrific things like honor their contracts. Makes perfect sense. That pretty much explains in detail why Matt is leaving the show. Thanks all of you for clearing that up. (Post #101, 'Matt Smith and practical reasons for leaving')

More specifically, however, this UK–US debate is used to put forward justifications for why Smith's departure may have a negative impact, especially for viewers in the United States who may not be as familiar with the show's frequent regenerations of actors. One fan notes, 'Conversely, things that work for British audiences don't necessarily fly in the US. And, like it or not, *Doctor Who* has a substantial US fan base, for whom this will be their first change of Doctor. It might be wise for the BBC to give some thought to their international audience' (Post #8, 'Matt Smith and practical reasons for leaving'). The implication here is that while British audiences will accept the regeneration as part of the programme's fifty-year history, American audiences may find it harder to cope with this change of Doctor. This assumption appears linked to the increased presence in the American market during Smith's tenure in the role (for example, setting episodes such as 'The Impossible Astronaut', 'A Town Called Mercy' and 'The Angels Take Manhattan' in the US), even though the show had previously aired on the Canadian Broadcasting Corporation, the Sci-Fi Channel and BBC America (see Porter 2012). One American fan, however, contests this view, suggesting that American viewers are equally able to accept regeneration and deal with the replacement of the actors. This poster refuses to demarcate

reactions along national lines, falling in line with the acceptance and renegotiation that many of the online fans articulated in relation to both Tennant and
Smith's departures:

> I don't know that you're giving US (and other international) audiences enough
> credit. Personally, as a USian, one of the reasons I love *Doctor Who* is because
> of the change. Many other fans I know started with Ten or Eleven but went
> back and caught up on previous Doctors, so it's not as if it's entirely unexpected.
> Even after 7 seasons, it still feels like relatively fresh TV. Perhaps non-British
> audiences love it for the same reason the native watchers do. It became popular
> on its own merits, so I see no reason to drastically change how the show is
> produced for those of us in other countries. You may find that you're getting rid
> of the reasons it's resonated with so many people. (Post #13, 'Matt Smith and
> practical reasons for leaving')

Debates over gender, age and national identity are common in fan cultures.
Here, however, such discourses are mobilized to discuss aspects of *Doctor Who*'s
narrative device of regeneration and to discuss endings and transitions in the
series more broadly. As a long-running series with a fifty-year history, *Doctor
Who* fandom is diverse, with some fans preferring the classic series and others
more focused on the post-2005 revival. As fans debate UK–US divisions or the
apparent split between fans of David Tennant and Matt Smith, their discussions
demonstrate the discourses that can be drawn on to defend fans' own positions
and to ward off potential anxiety about points of fissure or change in the series.
As the show moves into the realm of the Thirteenth Doctor and the era of actor
Peter Capaldi, such fan debates will continue to evolve (for an explanation of
how the Eleventh Doctor regenerated into the Thirteenth, see Jefferies, 2013).

Conclusion

This chapter has explored what Whiteman and Metivier call 'smaller endings'
to 'demonstrate the continuity of loss in fan cultures' (2013, 292). In examining
three instances of character departure – via narrative writing-out, real and
character death, and regeneration – the chapter suggests that these little
endings may indeed be quite significant for many fans. In adjusting, in a variety
of ways, to the loss of fictional characters, fans demonstrate that "The loss of
loved objects, however small or mundane, is a routine element of the emergent

production of self/of object, leading to a constant process of stabilizing and destabilizing' (Whiteman and Metivier 2013, 292). Fans may respond in a range of ways to the departure of characters, from sadness and grief through to using the departure as a springboard for broader discussions about gender or national identity within fandoms. In the next three chapters, this range of reactions will be revisited to consider more final forms of ending – the cessation of a televised narrative world entirely.

4

'The Constant in my Life':
The Reiteration Discourse

Having explored examples of 'little endings' such as the various departures of beloved characters or actors, the next three chapters focus on 'big endings' – fan reactions to the final episodes of favourite television series. These chapters explore how fans react when the cessation of 'a favorite program creates an emotional void and forced detachment from the program narrative' (Costello and Moore 2007, 135). This first chapter uses case studies of fans of the American political drama *The West Wing* (NBC 2000–6) and the mystery drama *Lost* (ABC 2004–10) to explore a 'reiteration discourse' where fans offer lengthy stories about their involvement with shows and post goodbyes to them at online forums. It considers the ways in which identity is closely tied to the fan object and how reasserting these fan relationships at the end of a show often worked to strengthen this sense of fan identity and to help fans deal with any potential threat to the ontological security provided by fan objects. Finally, the chapter examines how such fans draw heavily on notions of cultural value and 'quality' television in order to valorize their chosen fan texts and to validate their own prolonged attachment to such shows. Data collection for this chapter was, as in the next chapter, undertaken at the online fan community Television Without Pity (TWoP). Once a show ceases airing, it is archived (or put on permanent hiatus) in the Television Without Pity forum (http://forums.televisionwith-outpity.com/index.php?showforum=598). Threads cannot then be added to but can still be accessed online. Posts about *The West Wing* were initially collated in the period immediately after the show aired its final episode on 14 May 2006. A second period of analysis examined all posts made on the *West Wing* thread between July 2006 and July 2011 (http://forums.televisionwithoutpity.com/index.php?showtopic=3143108). At the time of completing data collection there were 14,518 posts in the general thread dedicated to the series *Lost*, of which

338 posts were gathered and analysed (from the Television Without Pity *Lost* Archives). For the purposes of this chapter, the majority of fan comments are drawn from the thread dedicated to the final episode of *Lost*, the two-part 'The End', which had 1,874 postings when it was archived by the site.

As outlined in the introduction, the finales of television shows are usually highly publicized media events, designed to attract high audience numbers and celebrate the ending of a television series. As Todd notes in her work on the final episode of *Friends*, 'The broadcast and online media surrounding the end of the *Friends* era positions the finale as an intertextual media event, which illustrates the influence of television on fans' social perspectives and cultural identities' (2011, 854). Her point is applicable to other TV finales which operate as complex mediated moments, often across a range of platforms. It has been argued that for finales to be seen as successful they need to be planned and carefully orchestrated to allow both fans and more casual viewers to be satisfied with the outcomes of the stories and characters and for them to feel that their investment in a series was worthwhile. Indeed, 'Much as a good death among humans necessitates it being both expected and prepared for ... the good end of a TV show requires foresight and planning' (Harrington 2013, 583). There are clearly industrial considerations here when considering the planned ending of shows such as *Lost* and *The West Wing* which fit Mittell's definition of 'a conclusion with a going-away party' (2013, paragraph 8). However, the desires of viewers and producers can diverge. While production teams may feel some sense of obligation to sate the desires of long-term viewers and offer them closure, there is also the unique opportunity to write a story without any pressure from networks or other industry agents to ensure that viewers continue to watch the show. According to Corrigan and Corrigan:

> A series finale can be understood then as the one episode that potentially offers the most artistic freedom for a production team, who no longer need to concern themselves with getting viewers to return next week. Instead of pandering to the audience's expectations, writers may take the opportunity to crystallize the aesthetic character of the production or indicate some aspects of personal experience involved in the series' realization. (2012, 91)

As noted in previous chapters, the textuality and industrial contexts of the ends of television shows must be kept in mind when considering fan reactions to these. However, it is in the audience that we can most clearly begin to understand the significance of these forms of ending of fan objects given 'the question of what it means to "miss television"' (Anderson 2005, online). The chapter thus explores fan reactions to the endings of television shows when these conclusions are deemed to have been appropriate, enjoyable and satisfactory both for the fans themselves and in terms of doing a series 'justice' and offering them a fitting end point. These reactions are understood as a form of reiteration discourse, when fans offer personal anecdotes or stories about their fandom and its importance to them, bid farewell to the show or other fans and when they work to reiterate the importance of a show to their own sense of self-identity, narrative and ontological security via positioning a series as important and as a worthwhile object of their affection.

'This is the night TV died': Saying goodbye to *The West Wing*

> *As I click off the TV from that last episode [of The West Wing], it will be very quiet in my apartment … Wondering what to do with myself now, I'll sit there in my recliner and speak to myself in a whisper—'What's next?'*
> Post #32, 'It's Official—*West Wing* to Conclude Sunday, May 14'

In the 'reiteration discourse' fans often responded to the potential break-up of their fan pure relationships with *The West Wing* by reasserting their self-identities, offering coherent stories of how the show had impacted upon their lives and often revealing large amounts of personal detail. These reiterations of self-narratives often took the form of lengthy postings of 'goodbyes' to the show on the Television Without Pity fan forum:

> I have grown up a lot over the run of this show. It's so great to have constants in your life, even if they are just fictional TV characters, and I will miss them all dearly. Not to be too sentimental about it, but the show started when I was at a very low ebb, and for a while it was really the best thing about my week (sad I know) … but since then things have changed in so many ways and in so many directions. (Post #277, 'Institutional Memory')

> It was so long ago when I first saw *The West Wing*. Through adversity, exams, marriage, residency, divorce, rediscovery, recovery, and now some sort of sanity, *The West Wing* and you people here on this forum have been my friends. The constant in my life. (Post #130, 'Tomorrow')

> Mid-way during the second season, my college friends and I started gathering to watch it. We'd cook dinners and sit silently, talking loudly and quickly during

commercials, hanging out until the evening news ... at least. This show was so much more than just a show, it was OUR show, you know? And now two of these friends are getting married this week, everyone is so different now ... This show ending is more than just another series end, something in my life has closed. (Post #35, 'Tomorrow')

"This is the end, beautiful friend ... "
Thanks *West Wing*. Thanks for entertaining me for the past seven years. Thanks for informing me about the world around me. Thanks for shaping my political views, and therefore me as a person. In a world of reality television and increasing cynicism all around us, thanks for the optimism and idealism. For the way with words, the emotion, and for the intelligence. But most of all, thanks for raising the bar. I can stand to look at it now. You have left an indelible legacy on all of us. 'Tomorrow' is the end of one chapter. Tomorrow is the beginning of another. Thank you.
"We had it good there for a while."
The West Wing 1999–2006 (Post #59, 'Tomorrow')

Such postings intertwine fan identity with the show but also ward off potential anxiety about the end of the fan object and the potential demise of the fan relationship with the series. By relaying their self-narratives these fans rearticulate their identities and form their experiences with the show into a coherent story. When a sense of self is threatened individuals often reinforce 'a sense of trust, predictability, and control in reaction to disruptive change by reestablishing a previous identity or formulating a new one' (Kinnvall 2004, 746). Thus, fans' reiteration of self-narratives is a way to strengthen and re-establish their fan self-identity, increasing their ability to deal with the end of *The West Wing*. Fan postings here suggest that ontological security can be linked to the temporality of television since routine can ward off ontological insecurity and anxiety. The knowledge that the series had routine scheduling in the television landscape offered a source of ontological security for fans since 'fixed schedules, in which the same program is put on at the same time of the day ... mean that audiences can come to find the overall shape of output to be ordered and predictable' (Moores 2005, 20). Thus, when this ontological security is threatened, there is a period of identity transition for the fan as 'the altered self has to be explored and constructed as part of a reflexive process of connecting personal and social change' (Giddens 1991, 33). The reiteration of the intertwining of the fan's self-identity with the history and narrative of the text here allows these posters to negotiate such a period of personal and social change.

Furthermore, the series itself encourages continued attachment as, although it has been argued that the show's 'political storylines have been constructed as repetitive mini-quests of the staff, without the guarantee of a happy ending' (van Zoonen 2004, 119), the final episode of the show did attempt to offer closure for each character, suggesting what the next stage of their fictional life would involve. Thus, in contrast to series that end ambiguously such as *The Prisoner* or *The Sopranos*, *The West Wing* leaves relatively few storylines in a state of uncertainty. Furthermore, by ending the show with the incoming Democratic Santos presidency which involved characters that fans 'knew', fans were presented with the impression of an ongoing narrative and a world that continues beyond the final frame. This continuation of the programme universe is dependent upon the established 'hyperdiegesis' of *The West Wing*, which consists of a 'vast and detailed narrative space, only a fraction of which is ever directly seen or encountered within the text' (Hills 2002, 137). Although this is most commonly seen in cult texts, *The West Wing* clearly displays – via its textual mentions of Senators, House Members, political chairs and chiefs, committees and subcommittees – a vast narrative space which involves characters and places the audience never sees. This hyperdiegesis 'displays such a coherence and continuity that it can be trusted by the viewer, presenting the grounds for "ontological security" … The fan-viewer treats the hyperdiegetic world as a space through which the management of identity can be undertaken' (Hills 2002, 138). Indeed, it is this hyperdiegesis that makes series 'cohere as ontologically secure worlds that can support discussion, speculation and cultural production' (Johnson 2007b, 66). Thus, even after *The West Wing*'s demise, its hyperdiegesis enables fans to draw ontological security from re-watching DVDs or reruns, engendering continuation of their fan pure relationship with the text. This is alluded to by one survey respondent who states that 'Sometimes I'm left wondering what characters "would be doing now." I think if a character has an intricate backstory – as do most of the [*West Wing*] characters – then fans are implicitly encouraged to imagine their futurestory just as intricately' (Lene). Similarly, an online poster links the concept of open-endedness to quality television, commenting that:

> … there are a lot of unanswered questions that each of us want fulfilled, but I believe that in the 'television for smart people' context, we know and love these characters and to an extent we each can decide and imagine where each will go in the future. I think that's what it's creator intended, for each of us to be content with whatever future each of envision. (Post #192, 'Tomorrow')

This sense of an ongoing narrative world indicates fans' links to specific characters. Furthermore, for some fans their 'interact[ion] with the mediated world' (Gray et al. 2007, 10) is often facilitated through the fan practice of 'shipping'. This term is short for 'relationshippers' and refers to fans' support for fictional romantic relationships in texts such as television shows, films or novels. Key examples include the characters of Mulder and Scully in the television series *The X-Files* (Scodari and Felder 2000), The Doctor and his companion Rose Tyler in *Doctor Who* (Hadas 2013), fans of the Buffy/Angel or Buffy/Spike pairings in *Buffy the Vampire Slayer* (Kirby-Diaz 2009) or the opposing fans of Team Edward and Team Jacob in the *Twilight* saga (Bore and Williams 2010). For shippers, fandom is often strongly based around practices that support this, such as re-reading texts for scenes or dialogue that support their chosen relationships. As discussed elsewhere (Williams 2011a), in the case of *The West Wing* the most commonly supported ship was the Josh/Donna (J/D) relationship which consisted, for the first five seasons of the show, of an employer (Josh)/employee (Donna) interaction, although the two characters were routinely depicted as having a closeness that superseded that of other senior White House staffers and their assistants. After suffering life-threatening injuries in a terrorist attack at the end of the fifth season, Donna leaves the White House in season six to work on a Presidential campaign, in direct opposition to Josh who also departs to work on a rival campaign. After Josh's campaign is successful, Donna is absent for the first few episodes of the show's seventh season after Josh rejects her application to work for the Democratic 'Santos for President' campaign. Eventually, she is hired on the campaign, casting Donna's character in a much more responsible role than she played at the White House and significantly altering the dynamics of her relationship with Josh. By the end of the series finale 'Tomorrow', the characters work as the Chiefs of Staff for the President and the First Lady respectively and are clearly in a happy romantic relationship. J/D shippers had often been opposed to the producers' and actors' intentions (Porter 2004) and, for example, 'after [creator Aaron] Sorkin left, the series' new behind-the-scenes commander-in-chief, John Wells, told [Janel] Moloney [who played Donna] that whenever Josh and Donna got together, the show would be over' (Avins 2006, 1). Despite this, the position of shippers appeared to be vindicated with the consummation of the relationship in the final episodes of the show.

However, as the final episodes approached, J/D shippers displayed clear anxieties surrounding the narrative depiction of the relationship. As argued, mediated objects can be instrumental in identity formation and the creation of self-narratives, allowing individuals to develop 'reflexive narratives of the self' (Giddens 1991). When objects that allow such identity work to be carried out cease to continue, there might therefore be potential instability caused by the move from an 'active' to a 'dormant' fan object which needs to be warded off. One way to limit the possible rupture of identity caused by the object's cessation is by reassuring oneself that the fandom of that object was legitimate and that the time and emotion invested in it was worthwhile. Thus, it may be that, while fans routinely clash over interpretations (Tulloch and Jenkins 1995), engaging in continual battles for textual authority, this may become intensified as the end of a fan object approaches. The following quotes indicate some of these anxieties. One online poster pleads that pro J/D shippers be allowed both 'closure' and 'fun' at the end of the series and given a satisfactory ending to the relationship. The argument that not fulfilling this request would be 'cruel', 'unfair' and 'mean-spirited' indicates a level of trust between fans and producers and a desire for the show's finale to satisfy their request and provide a sense of resolution. For these fans, failing to do so would indicate a breach of trust between fan and producer and fail to provide closure and the ability to 'move on' after the end of the show:

> Any ending for the show without a Josh/Donna union would be unduly cruel for all the fans that have not invented this romance out of thin air but, rather enjoyed and followed the insane amount of clues and innuendoes dropped by the writers over the past 6 seasons ... for the show to end without resolving that 7 year thread would be unfair at best, and mean-spirited at worst. This is it, this is the end. Let the audience have its closure and fun. (Post # unknown, 'It's official ... ')

Another poster notes, 'Do I want Josh and Donna to get together? Absolutely. In spite of it all, I believe that John Wells owes us that' (Post #117, 'It's official ... '). This need for 'closure', and the associated alignment of one's interpretation of a text with the officially sanctioned canonical events, enables fans to ward off anxiety about the move from active to dormant fan object, reasserting the validity of their reading of the text and avoiding any potential disjunction between their own understandings and the object itself. Thus, for example, J/D shippers had continually asserted that their reading of subtextual hints to suggest a romantic relationship would be vindicated. As the show approached its finale, these fans were eager that the show depict romantic developments and lamented the possibility that this would not take place:

I thought it was a good episode, but y'all, I am so sad. We've got a finite number of episodes left and I'm not seeing any development in the Josh/Donna relationship. I'm doubting at all we're going to get it. They haven't had a conversation that wasn't about work in months. (Post #42, 'Duck and Cover')

If they don't get together now, I think I will have to hunt down Wells and annihilate him. (Post #24, 'The Cold')

Just want to third, fourth or fifth the sentiment that if Josh and Donna do not end up together, I will set fire to someone's house (preferably not my own). Oh, also, I'll be in on the setting-fire-in-front-of-John-Wells' house business. (Post #65, 'It's official ... ')

However, even when narrative events such as the first J/D kiss ('The Cold') or their first night together ('Election Day Part 1') endorsed the interpretations of J/D shippers, other fans continued to argue against these developments. The reappearance in the last few episodes of the character of Amy Gardner (played by Mary Louise Parker) – who had dated Josh in seasons three–five – prompted debate, with one fan opining that 'I know I'm in the minority here and am prepared for the snark and flogging to come ... but I rejoiced in the previews when they showed Ms. Amy Gardner. I can only hope Josh comes to his senses in time' (Post #259, 'The Cold'). Furthermore, one questionnaire respondent reiterated the view that it was the end of the series that led to the canonization of the J/D ship, noting that 'really the producers decided to cater to the fans as the show concluded, Donna and Josh could never really be together, besides Josh belongs with Amy' (Victoria).

However, such interpretations were quickly dismissed by J/D shippers who suggested that 'Amy's return may push Josh towards Donna even more' (Post #262, 'The Cold') and 'I have a feeling Amy comes back like Joey came back; she's moved on. I just don't see Amy being an issue for Josh and Donna anymore' (Post #262, 'The Cold'). If *The West Wing* had ended without explicit canonical depiction of the J/D relationship, these fans would have faced greater threat to their sense of self-identity than those whose interpretations of the text proved correct. Thus, while the reignited fan debates regarding the validity of the J/D relationship or arguments over Donna versus Amy may seem superfluous given the impending end of the series, it may be that such deliberations actually become even more pertinent as there remains only a finite time frame in which fans can be vindicated. It is also worth pointing out that not all non-shippers were against the onscreen resolution of the J/D relationship. In the online thread devoted to the series' cancellation (titled 'It's official, *West Wing* to conclude Sunday May 14') many non-shippers sympathized with the desires of the supporters and their wish to have the storyline concluded:

> I don't want to see Josh and Donna together either, except to satisfy the shippers, who have been mercilessly teased for years. (Post #113, 'It's official…')

> I truly hope Josh and Donna get together for all you shippers out there. (Post #83, 'It's official…')

This suggests that, although there were some divisions between pro-J/D fans and nonshippers, for other online posters the ending of the show prompted a sense of camaraderie and being magnanimous about hoping that each fan got the ending and resolution that they wanted. Another reason why some non-shippers were willing to accept the J/D storyline was articulated through what can be described as the 'lesser of two evils'. As one poster summarizes:

> While I agree that I tired of the soap feel, I'd still rather see them and the other characters in whom I have invested 7 years of my life, plus rewatches of tapes and marathons of the DVDs. I know some people have grown attached to the 'new guys', but enough is enough with only 3 episodes left, there was no reason to waste it on the team work between St. Matt and Ernie [two characters introduced in season five]. (Post #57, 'The Last Hurrah')

Here, while the poster is not a J/D fan, seeing their relationship and characters onscreen is preferable to 'wasting' precious screen-time on newer characters who this poster is uninterested in. Again, as in many of the other fan comments, the emphasis on there being only a finite amount of time left for the show is clear. Anxiety about *The West Wing's* impending cessation is again expressed here.

However, given my dual interest in fan–object *and* fan–fan relationships, it is pertinent that many posters also bid farewell to the online fan community at TWoP, acknowledging that their involvement in *The West Wing* forum would inevitably lessen. Even fans who had not been regular contributors took the opportunity to 'de-lurk' and declare their fandom and to thank those who had contributed to discussions:

> I've been reading recaps here since halfway through S3, but I never posted before. Just had to say my own good-byes to the *West Wing* with a group of people who share my sadness at the end of this amazing show. (Post #47, 'Tomorrow')

I have never posted here, but I have always read this board ... from the very beginning ... read every post, silently joined every argument and taken sides ... and loved every minute of it. I felt compelled to post my first and final message now ... Thanks for the great years, guys. (Post #82, 'Tomorrow')

I have rarely posted but I have been an extremely loyal lurker. Thank you from the bottom of my heart to each and every one of you who's posts have helped me better understand and appreciate every episode of this wonderful show. (Post #178, 'Tomorrow')

By reiterating their membership of the Television Without Pity forums, fans reassert their sense of 'belonging' to the community, also acknowledging the impact of their fan–fan relationships upon their fandom. Such reiterations echo the goodbye messages posted regarding fan–object relationships, suggesting again that fans seek to rearticulate their fan identities by describing the importance of the text itself as well as the fan community that surrounded it. As one poster notes, 'I love that we have a place to express our joy, sadness, shock and at times anger. We are all a family, and are all certifiably nuts for our show. I'm a WingNut for life! So I thank you all for your thoughts, opinions, lessons and at times arguments' (Post #50, 'Institutional Memory'). In stressing that he/she is a 'WingNut for life', this fan responds within the 'reiteration discourse' to re-narrate their fan self-identity. For other fans *The West Wing* had been not only a point of entry into the Television Without Pity community but into online fandom more broadly. Many posters discussed this in a thread titled 'The Reflecting Pool: A Look Back at the Show'. One poster notes:

Because of the unique timing of the show's inception and my interest in it, *The West Wing* is responsible for my introduction to internet discussion, and, through that, to the concept of cyber-friendship and the cyber-cocktail party ... I have found a new home here and have been welcomed. We have shared so much of ourselves and I am the richer for it. Triumphs and tragedies, weddings and funerals, shoes, food, *double entendres*, the entire experience that is life is experienced here as truly as it is in the physical world. I lurk in many other show threads and post periodically in some of them, but this is the one in which I feel most comfortable, in which I feel safest discussing aspects of my life that could make me easily traceable to someone who wanted to get to me 'up close and personal'. It is because I instinctively trust that people who are drawn to this show, to the ideas it presents, to the conversations it provokes. (Post #58, 17 March 2006, 'The Reflecting Pool')

Such postings allow fans to cope with the 'emotional void and forced detachment from the program narrative ... [through] mutual consolation of others mourning the death of a series, or more positively, reviving the memory of a past program to keep it alive' (Costello and Moore 2007, 135).

The show was also often praised for allowing its viewers to learn and to change their views or to even embrace new experiences:

> I discovered *WW* around the time I moved to DC six years ago, and as I don't work in politics, I feel it helped me feel like I was a part of the city more than slowly acclimating myself would! I know it sounds odd, but I learn things from this show. It helps me clarify where I stand on certain issues. Ainsley's rant on the Equal Rights Amendment (in 17 People?), for example. It's the rare TV show that teaches you something instead of just diverting you. (Post #68, 19 March 2006, 'The Reflecting Pool')

> First post on TWOP after being a long-time lurker, so I guess let's just look past the fact that I'm a little late to the party and embrace the fact that I showed up. :-) I've been giving a lot of thought to why I've fallen in love with this show along with the rest of you, and reading through all of the comments here, as well as on the John Spencer memorial thread, have reminded me that the great thing about this show is that it means something different to everyone. For some, it's a look into an idealized (or perhaps at least more deal) way that our government should be run. For others, it's an escape into a world of literary genius, comic relief, drama and heart-rending relationships, with a little bit of politicking thrown in for good measure. I spent last week in Washington, D.C., and made a point of visiting the National Cathedral, and it was surreal being able to walk the same steps that President Bartlet did in 'Two Cathedrals' – far and away one of the most powerful and moving scenes for me. I only got hooked during the end of season four, so I remember the first time I saw that episode and the others from S1-S3 and thinking, 'wow, how could I have missed out on all of this the first time around?' Without *TWW*, that afternoon at the cathedral wouldn't have been nearly as meaningful, nor would my entire time in D.C. (Post #86, 20 March 2006, 'The Reflecting Pool')

For these fans, attachments transcended affinity for specific characters, instead impacting their political beliefs or prompting them to make changes in their real lives. As one questionnaire respondent noted, 'Like several of the characters, I left a more high-paying career for a more service oriented, low-paying career' (Rhian), indicating that our chosen fan objects are 'intrinsically interwoven with our sense of self, with who we are, would like to be, and think we are' (Sandvoss

2005, 96). Furthermore, intense identification with the fan object may actually *alter* fans' 'world view and self-image' since 'media fandom can potentially act as one motor of subjective/hermeneutic and social transformation' (Hills 2007b, 151). Indeed, some *West Wing* fans found that their engagement with the text prompted social changes and greatly impacted upon their self-identity. One poster reveals that 'I think I feel safe in saying that this show has changed the direction of my studies and, to an extent, the direction of my life ... this show helped me find the passion in government' (Post #279, 'Institutional Memory'), while another notes that 'The show caused me to a) Become interested in politics to the extent I now help out the DCCC on a local level. b) Move to DC for a year, just to see if it's like it was on TV—it is' (Post #212, 'Tomorrow'). It is clear that the show is indelibly interwoven with these fans' lives and histories, carrying deep meaning for them which transcends identification with characters.

Fans were especially keen to demonstrate their real-life political interest and to rearticulate this as *The West Wing* drew to a close. This may result from the cultural division between being a consumer or a citizen, with the former connoting passivity and indifference and the latter suggesting socio-political awareness and activism. If fan–object relationships reflect desirable self-identities, it is unsurprising that fans seek to align themselves with such culturally laudable characteristics. However, the reassertion of such political beliefs *after* the show's final episodes may also 'prove' that one's attachment to the show was worthwhile, that it was 'more than' just a television show and that it altered the fan for the better. The show engaged many viewers in performances of citizenship (van Zoonen 2004, 38) or caused them to become more involved in political activity (Riegert 2007, 218). This demonstrates that one's ongoing fandom of *The West Wing* facilitated transformation into a politically active and socially aware citizen legitimates that fandom, suggesting that fans are not passive but that their fandom may motivate them into valuable real-life action.

Related to this is another aspect of the 'reiteration discourse' – fans' insistence upon aligning *The West Wing* with 'quality television' in their discussions. The show meets many of the academic criteria for 'quality television' such as auteurship via the hyphenate figure of Aaron Sorkin (Crawley 2006), the workplace setting of The White House, serialized narratives (Feuer 2005, 31; Feuer 2007, 149), ensemble cast (Lane 2003, 32), a filmic-style musical score (Kaye 2007, 223) and cinematic association via actors such as Martin Sheen and Rob Lowe. It also received widespread critical acclaim, receiving thirteen

Emmy nominations in its first year and winning a total of twenty-four Emmy awards. It is also literary and writer-based, winning acclaim for its dialogue (Lawson 2005, xviii), realistically portrays government and national security (Clark 2005), uses aesthetically innovative flashbacks and multi-angled story-telling and attracts a largely upscale demographic (Crawley 2006, 63–70). The show has also been compared with 'a number of circa-2000 series that marked a new darkening of tone, deepening of subject matter or complexity of structure in American television' (Lawson 2005, xviii). Janet McCabe argues that *The West Wing* can be viewed as a 'milestone television series' since it provided, via its 'production, its creative pretensions, and the rhetoric surrounding it – a discussion about what constitutes a politics of quality TV' (2013, 6). She summarizes that 'Evoking ideas of quality in terms of authorship, stellar casting and acting (associated with legitimate theatre), high-production values and the latest television image-making technology, upscale viewers and serious high-minded (political) debate helped distinguish what made *The West Wing* stand out as a beacon in the highly competitive television marketplace' (McCabe 2013, 8). The television industry often draws upon the concept of quality television to promote shows, accord them value and attract affluent, literate audiences who can be targeted via niche advertising. In the UK, American shows are often characterized as 'quality television' as they 'help enliven the schedule, and sometimes even attract up-market viewers' (Rixon 2007, 101) and they have high production values although, conversely, the opposite is often true in the US, which tends to view British programmes as possessing higher production values and being well-made (e.g. *Masterpiece Theatre, Downton Abbey*). Thus, *The West Wing* was utilized by its UK broadcaster Channel 4 to position itself as an alternative, quality channel, to appeal to a specific demographic and to 'build a distinct corporate brand identity for itself' (McCabe 2005, 212). This was furthered when the show moved onto the Channel 4 digital channel More4 which positioned itself as 'a lively, outspoken and above all entertaining channel for discerning viewers who want more from digital TV than repeats, football and back-to-back acquisitions' (Wilkes 2005, online). More4 thus used *The West Wing* to 'brand itself as serious, challenging and intellectual' (Rixon 2007, 106).

Many fans clearly shared the view of academics, critics and broadcasters that *The West Wing* was 'quality television' and discussed this when they bemoaned the show's loss. In the thread dedicated to the final episode 'Tomorrow', posters suggest that the show was unique and incomparable: 'Television will never be the same again' (Post #147, 'Tomorrow'), while others suggest 'Tonight is the night TV died' (Post #75, 'Tomorrow'), and 'This was the crown jewel of tv drama' (Post #22, 'Tomorrow'). Comparisons with reality television and game shows are also made and these genres are aligned with lowest-common-denominator programming and passive, unintelligent audiences. One suggests that 'In a world that includes shows like *Deal or No Deal, The West Wing* made me believe network television could actually be worth tuning in for. Not that I'm a snob or anything, but there's no reason a show has to fall to the lowest common denominator' (Post #283, 'Tomorrow'), while another forum member posts 'In a world of reality television and increasing cynicism all around us, thanks for the optimism and idealism. For the way with words, the emotion, and for the intelligence' (Post #159, 'Tomorrow'). As seen in this distancing from reality television and game shows, fans position *The West Wing* as intelligent 'quality television' which challenged viewers. Such pronouncements indicate the fans' position as what sociologist Pierre Bourdieu (1984) called 'consecrating agents' who 'contribute to the formation of collective belief surrounding the value of symbolic goods' (Shefrin 2004, 270). By discussing *The West Wing* as 'quality television' that surpassed other shows, fans consolidate the view of the show as 'good', reinforcing the discourses perpetuated by the show's producers and academics who seek to elevate the programme to render it worthy of their critical scrutiny. However, why did fans continue to so vehemently draw on discourses of quality television, originality and intelligence even after the final episode of *The West Wing* had aired? Given the argument that fans use television shows to perform identity work and provide ontological security, it is perhaps unsurprising that they seek to align themselves with cultural objects perceived as 'good' or as worthwhile. By insinuating that the programme appeals to intelligent audiences and is diametrically opposed to the 'lowest-common-denominator' programming of reality television and game shows, these fans clearly associate themselves with such traits. By positioning themselves in opposition to the passive audience who happily consume lower-quality shows, they can employ *The West Wing* to reflect back a satisfactory self-identity. However, given the cessation of the show, such positioning also takes on the crucial role of validating their continued attachment to the show over a number of years. Systems of cultural value place all genres into categories of 'highbrow' and 'lowbrow' (Mittell 2004, 15), and if *The West Wing* is perceived as 'quality television' and those who are fans of it construed as intelligent, politically aware and so on, then the use of this object to perform identity work is legitimated. The reiteration of established narratives displayed by these fans thus demonstrates how 'fictional texts, characters, and textual fragments … serve as anchors or throughlines to fans' lives' (Harrington et al. 2011, 580).

Coping with losing *Lost*

That was intensely satisfying. If there is a page to take from 'how to end a series' that was it. There was some really delightful symmetry … the imagery of ending on a nearly precise beginning, with the plane passing overhead was really so well done …

Post #89, 'The End'

Like *The West Wing*, fans were well aware of the impending end of *Lost*. They had even greater foreknowledge of this since the show's ending was announced at the end of the third season with ABC's ' "bold and unprecedented" decision that *Lost* would run for three more seasons and end in 2010' (Askwith 2009, 176). *Lost* fans were thus in the relatively unique position of knowing for the final three years of the show that the end was in sight. The decision to set a finite point for the show's end was driven by commercial and creative imperatives since 'it came partly at the request of producers Cuse and Lindelof and was partly a pragmatic marketing strategy because ABC felt that providing the security of an ending would keep viewers watching the show' (Morreale 2010, 184). As *Lost* continued to provide a range of narrative twists and turns – incorporating flashbacks, flash-forwards and, in the final season, what initially appeared to be flashsideways to a parallel world – many fans and general viewers continued to wonder how a show that was predicated on a range of mysteries and enigmas would be able to successfully provide closure. As discussed in the next chapter, some felt that it did not and the reactions of rejection, disappointment and outright vitriol will be explored more fully there. Here I want to continue to examine fans who responded within a reiteration discourse and who, like *The West Wing* fans discussed above, articulated a range of positions to bid farewell to the series and to highlight its importance to their lives and sense of self-identity and narrative.

The narratives of the six seasons of *Lost* are too complex to outline in detail here (see the articles in Pearson 2009 for an overview) but for the uninitiated, the show followed the survivors of a plane crash as they explored a mysterious island. Across the six series, they encountered a shadowy group of scientists called the Dharma Initiative, a group of hostiles living on the island and a range of mysteries including the island's ability to heal and even resurrect, its capacity for time travel and a range of other enigmas. The show's final episode revealed that what viewers had thought were flashsideways to the parallel worlds of the characters were actually a form of 'waiting room' in the afterlife where characters could deal with their issues before accepting their death and moving on. The final scenes saw all the major characters from *Lost* reunited in a non-denominational spiritual space after their death and their acceptance of their need to move on. Some of these characters had died on the island (such as Jack and Charlie), while others had lived long lives after leaving the island (including Claire and Kate). However, they all reunited in their afterlives since their time spent on the island had been the most important experience of their lives. In this section I discuss the reactions of *Lost* fans who responded within the reiteration discourse, and the ways in which they discussed the final episodes of the series.

There are some overlaps with fans of *The West Wing*; for example, the similarity in the posting of short goodbyes to the show and its staff in the thread 'The End':

Goodbye, *Lost*. It has been a fun six years. (Post #4, 'The End')

That was effing beautiful. Two and a half perfect hours. Farewell *Lost*. You were the best. (Post #22, 'The End')

Thank you, *Lost*. You were one of the greatest shows ever, with a fantastic cast and crew. (Post #142, 'The End')

Lost fans tended to highlight issues of emotion in their discussions, echoing the dominant themes of the final episode itself. There were numerous instances of posters discussing the moments in the finale that moved them and which they found the most affecting. This emphasis upon emotionality reflects the episode's own focus on character relationships as well as allowing fans to share these reactions with others who responded in similar ways:

I was holding it together until Vincent [the dog] came to lie down next to Jack. Then I sobbed like a baby. (Post #17, 'The End')

I thought it was outstanding. Emotional as hell. I never cried as much as I did watching this show. Great performances and work. (Post #142, 'The End')

Oh bollocks. I have to get up in a few hours and I don't know HOW im going to stop crying. (Post #156, 'The End')

The description of crying is echoed by other posters who discuss their bodily responses to the finale. Here, while the ongoing questions of the show's narrative are acknowledged by some, their reactions are characterized by physicality and by affect. One fan posts 'I went to the store to get wine and Kleenex for the finale. I forgot the Kleenex. Im going to have one hell of a hangover tomorrow. Full-on ugly cry from beginning to end. Although the episode didn't answer all my questions, I feel oddly satisfied. Im even smoking a cigarette' (Post #158, 'The End'). Although the postings made online must be treated as performative texts, the reference here to crying and the allusion made to sexual satisfaction indicates the importance of physical responses to the ending of fan objects. The mention of smoking a cigarette (a stereotypical post-coital activity) and the possible dual readings of Kleenex tissues for cleaning up tears and other bodily fluids means that this post is rather explicit about the ways in which fans can react physically to the emotional impact of the ending of texts. Here is the discursive opposite to the concern of one *Twin Peaks* viewer examined by Henry Jenkins (1995) who feared that the series would end without satisfactory resolution and that fans were 'being treated to an excruciatingly slow fuck destined to end in a whimper of an orgasm' (1995, 64).

Other posters discussed their emotional reactions to the finale in different ways, mentioning the emotional impact it had on them via more humorous asides. One poster states, 'Thanks to all involved in this show. I'll have to wear sunglasses to work tomorrow, and for that, I blame you!' (Post #253). Another posts that 'I still don't know what the fuck went on, but since everybody technically got a happy ending, I can deal. I did not cry during any of the happy reunions. I didn't cry during Old Yeller, either. That's my story and I'm sticking to it … Everybody had a happy ending. That's all I really care about' (Post #44, 'The End'). This poster acknowledges their affective response through a form of ironic disavowal and distancing – the poster's claims that they didn't cry are immediately undercut, allowing other posters to acknowledge the sarcasm and to understand that this fan's reaction was like their own. This poster admits to not fully understanding the plot or resolution of the episode and focuses instead on the happy endings of the characters, demonstrating one of the key aspects of discussion that fans within the reiteration discourse drew on. The emphasis on a happy ending for the series and the characters expressed by online posters appears to contradict the tendency of respondents to my broader survey on television endings who were less motivated by a need for a happy conclusion. While only ten of sixty-six respondents indicated that this was important, the focus on conclusion and emotionally satis-factory resolution here suggests that, for those who liked the finale of *Lost*, the sense of a 'happy ending' was crucial. This focus on character over the plot and mysteries was welcomed by many posters after the final episode aired:

> Loved it. It was everything I wanted/needed it to be. Lots of really gorgeous character and relationship moments, a satisfying conclusion to the real driving mysteries, and a pretty brave and beautiful conclusion to the Sideways-verse. (Post #18, 'The End')

> I'm very pleased at how the finale made me feel. Of course, any science aspects of the show seem to have been abandoned. The reason for their shared struggles seemed to fade over the seasons until now, we see, that maybe it just didn't matter. (Post #42, 'The End')

> Its about the connections you make, not the answers. Its about the babies born. The friendships made, the parent you reconcile with, the faithful dog lying by your side. How lucky we are to experience some of these things. I think the show and the creators just wanted to remind us of that, and I was. (Post #118, 'The End')

For these posters 'the producers managed to satisfy the conventional desire for closure and maintain the frisson that had motivated the series. They opted for an emotionally satisfying closure that saw all of the major characters reunited, both with their loves and with each other' (Morreale 2010, 184–5). The show's tension between narrative mysteries and character development had been present throughout its run, with producer Carlton Cuse explaining that 'for us, we're making a character show. The thing that we spend the most time on are the character dynamics of a given episode, and what we're learning about these people' (cited in Murray 2008). Cuse also noted the link between character appeal and the ability to reach a broader audience, noting 'All the questions that we get asked about the show tend to be on the mythological axis … But if we were just focused on the mythology, we would have a small, genre cult audience of 5 million or 6 million viewers' (Cuse, cited in Abbott 2009, 17). These tensions must be understood with acknowledgement of the industry pressures on television producers to continually attract new audiences and simultaneously satisfy the established base of loyal viewers. This is often achieved via both episodic storylines as well as ongoing serial narratives, allowing newer viewers to easily understand what is happening, while also offering longer-term development of characters and narrative arcs. In the case of *Lost*, the need to satisfy a range of audiences was ever-present since it was a high-cost mainstream production with the pilot alone costing $10 million dollars to make (Abbott 2009, 14). It is, thus, the characters and relationships that were perceived to be of most interest to the broader viewership of *Lost* and the decision to end the show with a focus on emotionality, reunion and the personal, rather than on solving mysteries, begins to make sense. For fans who were happy with the series' resolution, this focus on happy endings and character was welcomed and the way that the narrative mysteries had become less important across the series did not undermine their narrative pleasure.

The focus on reunion and closure in the final scenes highlights how many finales include 'self-referential stylistic devices in their last scenes ... [to] highlight the relationship between text and viewer by enabling the viewer to read multiple levels of meaning' (Morreale 2003, 276). In his discussion of the *Lost* finale, Jason Mittell notes how:

> Curtain calls highlight a series's storytelling mechanics via the operational aesthetic without taking us away from the dramatic pleasures of seeing characters reappear, often with great emotional resonances ... *Lost* embraces a similar emphasis on returning to past people and places as part of the final season's thematic emphasis on remembering and letting go. Thus we get a guided tour of the island, returning to locations like the caves, the beach, the Hydra cages, and "New Otherton," but framed by the characters themselves articulating their memories of such places. These moments are designed to remind us of where we've been over the years of the series, as well as offer a bit of closure paralleling the characters' experiences of coming to terms with their pasts and future fates—we witness characters remembering their past experiences in each locale as a reflected proxy of our own narrative memories. (2013, paragraph 16)

Many online posters reflected such a sense of parallel remembrance and experience and noted, for example:

> So, aside from the superb acting, the finale gave the viewers one thing – emotional closure. Yes, I loved seeing my favorites reunite; but that should not have been the focus. IDK [I don't know]. I think it was better than *The Sopranos'* finale; but not by much. (Post #216, 'The End')

> I feel like this finale spoke directly to my heart, much more so than my brain. I don't think I can articulate much about what I saw tonight but it *feels* right. A very beautiful, soulful and completely satisfying ending. And I cant say that for any show finale ever. (Post #252, 'The End')

For these positive fans, the finale offered a chance to say goodbye to characters and to come to terms with the cessation of the show. In watching the characters themselves bid farewell to one another and achieve a sense of closure within the diegetic world, the *Lost* finale provided the chance for fans to mirror this. As Morreale notes, 'On a metalevel, the finale spoke to viewers as much as to the narrative plot and helped viewers, like the characters, remember the emotionally satisfying moments and then let go and move on' (2010, 185). For these fans, the threats to ontological security that can occur as the fan object ends its broadcast run of new episodes can be warded off by witnessing the onscreen conclusion of the storylines and seeing the characters they have watched for six years experience a similar process. Whereas *The West Wing* ended with a clear sense that the narrative universe would continue beyond the final frames of the show, *Lost* offers a slightly different promise. While the lives of the characters after the show ends remain largely unknown, it does offer the end of each character's story in terms of what happens to them after they die. In seeing the end of the characters' narrative 'lives', fans of *Lost* are offered a sense of completeness and closure. Such evidence echoes the sentiments of survey respondents who noted that successful series finales should offer closure and finality for characters and the narrative world.

Even fans who were equally interested in characters and *Lost*'s broader enigmas offered praise for the finale, often acknowledging the difficulty of the task facing the writers or countering that the quality of the episode had lessened their potential disappointment:

> There are people I truly missed from that final scene, but I have say all in all I am very at peace with the ending. A beautiful and touching ending that brought the show full circke. Bye *Lost*. Youre frustrating and make me want to occassioally split my head open with a spork to relieve the pressure but that ending was lovely. (Post #156, 'The End')

> So … I thought the time for questions was supposed to be over. I am more confused than ever! I still liked the finale, but I wish they had answered more … I had a lot of issues with the finale but I am still going to miss this show so much. It has been such a great ride! (Post #217, 'The End').

> I would have changed some things in the finale, and id have some requests for different angles on some storylines, for sure. But im more overcome with emotional parts than anything … (Post #266, 'The End')

Others, as with *The West Wing*, posted longer messages about the impact the show had on their self-narrative and identities across its six years. Again, this demonstrates how fans can work to guard against threats to fan identities by reiterating their fandom in order to strengthen their sense of self and ontological trust in the object:

> I cried. I am so happy. I really don't even care that I still have 20,000 questions. That was how you end a show. When I popped in my first *Lost* DVD one bored summer afternoon four years ago, I didn't realize I'd come to the point where I'd be the blubbering mess I was … Everyone involved should be very proud of themselves, and I am so happy to have been part of this cultural phenomenon. A full rewatch is in order for me soon, and I will be hardpressed to find something to rplace the hole this is going to leave. Bravo. (Post #281, 'The End')

This post demonstrates a range of ways in which potential threat is negotiated: the fan's own narrative is reiterated and the depth of attachment to *Lost* is made clear via the poster's admission that they did not foresee how much it would come to mean to them. This is reinforced by the final statement regarding the difficulty in finding a replacement fan object; rather than suggesting that this poster cannot 'move on', this claim works to 'prove' fan credentials and devotion and to reassert the importance of the series for this fan's sense of narrative and self. Finally, the statement that the poster is happy to have been involved in the cultural phenomenon of *Lost* echoes another common discourse employed by fans of the show: that it was a unique series that changed television and that its cessation was a major media event. While *The West Wing* fans discussed above also positioned the show as 'special' and as a 'good' fan object, the *Lost* posters draw more heavily on the notion that the show's ending was an important cultural occurrence; another poster comments that 'I am glad that I was alive for this epic event' (Post #3, 'The End'). The ending of *The West Wing* finale was seen by some fans as disappointing since it was not surrounded with some of the more usual accompaniments such as retrospective documentaries. Although such a programme was announced, it did not materialize, allegedly owing to issues over how much to pay the show's actors for taking part (*USA Today* 2006). In contrast, *Lost* was granted a two-hour retrospective and an extended final episode, running for two-and-a-half hours (including advertisement breaks), as well as a post-finale special of *The Jimmy Kimmel Show* entitled 'Aloha to Lost'. The show's climax was thus positioned as an important mediated event, demonstrating that finales are 'rituals of farewell that are accompanied by much fanfare and related programming' (Todd 2011, 857). In the case of shows such as *Lost* which are consecrated by the fanfare surrounding their finales, fans can come to view their attachment to a series as being vindicated and validated. As in the more recent case of *Breaking Bad*, whose finale was widely hyped as a television event, the ending of *Lost* was presented as an important TV 'moment'. Although some fans were more ambivalent about the narrative resolution, they were at least allowed a moment of celebration to reflect on the impact of the series and to 'participate in the ceremony of the finale: remembering the show's appeal, and recognizing the show's impact in their real lives' (Todd 2011, 858). In contrast, *The West Wing's* perceived 'fizzling out' and lack of fanfare offered little official opportunity for fans to engage in this type of ceremony.

Conclusion

As this first chapter on 'big endings' has argued, how television shows end is of huge importance for many fans. A successful episode has the potential to satisfy fans both emotionally and interpretively, as well as offering an avenue to reiterate their fan self-identities and narratives and work through a possible threat to their fan ontological security. A sense of 'coherence and closure' is needed 'for a good demise of both persons and texts' (Harrington 2013, 582), and for the fans discussed here, the endings of *The West Wing* and *Lost* were seen to satisfy these needs. For fans who are happy with the conclusions of favourite series, ontological security is threatened but there is the ongoing love for the show to help counter this. The acts of posting goodbyes to a series or vignettes and stories about its impact on the fan can help individuals with 'the sense of order and continuity [they] … attempt to maintain in relation to the events and experiences of everyday life' (Ritchie 2003, 2). When faced with the prospect of no new instalments of a favourite television series, fans often respond in highly emotional ways, discussing their reactions of sadness and grief. As Todd notes in relation to *Friends*, 'While the show will be broadcast in countless reruns, the end of the series indicates the end of audiences' on-going relationship with the Friends because there are no more new plot developments' (Todd 2011, 864). Many of the fans of *Lost* and *The West Wing* discussed here may have continued to watch the series via televised reruns, online streamlining or on DVDs and Blu-ray. As discussed in Chapters 8 and 9 and as I have argued here, the concept of post-object fandom is not intended to suggest that fandom ends when a series ceases to produce new episodes. Rather this chapter and the next seek to examine the affective reactions fans have to the potential rupturing of their fan pure relationships with a series and the potential threats to both ontological security and their sense of self-identity. Reactions to the lack of the ongoing narratives and new televisual instalments warrants attention whether these responses are positive or, as the next chapter will discuss, rather more negative.

5

'Turning off the Life Support':
The Rejection Discourse

While many fans greet the end of a series with sadness and grief, others actively seek the end of televisual fan objects and consider this to be a welcome relief. Continuing with the case studies of fans of *The West Wing* and *Lost*, this chapter considers such viewers as forms of 'anti-fans' (Gray 2003) whose connection to shows means they would prefer their cessation rather than any perceived decrease in quality, or versions of the show that violate their fannish expectation. While anti-fan responses have been explored by writers including Jonathan Gray (2003, 2005), Sarah Wagenseller Goletz (2012), Sarah Harman and Bethan Jones (2013) and Vivi Theodoropoulou (2007), this chapter explores how fans articulate these views when texts cease production. This 'rejection discourse' often sees fans adopting a critically defensive posture, articulating that shows are past their 'golden ages' (Tulloch and Jenkins 1995) and that they are glad to see their demise. This allows fans to distance themselves from a show, discursively positioning themselves as critical and non-emotionally involved and suggesting that a programme is past its best period and deserves to end. The invocation of forms of anti-fandom may offer a way for some fans to cope with, and re-narrate, potential ruptures to a sense of identity or self-narrative that the cancellation of a series may provoke.

The chapter offers empirical data on the negative fan reactions to the endings of *The West Wing* and *Lost*, both to the final episodes themselves and also to some of the episodes that preceded them. As in the previous chapter, fan comments are drawn from the Television Without Pity (TWoP) message boards. Drawing on Harrington's discussion of the 'ars moriendi for US serial television – in short, a good serial death' (2013, 586), this chapter considers fan reactions when bad textual deaths are experienced and when the ending of fan objects is perceived as violating the sense of ontological security that has previously been negotiated via fandom.

Fan negativity and anti-fandom

While media objects can be used to deal with transitions, fans sometimes end their fandom if they feel their fan objects have ceased to be as good as they had previously been (often referred to as 'jumping the shark' (Hermes 2005)). Fans can become dissatisfied with unwelcome narrative developments (Symonds 2003), unpopular characters such as *Star Wars*'s Jar Jar Binks (Hills 2003) or the violation of the object's established ideologies (Tulloch and Jenkins 1995, 145–63; Brooker 2002, 79–99). For instance, fan displeasure with *Buffy the Vampire Slayer* in its later seasons partly derived from the assertion that onscreen misogyny and potential homophobia violated the feminist ideologies of the show (Tabron 2004). This can occur across a range of television genres. For example, some fans of Australian soap opera *Neighbours* disagreed with a perceived lack of emotional realism (Williams 2010), critiquing characters that embodied 'attitudes they find socially undesirable and inconsistent with the values they find within [a] series' (Jenkins 1992, 116). However, such work has tended to emphasize how fans work to maintain community based on mutual displeasure (Harrington and Bielby 1995, 151), 'salvaging' unwelcome plotlines while simultaneously expressing their 'frustration and antagonism' (Jenkins 1992, 23) and has paid less attention to fans 'falling out of love' with a series. In the 'rejection discourse' that fans employ at the ends of series they adopt a critically distanced or defensive posture, articulating that programmes are past their 'golden age' and that they are glad to see their demise. Although such reactions are briefly alluded to via Jenkins' comments on the 'relief' felt by some fans when the original series of *Beauty and The Beast* ended (1992, 151), they have yet to be comprehensively examined in fan studies.

Anti-fandom has been defined by Jonathan Gray as those who 'strongly dislike a given text or genre, considering it inane, stupid, morally bankrupt and/ or aesthetic drivel' (2003, 70). Anti-fans not only engage directly with the texts that they dislike but their feelings can also be 'construct[ed] from paratextual fragments such as news coverage or word-of-mouth, reading, watching and learning all they can about a show, book or person in order to better understand

and criticize the text (and, very often, its fans)' (Sheffield and Merlo 2010, 209). Anti-fandom often results from apparently 'natural' oppositions between media texts or objects, such as football or other sports teams with rivalries (see Theodoropoulou 2007) or from seemingly disparate and unconnected fandoms such as the *Twilight* franchise and the rock band Muse, who were forced into antagonistic 'accidental anti-fandom' (Williams 2013a) when the band's music was featured in the films. Broadening the scope of study has moved some way towards responding to Theodoropoulou's statement that 'A further elaboration of such a notion of the anti-fan is certainly needed, so that we might better conceptualize and theorize it. Pursuing such a task can lead to a better understanding not only of the role of anti-fandom to the identity positions of the fan, but more generally of fandom's expression and appropriation' (2007, 326). This chapter contributes to such elaboration by focusing upon anti-fandom within specific fan communities when the object of fandom comes to a close. Fandom of television series can clearly 'continue through watching DVDs and re-runs, collecting merchandise, or ongoing conversations with fellow fans' (Williams 2011a, 266). Similarly, fans may move into or out of periods of anti-fandom across time – for example, a one-time fan of a television show or band may 'grow out' of them and move from a position of dedication to dislike or hatred (Williams 2013a, 337). However, the focus here is on how discourses of anti-fandom are utilized at the point of a show's cessation. This allows consideration of the fact that 'fans can become anti-fans of a sort when an episode or part of a text is perceived as harming a text as a whole' (Gray 2003, 73) but through the lens of broader understandings of how fans respond when beloved texts draw to a close.

'Putting the show out of its misery': *The West Wing*

It certainly felt like a love letter to those people who tuned in to see one of the final episodes of their program and its beloved long-running characters. And the individual letters are f, u, c k, y, o and another u

Post #146, *The West Wing*: 'The Last Hurrah'

Online fandom enables fans to 'quickly mobilise grassroots efforts to save programs' (Jenkins 2002, 161), such as a campaign to save CBS's *Jericho* (2006–8) by sending peanuts to the network (Barton 2014b) and the posting of

Mars bars to television network the CW to renew *Veronica Mars* (Paproth 2013). The possibility that fans may, in fact, campaign against their own fan objects has rarely been studied. However, in the case of *The West Wing*, some actively called for the show to be cancelled via the 'Don't Save Our Show' campaign. Tucker describes this as an 'entertainment form of impeachment' (Tucker 2004, online), outlining the petition's plea to NBC boss Jeff Zucker which 'respectfully request[ed] that you put the actors and the audience out of our collective misery and cancel it at the end of this season' (Tucker 2004, online). The show ran for a further two years after this petition was launched but its sentiments were echoed by some online posters, one of whom expressed that they 'would rather have no *TWW* than bad *TWW*' (Post #241, 'The Last Hurrah').

A range of discourses related to sickness, death and dying were utilized by fans who were negative about the end of *The West Wing*. Some reacted using discourses of euthanasia, alluding to 'putting the show out of its misery' (Post #124, 'The Last Hurrah') or lamenting that 'It's sad watching my favorite show die. I know the patient is on life support and not expected to live much longer, but I can't help watching it wither away' (Post #298, 'Two Weeks Out'). Such self-protective posturing allows fans to ward off any emotional upset when the show ends as they rationalize their affective ties away via the suggestion that the show had ceased to be worthy of their attention. These discussions over the perceived demise in quality relate to *The West Wing* fans' debates over what constituted the 'true' show. Such discussions were also commonplace within the Television Without Pity community before the cancellation of the show was announced, with posters debating what constituted 'real' *The West Wing*. This demonstrates that some online posters continue to view programmes they 'no longer really liked because they want to participate in the ongoing online dissection of the program, its characters and its writers' (Andrejevic 2008, 44). For example, many fans felt that those who supported a romantic relationship between the characters of Josh and Donna (so-called J/D shippers) were emphasizing the more 'soapy' elements of the show over the political drama (Williams 2011b) and such fans were perceived as 'mono-focused ... whose focus on romance blinds them to basic show themes and values' (Hadas 2013, 330). Those who vehemently opposed the romantic development of the Josh/Donna romance often clashed with the supportive shippers and this intensified as the show neared its final episodes. Such hostility echoes that within *The X-Files* fandom between those who supported the Mulder/Scully ship and those 'Noromos' who did not (Scodari and Felder 2000).

For some fans, emphasis on the J/D ship was not 'proper' *West Wing*, referring to it as the 'Josh/Donna "The Young and the Horny" daytime drama' (Post #47, 'The Last Hurrah') or a potential '*West Wing*, Tahiti Edition' (Post #130, 'The Last Hurrah') following the couple on their holiday. For these fans, such emphasis upon romance violates generic expectation that the show centres on political issues rather than personal ones. Indeed, one of the key distinctions operated at Television Without Pity was the dismissal of elements of the text deemed to be too 'soapy' and, therefore, too feminine. One poster argues that pro-J/D writer Deborah Cahn 'has a real tendency sometimes to wander off into soap land' (Post #156, 'Institutional Memory'), while another pleads that the J/D relationship not be 'drag[ged] […] out so that it resembles some kind of third rate soap opera' (Post #67, 'The Cold'). Another fan comments that 'I am looking forward to more politics not an additional "*Legally Blond*" [sic] episode . . the show is about politics first, people second … The remaining time left for this series is so precious, and I sincerely don't want [soap opera] "*Days of our Lives*"' (Post #180, 'The Cold'). Although these fans devalue the soap genre, the possibility of *The West Wing* as a 'prime-time soap opera' has been considered by Liesbet van Zoonen, who argues that the show displays soap narrative hallmarks such as 'a core location, the focus on a community of people trying to get by, the emphasis on the human side of public affairs, the multiple storylines, and … the core tension between two "families", Republican and Democrat' (2005, 118). However, for non-shippers, comparison with soap opera is to be discursively avoided and the alignment of personal, character-based stories with the feminized and culturally devalued continues. Soap opera has long been seen as a 'woman's genre' given its emphasis upon personal relationships and interactions, verbal interaction and its open-ended storytelling techniques (Brown 1994). This anti-soap opera discourse can thus be seen as indicative of a wider battle within this *The West Wing* fan community between the personal and the political, with specific strategies employed to denigrate culturally feminized readings of the text, since there is 'a common association of the feminine with vulgarity and excessive emotion' (Bird 2003, 141). The personal versus political discourse can be clearly aligned with feminized and masculinized readings of the text, which is not uncommon within fan cultures. For example, as Susan Clerc notes, fans of *The X-Files* engaged in such divisions since 'men used the character interactions to illuminate the plot and referred to outside information to solve narrative problems; women used the plot to illuminate aspects of the characters' internal lives and worked within the universe established by the series' (1996, 41). Furthermore, many fans opposed the possibility of a Mulder/ Scully romance in *The X-Files* as they 'worr[ied] about the show drifting into the realm of soap opera' (Scodari and Felder 2000, 241). Such gendered divisions can also be seen in Jenkins' discussions of *Twin Peaks* (1995) and *Star Trek* (1992) fans, and are alluded to in MacDonald's work on *Quantum Leap* fans, and the fact that male posters disliked discussion of attraction to characters, onscreen relationships or the posting of real-life events and stories (1998, 148).

However, in addition to the genre-based anti-soap opera sentiment, other discourses were deployed to argue against the validity of the J/D ship as the show neared its end. Fans comment, variously:

> I don't buy into [Donna's] new role, and I'm totally offended that Josh would have a relationship with her which is unprofessional and possibly unethical. (Post #266, 'Institutional Memory')

> I'll skip commenting on the Josh/Donna crap because I find it to be exactly that, modified by 'boring'. (Post #101, 'Election Day Part One')

> I personally would rather not see Josh and Donna on the beach canoodling. I almost get a little squeamish seeing them 'together', almost like a brother and sister. (Post #75, 'The Last Hurrah')

While these fans offer different reasons for their dislike of J/D, each works to discursively position the ship as 'wrong' and to attempt to enforce the dominance of their own fan interpretation. By variously suggesting that the ship violates moral and ethical boundaries, is tedious or nauseating (even discursively aligned with incestuous behaviour due to some fans' reading of the J/D relationship as familial rather than romantic) such fans seek to impose their textual readings and to imply that those who support J/D are misguided. Given that the final season of *The West Wing* itself officially sanctioned the relationship, non-shippers could no longer rely upon the ambiguity of producers' statements as 'evidence' to verify that the romance existed only in the minds of shippers.

However, given that these fans were aware that their fan object was coming to an end, why did it remain so important for them to compete over textual interpretations and to struggle to enforce certain reading practices? Why were debates over the narrative representation of a fictional relationship so important at this specific point? As argued, mediated objects are instrumental in identity formation and the creation of self-narratives, allowing individuals to develop 'reflexive narratives of the self'. When objects that allow such identity work to be carried out cease to continue, there might therefore be potential instability caused by the move from an 'active' to a 'dormant' fan object which needs to be warded off. Fan debates over the appropriateness (or otherwise) of the Josh/ Donna relationship allowed final attempts to be made to limit the possible rupture of identity caused by the object's cessation by reassuring oneself that the fandom of that object was legitimate and that the time and emotion invested in it was worthwhile. Thus, while fans routinely clash over interpretations and engage in continual battles for textual authority, this often becomes intensified as the end of a fan object approaches. As Mittell points out, 'The knowledge of a series's upcoming finale recasts fan expectations for the final season, and potentially serves to overshadow the various ways fans have engaged throughout a long-running season' (Mittell 2013, paragraph 9). Thus, although noted in the discussion of fans who responded through reiteration of their fandom and who wanted to see an emphasis on characters and relationships, for others this focus on personal issues was disliked even more intensely by some fans and their 'deliberations actually become even more pertinent as there remains only a finite time frame in which fans can be vindicated' (Williams 2011b).

Furthermore, many fans felt that episodes focusing upon the Presidential campaign between the Democrat and Republican candidates to replace Bartlet were not 'proper' episodes of the show:

> Well, that was pretty good. It was interesting. But what show was it? It certainly wasn't *The West Wing*. (Post #2, 'Message Of The Week')

> Wow the only thing missing from *The West Wing* tonight was 'THE WEST WING'. (Post #6, 'Message Of The Week')

> It just isn't the same show without all of our original characters. It might not be a bad spin off but, it simply isn't *TWW*. (Post #57, 'Message Of The Week')

Acutely aware of the finite amount of time left to enjoy the narrative diegesis of the series, some fans react angrily when this time appears to be 'wasted'. Others were slightly less critical and felt that the new direction was still 'true' *West Wing*. One poster noted, 'Seriously, can we stop with all the "This isn't *The West Wing*" stuff? I get that there are a lot of people dissatisfied with the direction of the show right now and would prefer that it had never shifted away from Jed and the gang ... But this is the show. It's still called *The West Wing*' (Post #227, 'Message Of The Week').

However, such debates intensified and occurred with increasing regularity as the final episode approached. When the antepenultimate episode 'The Last Hurrah' was screened fans were outraged that it focused upon the incoming administration and barely featured long-term characters:

> OMG what an amazing waste of one of three final episodes of this show. Appalling. John Wells is just incapable of getting it, isn't he? Of course there will be storylines left hanging, but these all rank among the top of the Who Gives a Fuck list? (Post #11, 'The Last Hurrah')

> With three episodes left the focus of characters created by the new writers is egotistical and selfish. Nobody cares, get over it. (Post #67, 'The Last Hurrah')

> it certainly felt like a love letter to those people who tuned in to see one of the final episodes of their program and its beloved long-running characters. And the individual letters are f, u, c k, y, o and another u. (Post #146, 'The Last Hurrah')

Such vitriolic statements indicate the level of fans' attachment to the original characters and premise of the show and the sense of disappointment and betrayal that they feel regarding such episodes. However, the emphasis upon the fact that there are only a few episodes of the show left also demonstrates an anxiety that the narrative can never fully sate their need for resolution of events. These statements further indicate a level of blame toward the writers and producers, suggesting that they are not only incapable of writing satisfactory conclusions to the story but are deliberately antagonizing fans in their insistence that storylines involving new characters are what the audience wants to see. This is not to say that John Wells or the other writers are actually behaving in this fashion. Here, anti-fandom is articulated in terms of quality television and 'golden ages' and these discursive fan strategies must be read as symptomatic of their debates and struggles over what constitutes *The West Wing* and what types of episode are 'good' or 'bad'. Anti-fan discourses are employed to single out aspects of the show that are seen to be inadequate, offering insight into one example of how fans make value judgements about text and allowing, as Gray puts it, 'meaningful re-entry points to discussing quality, values and expectations, allowing us to focus on the range of everyday viewers' values, and on how they interact with media consumption, use and meaning' (2003, 73).

However, such distinctions do not only result from the impending demise of the show. One poster notes 'Yay, we've gone back to a year ago this time. Because those episodes were so great' (Post #27, 'The Last Hurrah'), indicating that episodes in prior seasons that focused upon the Santos campaign were equally unpopular and perceived as 'inauthentic' *West Wing*. Here, in order to protect their fan/object relationships (and their ontological security and sense of self-identity), some fans refute any potential threat caused by the ending of the series by reiterating that they foresaw that the fan object was already decreasing in quality. This suggests that such discursive manoeuvres may be a way for fans to protect themselves against threats to their fan identities. Some fans claim that such flaws lead them to be relieved that the show is ending, commenting 'Just when I thought that it was a travesty this show was going off the air' (Post #92, 'The Last Hurrah') or, after the final episode, 'Dissenting here. I thought it was just dull. They clearly had nothing more to do or say. Such a boring finale helps me get over my sadness that the show was ending' (Post #86, 'Tomorrow'). However, as discussed above, such debates allow fans to make defensive statements which enable them to deal with the loss of a previously valued fan object. If episodes such as 'The Last Hurrah' or 'Tomorrow' can be dismissed as violating or denigrating what was enjoyable about the show in the first place, the show's demise can be rearticulated as a welcome relief, enabling fans to cope with potential disruption to their identities, self-narratives or ontological security.

Discourses of good/bad episodes and the 'proper' show are often related to issues of authorship, a cinematic concept that endures within television studies. Similarly, *The West Wing* fans commonly distinguish between the show's earlier seasons, helmed by show creator Aaron Sorkin, and seasons four to seven, led by John Wells:

> That was a truly outstanding episode. It reminded me of the best days of the show (cough, Sorkin, cough). (Post #28, 'The Cold')

> Aaron Sorkin would have done better with this because Aaron Sorkin is a better writer/conceptualist and hears nuance a hell of a lot better than John Wells. (Post #148, 'Requiem')

Such dividing of shows into golden ages is not uncommon but *The West Wing* fans routinely project their disappointment onto Wells while seeking to privilege and elevate the figure of Sorkin as auteur or 'hyphenate' (Thompson 1990 cited in Hills 2002, 132). The associations of auteurship with an ideology of quality have long been noted (Brower 1992, 171; Hills 2002, 133) and fans thus associate *The West Wing* with 'good television' via their alignment of the 'best' episodes or seasons with Sorkin. Such a distinction between art ('high' culture) and commerce ('low' culture) is common within fandom (Shuker 1994, 16). Such distinctions became more pronounced as the series neared its end, with fans frequently bemoaning the opportunities wasted by both John Wells – sometimes referred to as 'Wellsatan' (Post #92, 'The Last Hurrah') – and another widely derided writer Lawrence O'Donnell:

> firing Lawrence O'Donnell woulda been a good budget cut. (Post #91, 'The Last Hurrah')

> Lawrence O'Donnell should never write anything ever again. Not even a take-out menu. (Post #22, 'The Last Hurrah')

> I didn't want this feeling of being manipulated by John Wells – he just went for the sucker punch again and again and again. There was no story here – just endless manipulation of my emotions as I watched the finest series that has ever graced American Television come to an end. (Post #20, 'Tomorrow')

> John Wells … Well I know not to seek out anything that you had a hand in making! I know you tried, but it just didn't work. (Post #92, 'Tomorrow')

> I can't say I'm disappointed because this was pretty much what I expected, but I thought it was glacially paced and dull; where Lawrence O'Donnell is dry and dull, John Wells is soppy and dull. (Post #118, 'Tomorrow')

These distinctions between good and bad writers relate to discourses of quality television but also suggest an anxiety that the show may never fully resolve all of its narratives, leaving the fan unfulfilled once the final episode airs. Although the hyperdiegesis of *The West Wing* enables fans to imagine a narrative world beyond the final frame, events that are not rendered canonical in the final few episodes will never be realized, potentially undermining fans' sense of ontological security. Furthermore, berating the writers for unpopular episodes also shifts the causes of loveshock onto outside sources, allowing fans to deal with their potential feelings of loss by apportioning blame.

The failure of answers: Genre, gender and professionalism at the end of *LOST*

I think the show will end exactly as it began. There'll be people who love it, there'll be people who hate it. There'll be people who'll be confused by it, there'll be people who love being confused. It'll end on its own terms
Lindelof cited in Morreale 2010, 184–5.

Well, that's six years I'd like back. (Post # 82, 'The End')

As outlined in Chapter 4 the ending of ABC drama *Lost* was, like *The West Wing*, expected although its ending came at the explicit request of the producers (Morreale 2010, 184). The show's ending was thus known to fans throughout the final three seasons, ensuring that they were not surprised by the sudden cessation of the programme as fans of other suddenly-cancelled programmes such as Joss Whedon's *Firefly* may have been. While the cancellation of *The West Wing* had been long rumoured, its fans had mere months to prepare for the end in contrast to the slow demise of *Lost*. Indeed, this foreknowledge and expectation of *Lost*'s ending may have been one way for viewers to negotiate their feelings about this since 'the long lead time viewers have to expect such a breakup may mitigate its negative effects' (Eyal and Cohen 2006, 516). The fans discussed here may well have been able to deal with potential threats to ontological security by focusing on the alleged decline – the slow 'death' – of the show across its last three series. As discussed in the previous chapter, some viewers responded positively to the series finale. However, reaction to the finale was mixed, with many fans expressing deep disappointment or offering fairly stinging critiques of the show. While series co-creator Carlton Cuse noted that 'I don't think we honestly believe we can make every single person happy with the ending of *Lost*. Nor should that be the goal' (in Windolf 2010, 93), the intensity of the rejection discourses deployed by some fan viewers deserves scrutiny.

The disappointment and disillusionment of many *Lost* fans had begun years before the final season and offers perhaps one of the most vitriolic examples of antagonistic fan–producer relationships. Derek Johnson refers to this as 'fan-tagonism': 'an interpretive, evaluative, and hegemonic struggle between internal fan factions and external institutions, through which acceptable relationships between fan, text and producer are continually articulated, disarticulated and rearticulated' (2007b, 63). For instance, the show's Executive

Producers Damon Lindelof and Carlton Cuse were often disparaging about certain types of fans. This highlights how, despite increases in fan participation and the fact that 'the figure of the listening production team is important to the popularity of [*Lost*]' (Ross 2008, 207), production institutions still seek to control and 'innovate new strategies for managing and disciplining the audience that they bid enter' (Johnson 2007b, 74). For example, Lindelof commented that 'we find that the [message] boards can be really toxic. Nobody goes on the boards to say, "Wow! That was awesome!" Traditionally, they go on the boards to nitpick' (Murray 2008) while he also posted at a non-Television Without Pity fan board in response to criticism of the show:

> I really don't care if you believe we've 'pulled it off' or not. Your negativity stands out as a harsh contrast to the spirit of what is essentially a fan board. I'll bet they'd LOVE you over at *Television Without Pity* as you seem to have none … So all due respect, either keep watching and try to be nice every once in a while … Or as I've suggested before, go check out CRIMINAL MINDS. It's awesome and they solve THEIR mysteries every week. (Cited at TWoP, 'The Bitterness Fiesta', Post number unknown)

Fans at Television Without Pity similarly expressed dislike of Lindelof and Cuse, perceiving them to be insincere and lacking respect for the fans: 'I do have to wonder if Demon and Curse were more invested in fandom if perhaps we'd forgive some of the writing. A likable creative team can get away with a great deal more. However, whenever I've read an article with the creators, it sounds as if they are laughing at viewers' (Post number unknown, 'The Bitterness Fiesta'). It is this apparent disconnect between the textual content of the show and the producers' extra-textual comments that fans also object to, owing to the implication that the producers are not in control of the narrative world they are responsible for. Jenkins noted a similar fear among online fans of *Twin Peaks*, a series predicated on secrets and the central mystery of who killed schoolgirl Laura Palmer. He cites one fan who noted, 'Look for dozens of questions to remain unanswered, for the series to end with hundreds of plot threads dangling into a TV vacuum', while another posted, 'Am I the only one experiencing a crisis of faith? I waken in the middle of the night in a cold sweat imagining a world in which no one knows who killed Laura Palmer' (cited in Jenkins 1995, 62–3). Such anxieties can be seen in *Lost* fandom where fans who are invested in the diegetic world of *Lost* lose faith in the creators' ability to satisfactorily resolve narrative mysteries or to sate their expectations for the series:

What's making me bitter is the growing suspicion that the writers don't have an explanation for anything at all ... All this mystery is only fun for me so long as I think it has meaning. If they're just making things up as they go along, just throwing in any old spookiness, then the laugh's on the viewer, and I lose interest. (Post #126, 'The Bitterness Fiesta')

Furthermore, in contrast to previous work on fandom, they appear to actively dismiss the use of fan theories and ideas as lazy and as further evidence of the producers' incompetence. For example, posters note:

I think in 20 years [*Lost*] will mark the first time that creators and writers of a major network show took their plot points almost entirely from the Internet and random fans comments, and instead of having testicular fortitude along with a unifying vision and following through on that, they made a convoluted mess from putting together a mishmash of ideas and plots. (Post #12,512, 'The Bitterness Fiesta')

It bugs me to no end when D&C use the 'fans didn't like it' defence ... I think the fans would rather prefer (1) better writing, (2) continuity and NO RETCONS, (3) a cohesive plot whether its mystery, science or supernatural – just pick one for chrissakes. (Post #12,357, 'The Bitterness Fiesta')

These fans expect producers and writers to be in control of their own narrative construct and to possess the ability to tell a clearly defined and planned story. Writers are expected to understand that 'a good death resolves the narrative of one's life in an appropriate and meaningful way' (Harrington 2013, 582) and that the death of a series must be equally appropriate. For viewers who responded within the rejection discourse, the show's final episodes confirmed their sense of 'fantagonism' and narrative anxiety and they often linked their sense of disappointment to discussions around professionalism (or lack of) on the part of the writers and to the perceived failure of the narrative. While some fans were happy with the show's ending and others acknowledged the difficulty of the feat of trying to wrap up six years of storylines, other posters at TWoP were keen to express their negative views.

There were debates over the finale not being specific enough to what *Lost* had stood for as a television series. In the accusation that the final storyline could have been applied to any long-running show, there is the suggestion of a generic and unimaginative conclusion to the series. Such reactions echo the sentiments expressed by my survey respondents who indicated that the ending of a television programme must be 'true to the series'. An overwhelming majority of respondents felt that this was important (fifty-six of the sixty-six respondents), while it is clear that, for the *Lost* fans on the TWoP forum, the finale had not been faithful enough in reflecting the show. One online poster notes:

> Well done fan service for people who don't care if the plot makes any sense. Yes, it was great to see old characters return, and all the reunions. But this last 'story' where everyone meets in the afterlife could have had the characters names filed off and replaced with different characters to end ANY long-running TV show. What made this *Lost*? What connected it to the mysteries of the island? *Buffy* could have ended this way. (Post #238, 'The End')

For these fans a series finale must be true to the narrative that they have committed to and must be specific to that show. A resolution that is too general or seems like it could be used to end another show is thus rejected. Here, there is the threat that the show itself is not 'special', that its narrative can be ended in a generic way and that the time the fan dedicated to the show has been potentially wasted. A fan's sense of identity and self can be threatened; there is the potential for feeling that one's investment has been misplaced and that a series was not what the fan 'thought it was'. Such broken narrative promises or perceived violations of a series' established themes and ideologies can present a threat to fans' sense of ontological security and their narrative of the self by presenting the possibility that the fans' understanding of a series was 'wrong' or that they have been misled by the producer's intentions.

For others, there were questions over what the final episode – and the final season's use of flashsideways to what appeared to be parallel storylines – actually meant:

> UM. WHAT?
> … the end just totally erased everything. What was the point of the sideways? What was the point of anything? (Post #58, 'The End')

> ***SHAKING HEAD***
> WHAT?
> Were we just in purgatory for 6 years? Im confused. I don't get it.
> Maybe I'm just way stupid, but … what the hell? (Post #33, 'The End')

> What the devil was that? So, we had three years of flashbacks, two years of flashforwards and now one year of a flashafterlife? There was no point to the flashafterlife. It added NOTHING to the story. Not one bleeding thing … In short, that was a bad ending. (Post #392, 'The End')

There was much fan debate over the 'meaning' of the last episode, especially given the popularity of a theory about the characters having died in the plane crash that opened the series in its first episode and the island being a form of purgatory. This popular interpretation had been dismissed by the writers early in the first season of the show and its apparent return, albeit in a different form, in the finale contributed to confusion and frustration for some posters. One noted that 'I am very disappointed in this series finale. I feel like the writers could've come [sic] much harder than the they're all dead conclusion' (Post #32, 'The End'). Others expressed confusion and disappointment over the 'purgatory storyline':

> The writers created a tangled vine they could not untangle. Some viewers might have thought the writers had a destination in mind for all those characters and subplots, but apparently not. This could have ended with such surprise and gratification, but it seems as if they took an easy way out. They knew this was the last season, what the f???? I thought it was purgatory in the first season, and that might have been a better story line than what we got. (Post #364, 'The End')

For other fans, the finale seemed to confirm their fears that the showrunners had no master plan for the series. As Askwith noted in 2009, fans were already anxious that *Lost's* writers and showrunners had no long-term plan, or – even worse – that the writers might be 'making it up as they go along' (2009, 160). This fear was stoked by the claims of ex-writer David Fury that there was, indeed, no plan, and this 'suggested that the numerous references, clues and suggestions would never add up to answers and made a mockery of the fans' post-episode analysis, debate and speculation' (Askwith 2009, 164). The producers themselves were acutely aware of these accusations and, as early as 2005, were acknowledging the notion that there was no master plan for the series. Executive Producer Damon Lindelof commented that 'The "making it up" part is just our acceptance that this is a collaborative process, that the show is about writers and actors and directors and all these voices ... That's the sense in which we're making things up' (cited in Pearson 2007, 247). After the final episode, fans rejected the finale for these very reasons:

> This finale is exactly why I stopped watching after season three. It is obvious that the show runners have been making this shit up all along. Whatever dudes. All of you made a bundle and now it is over. (Post #34, 'The End')

THAT?
SUCKED.

It was just awful. Ham-handed, heavy-handed, pitiful. I can't believe that mess they made of this. And Dartlon lied … saying it wasn't some purgatory/death thing. Oh year? Liars …

'Had the story planned from the beginning?' Liars. (Post #212, 'The End')

What was the smoke monster? Where/why did it come from?
What was the vase Desmond was playing with in the cave?
What was the light? Why did anyone have to protect it?
Why weren't any questions answered?
Oh yeah, because there aren't any. The writers made this crap up as they went. (Post #300, 'The End')

We've been had by the writers. They had no ending for the series so they manipulated us into thinking it was a great finale with all the feel-good reunions in the finale. This was a substitute for the lack of clarification and answers that we were promised. BAAAAAAAAAAAAAD Robot. I mean, BAAAAAAAAAAAAAAD ENDING! Pardon me. I need to go gargle with mouthwash to get the bitter taste out of my mouth. (Post #335, 'The End')

The finale's lack of resolution to the questions that these fans deemed important is used here to dismiss and critique the show itself and the writers, and is used as proof that *Lost*'s 'inexplicable twists and turns … were now beginning to serve as proof that the writers had no long-term plan in mind, and that the show's endless mysteries would never be resolved in a satisfying manner' (Askwith 2009, 161). The writers are explicitly insulted as 'liars', being unprofessional in their duping of the audience and promising answers to questions that they could never provide. For these fans, it is the mysteries and the puzzles that have been the focus of their viewing interest, while the focus on relationships and characters enjoyed by the fans discussed in the previous chapter is dismissed and derided. Again, this reflects ongoing issues in some parts of the *Lost* fan community regarding the disconnect between fans and the writers since producers Cuse and Lindelof had long emphasized in extra-textual material that character was the heart of the show, rather than the mysteries and monsters (see Cuse cited in Murray 2008). For the fans at TWoP the finale confirmed this:

Exactly what I expected. They copped out completely from all mysteries and went for BS spiritual uplift … None of the mysteries and puzzles meant anything. Remember all the speculation about the numbers alone? (Post #74, 'The End')

Overall, very disappointing. They went the sappy route and relied on character moments, a la [*Battlestar Galactica*] and its stupid ending, without bothering to answer any of the major questions.

What was the white light at the centre of the island? *Who cares?*

What was the sickness? *Doesn't matter!*

How was Sayid brought back from the dead? *Lalalalalalalala, not listening!*

Rather than answer any of that, we had to endure boring flashsideways that turned out to be precisely meaningless ...

Ugh. It was a fun ride but THAT's what they were building towards for six years? (Post #268, 'The End')

There is a sense among some of the posters that a focus on characters is used to distract viewers from a lack of answers to the narrative questions and to cover up perceived holes in the plot. For example, they post:

Remember when writers say 'character study' they really mean 'lack of consistent plot' ... It could have been worse. (Post #305, 'The End')

Lindelof and Cuse said that in the end the story was about the characters. Thing is, Moore said the same thing about [*Battlestar Galactica*] and God, know that show had a bad ending. It seems to be that 'it's about the characters' is code for 'We have no idea how to end this show or even end it logically so here is a bunch of stuff.' Guess what, gentlemen, you had a mystery show. The plot mattered. It mattered very much and you dropped the ball. Christ, that show could have ended so much better. (Post #392, 'The End')

Here, the online posters offer different sentiments from those expressed by fans who responded to the survey. In the survey responses forty-one people suggested that an opportunity to say goodbye to characters, as in the final *Lost* episodes, was important. The online posters, in contrast, privilege the narrative enigmas and questions over character. The distinctions made here between a focus on character and on the mysteries and puzzles are linked both to issues of genre and also to a more subtle process of gendering specific readings of the show. As discussed previously, there were ongoing debates across *Lost*'s six seasons regarding its generic status and clear manoeuvres were made to avoid it being associated too heavily with science-fiction or fantasy genres: 'While acknowledging the show's relationship to genre television, *Lost* creators [J. J.] Abrams and Lindelof clearly demonstrate that for the network it was necessary to downplay the show's [science-fiction] heritage' (Abbott 2009, 17).

Fans, however, while aware of these industry tensions often refuse to compromise their own ideas of what a show such as *Lost* should be and tend to foreground those aspects of the programme that attracted their dedicated viewership in the first place. Many of the disgruntled posters at TWoP refused to reject the show's fantastic origins – as the above quote's reference to *Lost* as a 'mystery show' demonstrates. While many of the more satisfied viewers are content to accept the focus on emotionality and character, those responding with rejection refuse to do so. There is an implicit sense in some of the online postings that viewers who accept this focus are 'going along' with the official position on the show, as put forward by Cuse and Lindelof, and the network ABC. Again, there are parallels with ABC's earlier drama series *Twin Peaks*, this time in relation to the tension between characters and narrative puzzles or questions. Perhaps paradoxically, ABC's strategy with *Twin Peaks* appears to have been the opposite of its focus with *Lost*. While *Lost*'s science-fiction associations and mysteries were downplayed by the network, with *Twin Peaks* they were keen to focus on the central enigma of 'Who Killed Laura Palmer?' at the expense of the show's soapier elements: 'Whilst ABC were pushing for the mystery of Laura's killer to be solved up-front, Lynch and Frost saw a number of TV genres mingling in the series, ideally diminishing the need to solve the central mystery' (Williams 2005, 48). Such tensions are present across different fan objects that pose narrative enigmas. However, the *Lost* fans at Television Without Pity who maintain a focus on the mystery origins of the show discursively position themselves as more discerning viewers, who are not as easily pacified by the emotional soothing of the finale. As one poster, who also continues with the notion that there was no overall plan for the show, notes 'Major disappointment! What the finale exposed is that the writers never had answers that we crazed. they threw out some cool mysteries over the past 6 years but they were never able to came up with a coherent explanation. The final revelation in the church, while offer some comfort for the audience, is a cop out' (Post #385, 'The End'). Here, the audience who is comforted by the 'happy ending' of the character reunion is acknowledged but disparaged; the ending works to pacify those who need emotional closure but fails to offer an acceptable rationalization for the unresolved plotlines for viewers more concerned with the cerebral and logical.

The issue of genre is closely linked to gendered readings of the show and, while the gender of online posters is impossible to determine with any certainty, there is an implication that fans such as those discussed in Chapter 4, who focus on culturally feminized aspects of the show, such as romantic relationships and character development, are unwelcome. Stacey Abbott has drawn attention to the way in which these relationships formed a crucial part of the show's appeal for some viewers: 'This expression of fandom is completely character driven ... By placing a large group of people onto a deserted island for an indefinite period of time, it is natural for audiences to begin to consider what relationships might emerge' (2009, 18). While this strategy did work in terms of attracting both mainstream and cult audiences to *Lost*, it was not welcomed by all fans. Indeed, there is a clear sense in some of the postings that the series finale sought to placate and reward those who supported specific romantic pairings, at the expense of solving the series' mysteries. Posters note, for instance, 'Well, tonight's ending was for *Lost* fans who shipped the right couple. If you are not one of them then you are fresh out of luck' (Post #293, 'The End'); and 'Kate and Jack have no chemistry whatsoever' (Post #105, 'The End'). As in *The West Wing* discussions, the alignment of personal, character-based stories with the feminized and culturally devalued continues. The opposition of character versus mystery among *Lost* fans indicates that specific strategies are employed to denigrate feminized readings of the text. Indeed, the personal versus political discourse can again be clearly aligned with feminized and masculinized readings of the text. As the frequent discussion of an over-emphasis on character indicates, many *Lost* fans drew on gendered discourses to support their critique of the show's final episode and its depiction of relationships and emotionality at the expense of offering answers to the narrative enigmas.

The discourses drawn on here regarding authorship and professionalism, gender and genre and being 'true' to the show that is drawing to a close demonstrate some commonality of fan discussion and practice across different television fandoms. Indeed, viewers of many shows 'feel cheated for investing their time and emotions in a show incapable of delivering on its own promises' (Askwith 2009, 167) and dissatisfaction with a series finale is not limited to *The West Wing* or *Lost*. The ending of *The Sopranos* was controversial for cutting to black in the middle of a scene, indicating the creator David Chase's refusal 'to wrap his series in the neat package that American audiences have come to expect with serialized or dramatic television programming' (Corrigan and Corrigan 2012, 97). Debate still rages over the abrupt ending of *Twin Peaks* which saw the lead protagonist Dale Cooper possessed by the evil spirit BOB (Nochimson 1997, 94–7), while in 1967 the ending of the mysterious series *The Prisoner*, 'which made a certain nonsensical sense, enraged viewers who wanted a coherent narrative resolution' and who expected 'that the central narrative enigma would be solved in a logically coherent manner' (Morreale 2010, 184). Indeed, for every fan who is happy with narrative resolution and who mourns for the ending of a show, there is one who takes a more critical stance, bemoaning the narrative shortcomings or failures and, in some cases, actively celebrating the end of a series. As this chapter has shown via two examples, fans who react within this rejection discourse often adopt forms of anti-fandom to articulate their dissatisfaction with a show that they previously loved, drawing on their knowledge of the narrative, writers or the wider production context to articulate the reasons for these feelings. When their fan identities or narratives face possible threat, they respond not by reiterating or rearticulating their fandom and its importance to them, but instead by highlighting the distance that has developed between themselves and their chosen television shows, warding off and protecting themselves from disruption or emotional upset by rejecting the fan object and performing disavowal and critique.

Conclusion

For these fans of *Lost* and *The West Wing*, discourses of anti-fandom are used to articulate a sense of rejection at the end of the series. They are those who have, at other times, occupied the role of more appreciative and positive fans, highlighting that 'anti-fans must find cause for their dislike in *something*. This something may vary from having previously watched the show and having found it intolerable; to having a dislike for its genre, director or stars; to having seen previews or ads, or seen or heard unfavourable reviews' (Gray 2003, 71). These posters exemplify fans who have become dissatisfied with certain aspects of the show (e.g. the writers, the storylines) and who have chosen to occupy positions of anti-fandom that are 'performed with close knowledge of the text and yet be devoid of the interpretive and diegetic pleasures that are usually assumed to be a staple of almost all media consumption' (Gray 2005, 842). This intimate knowledge of specific shows is highlighted by the fact that, while rejection can be seen across the two fandoms examined here, the discourses of dislike and anti-fandom are specific to each show. Thus, while *West Wing* fans were conscious of a split between the personal and political aspects of the show and *Lost* fans appeared to share a similar concern regarding the character and mystery division of their show, the latter's issues around narrative premeditation were the most pronounced. This may well be an issue of genre – *Lost*'s borrowings from fantasy and science-fiction and its status as a 'cult blockbuster' series (Abbott 2009) always set up mysteries that it promised to resolve, whereas *The West Wing*'s political drama never offered such complex enigmas to its audience. However, it does demonstrate that disparate fan cultures may share broad axes of distinction and rejection, even if these are closely linked to the different implied promises set up by the producers of favourite fan objects. In the case of *Lost*, such disappointment did not necessarily diminish over time; in 2013, *Lost*'s Damon Lindelof shut down his Twitter account, allegedly in response to the ongoing negative tweets he received about the series finale (O'Brien 2013). This was, apparently exacerbated by the ending of Vince Gilligan's drama *Breaking Bad*, which was widely heralded as the 'right way' to end a series; disgruntled *Lost* fans bombarded Lindelof with tweets critiquing the ending of that programme. As Lindelof (2013) himself noted, 'my Twitter feed was pretty much a unanimous run of, "Did you *see* that, Lindelof? *That's* how you end a show"'.

The ongoing consternation over *Lost*'s finale and the responses of many *West Wing* fans suggest that it is important to consider how some fans may, rather than displaying sadness or grief, demonstrate pleasure or relief at the end of once-beloved television shows and that they might work to distance themselves from their fandom. Furthermore, this allows broader understandings of anti-fandom and how it operates across fandoms at different times. If, indeed, 'In the context of television both creatives and fans imply that endings ultimately belong to fans – a good death is one that satisfies the fan community and thus serves as a final gift from the writers/creators' (Harrington 2013, 590), we must consider the discourses used when fans reject a specific ending, and the implications this has for their use of fan objects in fashioning self-identities and narratives and negotiating their sense of ontological security.

6

Moving On? The Renegotiation Discourse

In contrast to the more decisive responses of rejection or reiteration already discussed, the fans explored in this chapter deal with the ending of favoured shows through a process of renegotiation, coming to terms with the end of the fan object and discussing how their interactions and relationships with the text change. For these fans, discussion of other fandoms is often key and the notion of multi-fandom – being a fan of multiple texts at the same time – is explored here to consider how 'being a fan' more broadly can provide security and ongoing avenues for identity work, even when one particular fan object changes form. As Mark Duffett notes, 'fandom is a continual process. Some move nomadically from one phenomenon to the next and therefore experience their fandom as a kind of lifestyle ... Others are dedicated to singular objects' (2013, 279).

Although the case study of *The West Wing* that has been drawn on in prior chapters is discussed, here the focus shifts to other examples of television shows that have ended. The chapter makes particular reference to how fans 'move on' to fandom of other texts created by or starring those associated with the show that is ending, examining the forms of 'pre-view' (Gray 2008) that fans engage in. It then specifically considers the survey responses of fans who followed specific actors, writers and producers such as Joss Whedon, Aaron Sorkin and John Barrowman across a range of fan objects. In examining how this allows some fans to move on to other forms of fandom, while both continuing to respect and maintain their previous connections to television shows, fans' use of a range of media texts is explored.

While fans who responded positively to the endings of series have been seen to draw on a discourse of reiteration and reassertion of their fandom and those who were more critical and distanced responded within a rejection discourse, for many other fans responses fall somewhere in the middle. As this book demonstrates, fan reactions to endings, whether big or small, form a continuum with multiple overlapping responses or vast differences across various fan objects and points of engagement. In this section, those whose reactions were more moderate than outright dislike or dismissal, or overt declarations of sadness, are considered as fans who respond through a process of renegotiation. These fans are those who acknowledged that, while fan objects have been of huge importance to them, their interest will inevitably lessen and the object will cease to be so influential in their lives. They are more likely to view their devotion to a specific television show in the context of their broader engagement with media objects, although this does not diminish the affective ties that they have had to a specific series. Nor are these fans in some way 'inferior' or less dedicated than those who deal with potential threat to their fan selves by protecting themselves via reiterating their connection and reasserting their loyalty (as in the reiteration discourse) or by avoiding possible threat through critical distance and rejection. Rather, the fans discussed in this chapter offer a way to consider those whose responses are more multifarious than outright rejection or grief and upset.

'My interest will probably wane': *The West Wing*

The sample of fans of *The West Wing* discussed in previous chapters also demonstrated the reactions of those who dealt with potential threats to their fan pure relationships, ontological security and sense of self-identity and narrative by accepting the demise of the shows and preparing to move on to discover new fan objects. In the case of *The West Wing*, some of the respondents to the survey conducted before the final episodes aired noted:

> It had a good run. It was fun to watch, and I'll have to find something new to do on Sundays at 8:00 pm … I'll inevitably lose interest when a new show catches my eye. I'll probably stay involved for a year or so before moving on to a new fandom. (Lucy, Questionnaire respondent 2006)

> I'm sure it will fade away after a while. There is talk of a fan fic virtual season. I might try to read that. I'll still beta [proof read] for my friend until her story is completed (it's a long one.) After that, I'll probably start finding other interests/ shows to follow. (Rhian, Questionnaire respondent 2006)

Both of these respondents suggest that that show's impact on them will decrease once the run of new episodes comes to a close and when newer objects of fandom catch their attention. While Lucy notes that this is likely to be an accidental but inevitable conclusion – that a new show will 'catch her eye' without her actively seeking one out – Rhian suggests a more active decision to discover new fan objects. Rhian's declaration that she will eventually 'start finding other interests/shows' indicates a more enthusiastic desire to find other objects to follow. This transition, however, appears to be gradual since Rhian intends to continue her *West Wing* fandom for the near future after the series ends through reading fanfiction or beta reading fiction for a friend (see Chapter 8). Rhian's movement towards new fan objects shares parallels with what Matt Hills terms 'cyclical fandom' where fan experience 'combines a self-reported level of affective "intensity" and activity with cyclical shifts away from discarded fan objects and toward newly compelling objects' (Hills 2005a, 803). However, while both of these respondents recognize that they will 'move on' from the show, there is a clear indication that this process of acceptance will take time to work through in order for them to deal with any possible threat to the sense of ontological security and fan self-identities. As noted, Giddens' work on pure relationships suggests that after a break-up, difficult emotions must be worked through and a period of 'loveshock' can occur. Such 'loveshock' has a "psychological traveling time", which may take a period of many months to work through' (Giddens 1992, 103). The responses of fans here suggest that a 'psychological traveling time' is necessary to come to terms with the ending of *The West Wing* before, eventually, reducing the level of fandom and moving on to other, newer interests.

Other fans also concede that their interest will fade, commenting 'I doubt there will be much point in reading the sites, my interest will probably wane' (Kate, Questionnaire respondent 2006) and 'I'll continue to visit message boards because I've met some really great people, but I don't think it'll be as much as it used to be' (Caroline, Questionnaire respondent 2006). For these two survey respondents it is the potential loss of the fan forums that appears to be most threatening; there is little sense here that relationships formed on these sites will transcend the communal experience of watching and enjoying the show as in the *Buffy the Vampire Slayer* and *Angel* fans explored by Gatson and Zweerink (2004) and Whiteman and Metivier (2013). Instead the overarching sense is that the lack of new episodes will cause online involvement to decrease and many fan–fan pure relationships to come to an end. Such fans have already begun to renegotiate their identities accordingly, acknowledging that eventually *The West Wing* would no longer have such meaning for them and, we can extrapolate from this, no longer provide such high levels of ontological security. Equally, other fans renegotiate their fan–fan relationships, suggesting that while the fan community was important to their fandom, this will necessarily become less crucial to their sense of self-identity and self-narrative. One poster on the thread dedicated to the final episode of *The West Wing* comments, 'also a thank you, but hopefully not goodbye, to the people in this forum who also entertained me and made me smarter. On top of everything else, *TWW* was my first Television Without Pity show, and although I've been a-wandering through other shows/forums, this one will always hold that nostalgia for me' (Post #117, 'Tomorrow').

For others the opportunity to move on to other fan objects that had a connection to *The West Wing* was discussed. This allows fans to bid farewell to the original fan object while maintaining some link to it via overlaps with new ones. In the case of *The West Wing*, this was commonly articulated via the intention to watch *The West Wing* creator Aaron Sorkin's new series *Studio 60 on the Sunset Strip* (NBC 2006–7), which premiered on the NBC network on 19 September 2006. In addition to being created and written by Sorkin, the show had another key link to *The West Wing* via the actor Bradley Whitford, who had played Joshua Lyman and who had been cast as Danny Tripp, one of the lead characters in *Studio 60*. *Studio 60* had other potential fan 'structural links' (Hills 2002, 81) via the casting of actor Timothy Busfield (who played White House reporter Danny Concannon in *The West Wing*) and the presence of producer Thomas Schlamme. The series had also been widely promoted via its connections to *The West Wing* in its first trailer, which showed how the programme would reunite:

> *Studio 60*'s writer–director pair of Aaron Sorkin and Thomas Schlamme, best known for creating one of television's most awarded shows, *The West Wing* (as the preview opens by telling us). Certainly, with the momentary idolatry given within the preview's frame to Perry and Whitford's characters, an immediate and obvious parallel is drawn between them and Sorkin and Schlamme, themselves absent from television (as a team) since leaving NBC's *The West Wing* under strained circumstances several years before … And by assembling such a cast and crew, NBC can imply that they too have spared no expense to turn their network around. Few show creators in television history could claim the role of 'quality television' producers as easily as can Sorkin and Schlamme, hence allowing NBC to stamp the show immediately as 'high quality'. (Gray 2008, 44–5)

Likely informed by such 'pre-views' (Gray 2008) before the series began airing in September 2006, some *West Wing* fans indicated that they intended to move on to the new show. For example, two questionnaire respondents from before the show's finale in 2006 noted that 'I'm already part of a few communities on LJ for *Studio 60* ... I watch [*Sports Night*] on DVD as much as I do [*The West Wing*] and *Studio 60* will be the #1 priority on my Tivo come fall' (Nancy, questionnaire respondent, 2006), and 'Before I got involved with *West Wing* fandom, I didn't know much about Aaron Sorkin. Since then, I have become a fan of his writing, and plan to watch *Studio 60* from the very beginning' (Rhian, questionnaire respondent, 2006). Some online forum members appeared to be decisive about their moving on after the show finished; one commented after *The West Wing* finale aired, 'Great show, great ending. On to *Studio 60*' (Post #78, 'Tomorrow'). For other fans, however, progress was less assured and their reactions were more complex, prompting some lengthy posts about their responses to the end of the show. For instance, one poster disclosed:

> I am sad. I will take me a long time to find other show to watch. Before '*TWW*' the only one which i watched every single episode was *Hills Street Blues*. I just want to say Thank you so much to everybody who worked in the show. The fact to watch TV and get a great time of entertainment to this level make my day after the stress of my day by day. My only hope we can have some specials of the show in the future. Also my only hope to watch something new and good is *Studio Seven* [the original name for the show *Studio 60 on the Sunset Strip*]. (Posted #95, 'It's Official – *West Wing* to Conclude Sunday, May 14 ... ')

While this poster hasn't experienced intense fandom only with *The West Wing* and also identifies as a dedicated fan of police series *Hill Street Blues*, the grappling with moving on from the show is clear here. There are echoes of the common sentiments expressed by fans who responded with more straight-forward reiteration of their fandom, such as thanking those who made the programme, but there is also a strong sense of readjustment and hesitancy in moving on, with an expectation of it being difficult to find a new object of fandom. While *Studio 60* is held up as a potential new source of 'good television', this post reveals the complex reactions of fans when favourite programmes end and how the decision to find new objects of interest must be negotiated. The expression of hope from this poster regarding the possibility of special episodes of the series indicates some desire for resurrection of the series, albeit a temporary or one-off revival. As discussed in Chapter 8, fan desires for resurrections of favourite programmes are often contradictory, indicating a broad range of anxieties and hopes around a particular show. Here, however, this poster suggests that the possibility of a return to the narrative universe offers the opportunity to ward off and protect against any threats to self-identity or ontological security. For this fan, who expresses that the show offered an escape from the 'stress' of everyday life, there is a very real sense that the ending of *The West Wing* will be an emotional experience. In the hopes for both new episodes of the series and the success of Aaron Sorkin's new show, this fan negotiates this threat, acknowledging the importance of *The West Wing*, while also drawing on other texts for comfort and security.

As noted, such posts echo aspects of the reiteration discourse discussed in Chapter 4 in their declaration of missing the show and the posting of goodbyes. These fans accept that they will move on to other forums and shows but still privilege *The West Wing* as being crucial in the formation of fan self-identity. Indeed, fans often form links of similar fan objects, either devoting themselves to various objects simultaneously or wholeheartedly to one object before moving on to another (more serially monogamous fans, perhaps?). For example, in discussions of *The West Wing* creator Aaron Sorkin fans often cited his other work as favoured fan objects or suggested that this would help them to get through the end of *The West Wing*: 'I definitely plan to watch [*Studio 60*] this fall. In fact, I expect it to live up to the Sorkin/Schlamme legacy and therefore plan to record-to-keep it' (Lene, Questionnaire respondent 2006). Furthermore, the fact that ontological security can never truly be eradicated by the demise of one singular TV show may also be reflected in fans' movement to new shows such as *Studio 60*. As well as enabling them to transfer fan 'subcultural capital' (Thornton 1995) between fandoms, the enthusiasm of many fans for *Studio 60* is indicative of the fact that television *as a whole* provides ontological security owing to its routine via 'schedules, genres and narratives' (Silverstone 1994, 15). In such cases, fans' 'ontological security is not a matter of feeling safe through routine, but of being able to cope with changes in routine' and dealing with 'upsets and disturbances' (Craib 1998, 72) to their sense of fan identity. Thus, if the end of one show forces fans to renegotiate their self-identities and narratives, it is undoubtedly the 'basic trust' or 'primary ontological security' (Laing 1960, 39) established in early childhood that equips them to cope with this. Thus, it can be argued that ontological security means that, despite the loss of one fan object, a replacement can usually be found that, over time, may develop into a new fan–object relationship and come to offer similar rewards as the previous object.

However, other fans of *The West Wing* suggested that they would not so readily transfer their interest or affection onto other programmes. They note 'I am done with episodic television, I am not getting roped into another one of these but I don't regret jumping in with both feet seven years ago and not looking back' (Post #108, 'Tomorrow') and 'In an effort to return to a normal life, I hope I don't get sucked into another episodic show any time soon' (Post #121, 'Tomorrow'). The language used by these fans in their invocation of being almost helplessly 'dragged into' fandom of a series suggests the emotional and affective connections that they have developed to a series. The use of terms such as 'getting roped into' or 'sucked into' indicate the strength of feeling that these fans have, but also suggests some anxiety about the impact that fandom has had on them. Without wanting to pathologize such fans or to reinstate stereotypes of fans as vulnerable and easily influenced (see Jensen 1992), their own use of such terms suggests the strength of their involvement as well as a desire to avoid such attachments in the future. While none of these posters appear to regret their intense fandom, the impact of the series' end on them is articulated as almost 'too much' and too upsetting. In this case, such fans express that such involvement and attachment is to be avoided in the future in order to prevent being 'roped into' another fandom to the same level of intensity.

Similar sentiments were expressed by some of the survey respondents to the questionnaire conducted in 2013. For example, one respondent commented, 'There is only one fandom I participate in, others I have an interest in but don't want to get so emotionally involved as I know it will end. More than anything I just want a satisfactory ending, time to tell the story or close the narrative'. As with the fans discussed in the chapter on discourses of reiteration, the desire for a satisfactory ending is clear here. For this respondent, however, the foreknowledge of a forthcoming ending can work to prevent complete immersion or connection to a fan object. This fan suggests that one way to ward off potential threats to ontological security or to their emotional involvement with a series is to avoid such intimate connection in the first place. In some cases, threats to self-narrative and identity can be weathered by trying to avoid the 'moments [that] disturb and disorder our assumptions about the world, and our place in it' by 'distancing that which could potentially threaten the social order and continuity of human existence' (Ritchie 2003, 2). Although these fan comments may refer to a desire not to invest owing to time constraints, they also suggest that the trauma of the ending of the fan object may be so great that fans cannot comprehend being able to form such close attachments to another object. As well as appearing to seek to protect themselves against the trauma of the cessation of this source of ontological security and self-identity, these fans also demonstrate the depth of their attachment, displaying their emotional ties and forms of affective capital.

Another fan who replied to the 2013 survey discussed their initial resistance to becoming involved in another fandom after the ending of their favourite series *Stargate*:

> When *Stargate* was cancelled, I felt as if I might have time not for other things, not spend so much time in front of the computer anymore. Maybe take up drawing again. Fandom is about going to conventions, reading and writing fanfictions, talking with other fans all over the world online, etc. I thought I would give all this up not and go back to 'real life'. Then *Torchwood* came along and I started all over again – joined new forums, met new people, found also some old friends again, became a fan of new actors, started to travel to the UK ...

While there are no obvious overlaps (beyond generic similarity in the fantasy/science-fiction genres) that would have led this fan between her *Stargate* fandom to being involved with *Torchwood*, it is apparent that for fans such as this the desire for involvement with a fan object is strong. Despite initial resistance to such attachment, the rewards offered by intense involvement in fandom such as meeting fellow fans, discovering new objects of fandom and so on appear to outweigh the disappointment that follows the cancellation of a single fan object. Since ontological security refers to 'the psychical attainment of basic trust in self-continuity and environmental continuity' (Hills 2012a, 113), ontological security in these cases can be attained from a broader fandom of multiple objects and wider engagement with the media and cultural field.

Following the actors and producers

The section above has touched on fans who follow particular elements of a favourite television series onto other shows once the original object of fandom draws to a close. This can be a producer or writer such as Aaron Sorkin, but it can also, as the example of actor Bradley Whitford's move from *The West Wing* to *Studio 60 on the Sunset Strip* demonstrates, be related to those who fans see onscreen. Given, as discussed in Chapter 3, the close affective ties fans can feel to characters, it is perhaps unsurprising that some choose to follow those who play them across different fan objects. This section turns to more specific examples of how some fans follow actors or producers and writers from one television show to another. The continuation of an element of a series is one way in which fans can work to renegotiate and re-narrate their self-identities when the ending of a show or contact with beloved characters is threatened. For example, in their study of *Friends*, Eyal and Cohen argue that, for some fans, the ending of the series was not as upsetting as it might have been since the character of Joey Tribianni (played by Matt LeBlanc) was starring in a spin-off series called '*Joey*'. They suggest that this knowledge 'could have contributed to the generally low levels of [parasocial breakup] reported in this sample' (Eyal and Cohen 2006, 516–17), since fans were aware that one element of *Friends* would continue and could be followed. A similar situation may have occurred for fans at the end of *Breaking Bad*, since its spin-off series *Better Call Saul* (AMC 2014–), which features several of *Breaking Bad*'s characters, had already been announced. However, I want here to consider another way in which this may work for fans: the process of following favourite actors or writers from the fan object that has ceased production onto new projects that share no 'official' textual overlaps with the original series (i.e. programmes that are not direct spin-offs or prequels).

Examination of how fans move on after programmes end can also shed light on how objects of fandom are 'found', since fan studies' 'focus on attachment and affect has somewhat marginalized the matter of exactly how fans "find", or alight on, what subsequently become their favoured fan objects' (Hills 2005a, 802). Although we must 'treat "becoming a fan" narratives very carefully as documents of experience' (Duffett 2013, 154), considering how fans discover new objects of fandom allows a greater understanding of the multiple intersecting interests that fans often have. Matt Hills argues that the concept of 'cyclical fandom suggests that reified approaches to singular fan cultures, focused on singular fan objects … may require theoretical amendment and refinement' (2005a, 819) and that it can shed light on how and why people move between fan objects and discover new ones. There is clearly a range of ways in which people do this – suggested television shows or bands by friends or family, a random recommendation of a DVD or download on an online retailer such as Amazon, a chance glimpse of something intriguing on television one evening. Here, however, the concept of the renegotiation discourse can be used to examine one avenue of fan discovery by allowing us to consider how fans maintain links between fan objects while uncovering new potential ones.

The data generated by the surveys conducted in the summer of 2013 offers a range of insights into how fans chose to move on with favourite elements of a chosen series. For some, this resulted from a broader attachment to any aspect of the series and a general sense of loyalty to those who had been involved in it. In some cases, actors were the key focus for this continuing-yet-different fandom, since they allowed fans to follow points of interest onto new objects of fandom. One fan notes that:

> I follow Alex O'Loughlin who was in *Moonlight*, went to *3 Rivers*, and then to *Hawaii 5-0*. I also follow Jason O'Mara who was in *Life on Mars*, *Terra Nova* and *Vegas* – all 3 of his shows have been cancelled and I loved all of them. I will continue to follow them in whatever projects they are involved in.

Such responses, however, indicate the complexity of such following and the ways in which the new fan objects can replace existing fan objects. One fan replies 'I watch *Bones* because it has David Boreanaz in it, but that was just a hook that got me to watch the first few episodes. I think I like the actor much more in *Bones*, than I ever did in *Buffy* or *Angel*. Here, the new series has worked to supersede the fan's attachment to the actor in his previous programmes, offering a character performance by the actor that has come to be preferred. The same respondent goes on to note, 'I watch *Castle*, but not because of Nathan Fillian's role in *Buffy* or *Firefly* – its more in spite of them. I didn't really like *Firefly*. (Yes, I'm a philistine.)'. In this case, as with the fandom of David Boreanaz, there is a connection to a broader fandom of Joss Whedon's programmes but, again, the actor's most recent role is the preferred one for this fan. Another fan discusses a more straightforward following of actors from her favourite show, *Being Human*, noting:

> I was already a fan of Russell Tovey (he was the reason I started watching in the first place), so always watch anything he is in (*Him & Her*, *The Job Lot*, etc. since he left *Being Human*). I have seen a film starring Lenora Critchlow (*Fast Girls*) partly because she was in it and partly because of Noel Clarke's involvement. I would watch anything written by Toby Whithouse, although I would have watched his *Doctor Who* episodes even if he hadn't created *Being Human*.

Here, fandom of both *Being Human* and *Doctor Who* are discussed, highlighting the overlaps between different fandoms that share creative personnel such as the writer Toby Whithouse and the fact that *Doctor Who* actor Noel Clarke (who played the character of Mickey) was involved with a movie also featuring *Being*

Human actress Lenora Critchlow. Meanwhile, fandom of the actor Russell Tovey both pre-dates and succeeds the interest in *Being Human* that this fan discusses. Here, a range of fandoms comes together across the fan's media interests. Such overlaps between fandoms show how 'multiple fandoms are linked through the individual's realization of a self-identity. These multiple fandoms and interests in different media forms may cohere in intriguing ways. Particular discourses might be shared across what, at first glance, appear to be very different objects of fandom' (Hills 2002, 81).

Actor John Barrowman was often discussed in the survey results, with many fans of *Torchwood* keen to maintain their links to the show and their favourite actors from it. *Torchwood*'s ambivalent status, as discussed in Chapter 8, played a part here since fans were uncertain about whether *Torchwood* had been cancelled or not. As long as a return was not assured, however, following Barrowman onto other fan objects was a way of discovering new fandoms while sustaining links with the origin fandom. One respondent comments that 'I started watching *Arrow* due to the involvement of one of the *Torchwood* actors. However, I have liked the series in it's own right, simply a case that with it being on a pay-per-view channel I probably wouldn't have heard about it without his involvement', while another notes, 'Still a fan of *Dr Who*, where *Torchwood* came from. Also a fan of *Arrow* as the actor John Barrowman from *Torchwood* stars in it. The show *Frankie* because of Eve Myles, another actor from *Torchwood*'. Another respondent who identifies as a fan of *Torchwood* and of Barrowman specifically, identifies the actor as relatively unique in the following that he has acquired and attributes this to his presence across a range of media and genres (Williams 2013b, 159–60). They note that 'John Barrowman has quite a following which tends to be different from the average actor, since he is involved in so many other aspects (music, theatre, presenting, etc.)'. While this does allow fans to be attached specifically to one aspect of his career, this broad presence in the media has also contributed to an increased ability to follow the actor in his post-*Torchwood* endeavours. As the fan summarizes:

There are separate groups who might prefer just one of those things that he does, but generally it crosses over to his other work. I know of some fans who will only watch the episodes in a new series he might be in (such as *Desperate Housewives* or *Arrow*). I have watched these other series and found new shows to like that I wouldn't have been aware of otherwise. One firm favorite was *Hustle* – I wasn't familiar with this series and usually will go back and watch the whole series if I can for context. Often I find I enjoy these series on their own merits.

Here, fandom of Barrowman begins a chain of new media texts to be watched and engaged with (albeit with varying levels of attachment), such as *Arrow*, *Desperate Housewives* and *Hustle*. For some fans, it is only Barrowman's appearances that cause them to view a programme and, in these cases, his connection does not equate to long-standing new fan attachments. For this fan, however, the case of *Hustle* offered a chance to find a new 'firm favourite' and the opportunity to discover new series via the link to Barrowman which could then be enjoyed as independent series and assessed on their own qualities. Cases such as this suggest that, for some fans, the sense of ontological security gained from their fandom results from their fandom of a specific actor or actress, rather than a particular television series. In this case, being able to continue fandom of John Barrowman after *Torchwood* is put on hiatus allows this fan to maintain their sense of identity as a fan, as well as gaining ontological security from following his ongoing career. Given the often intense attachments that fans can form with celebrity figures, it makes sense that fandom of specific media personalities would allow the same rewards as a 'pure relationship' (Giddens 1992) with a text.

For other fans, an attempt is often made to follow favourite actors but loyalty to their future projects is not assured if their new shows do not appeal to the fan. One *Stargate* and *Torchwood* fan discussed their feelings about this issue:

> [*Stargate* actor] Richard Dean Anderson is pretty much retired now and doesn't work as an actor at the moment. So not much new from him. I have tried to watch some new work of the other *Stargate* actors but nothing interested me much and I wasn't a big enough fan to keep going. So I lost interest to follow what they do now but once in a while I hear updates from friends. Much to my surprise, I have become a huge *Arrow* fan now. I started to watch only for John Barrowman (from *Torchwood*) who plays a recurring character (the bad guy), but quickly I fell into love with the whole show and all of its actors. It's my new fandom at the moment!

This lengthy response indicates the range of fan attachments at work and the fact that fans are often interested in multiple fan objects that maintain their interest and allow them to move on to other texts. For this fan, fandom of *Stargate* and *Torchwood* is discussed in equal terms, but while one – the *Stargate* fandom – has failed to yield any meaningful new attachments, the initial interest in *Arrow* via fandom of *Torchwood*'s John Barrowman has led to 'falling in love' with the show to the extent that it is referred to as the respondent's primary 'new fandom'.

Precisely *why Arrow* has provoked this attachment is not articulated here (it is an apparent 'surprise' for this fan), seemingly reinforcing Hills's observation that fans' accounts of their 'becoming a fan' stories are often 'strikingly self-absent' (Hills 2002, 6–7). However, studying how fans follow actors and writers does offer one way to trace how fans 'find' their fan objects and how the 'intertextual or generic links' (Hills 2002, 82) between different objects operate.

While actors were often discussed in the survey responses, many fans emphasized the importance of producers or showrunners in their decision to move on to new fan objects. One respondent commented:

> Most often, I find that I will like shows that are created or written by people who were involved in shows that I loved before. When it comes to shows starring the same actors, it is always a pleasure to see them (and to know they found work), but it is more hit or miss as to whether I will become a fan of the show.

As with the comment above from a fan who lost interest in the ongoing work of *Stargate* actors, this fan clearly states that their fandom of the programmes that actors move on to is not assured; rather, it is contingent and clearly related to a range of factors that the fan does not discuss. In contrast, the fan suggests that it is creators and writers who offer the more certain chance of a new fan object via their involvement and connection to objects that the fan previously 'loved'. In other responses the involvement of a specific 'Executive Producer-Creator-Writer figure' (Hills 2002, 132) or 'hyphenate' (Thompson 1990, 36) was often a big draw for fans and names such as Joss Whedon, Aaron Sorkin and Steven Moffat were mentioned in several responses as being key motivators in fans following their movement and drawing links and points of commonality across fan objects:

> Well, I watched *Dollhouse* because it was a Whedon show (besides the *BSG* connection) [Actor Tahmoh Penikett had lead roles in both *Dollhouse* and *Battlestar Galactica*] but I generally choose to watch new series according to showrunners that I'm familiar with.

> I tend to follow writers, but much of the stuff Shawn Ryan has put out since *The Shield* was cancelled. Glen Mazzara's *Walking Dead* is pretty good, but I like the graphic novels more. Kurt Sutter's *Sons of Anarchy* possibly comes closest to re-capturing *The Shield*. I find Alan Ball incredibly fascinating, mostly because *Six Feet Under* and *True Blood* seem so different from each other. I only started watching *True Blood* because of Alan Ball, and I think he may be the reason why I started to engage with it more closely. Otherwise, I possibly would have dismissed it early on.

> *The West Wing* inspired me to watch Sorkin's *Newsroom, Studio 60* and *Sports Night*. That show also featured Josh Charles, which was a significant factor in me watching my currently airing favorite show, *The Good Wife*. I'll probably check out the new show by the creators of *Merlin*, but I don't think it will be quite the same.

Familiar auteur figures appear to offer a guarantee both of a form of 'quality' and a promise that if the fan enjoyed their previous work their new projects will also appeal. As discussed in Chapter 4 in relation to *The West Wing*, 'auteurism brings with it an ideology of quality' (Hills 2002, 133) and is often part of the way that new television shows are pre-sold and packaged, 'offered up as an official extratextual/publicity narrative' (Hills 2002, 133). Jonathan Gray argues for the importance of such paratexts since 'many interactions that we have with texts will be set up and *framed* by the hype that we consume; more than merely pointing us to the text at hand, this hype will have already begun the process of creating textual meaning, serving as the first outpost of interpretation' (Gray 2008, 34).

The presence of certain writers or producers is often used to 'hype' a new television series and such manoeuvres are an established part of the contemporary television landscape. It is therefore unsurprising that fans appear drawn to specific writers and directors as they move across different fandoms. For fans who feel well-served by such figures on previous shows a sense of trust and familiarity can be maintained when potential threats to their sense of fan identity, self-narrative and fan ontological security are posed by the ending of one series. Following a showrunner onto new projects means that the fandom does not entirely cease; instead, aspects of it can be carried onwards via familiar writers, directors or producers. One fandom is thus not replaced by another. Rather it allows overlaps and commonalities to be discussed in relation to both the new and the previous fan object. As one survey respondent stated: 'I want to stay in contact with all the friends I made during my fandom years. Everyone has also moved on to new fandoms now, but still we all like to look back and reminiscent. So our new fandoms and our old fandom always mix and the old one will not be forgotten'. Furthermore, as the final quote above demonstrates, fandom of auteurs and actors can sometimes be inextricable; for this fan a love of Sorkin's work leads to an interest in the actor Josh Charles which leads to a current favourite series *The Good Wife*.

Other survey respondents discussed this in more depth, demonstrating how following a specific showrunner leads to fandom of actors who then offer other avenues for new fan objects and entry into new fandoms:

I am a Whedon fan and a Moffat fan. Anything related to these two writers I will watch. Often, I become fans of people who have been in a Whedon or Moffat series, and then I wind up watching other things they are in. This is how I wound up watching ABC's *Castle* (Nathan Fillion was in *Firefly*). I watched *Flashforward* in part because Jack Davenport (from Moffat's *Coupling*) was in the show.

I decided to watch *Firefly* in the first place because it was by Joss Whedon, whose brain I fell in love with thanks to both *Buffy* and the *Angel* spin-off. I also then went on to watch *Dollhouse* because of Whedon (again, tragically cancelled), *Chuck* because of Adam Baldwin (where yes, I participated in campaigns to keep it going because it was awesome) and *Castle* because of Nathan Fillion (which is still going despite possibly already running its course). Oh, and *Avengers Assemble* of course because of Whedon, but also because I'm a Marvel fangirl.

The movement between fandoms is not always linear and may, as this fan outlines, incorporate multiple fandoms and interests that overlap and intersect across actors (such as Jack Davenport or Adam Baldwin) and producers (e.g. Joss Whedon, Steven Moffat). For this fan, the links followed across fandoms incorporate a range of programmes and move across genres and media forms. The sense here is that these fandoms co-exist and become more or less important and central to the fan at different points; the movement of renegotiation is not simply an interest in one programme due to one factor but, rather, a more complex and wide-ranging interest across the media, albeit one that demonstrates clear 'intertextual or generic links' (Hills 2002, 82). This echoes Lather and Moyer-Guse's finding that when faced with temporary lack of contact with the series during the writers' strike in 2008, fans of *Friends* were 'most likely to increase time spent with other media, rather than increasing nonmedia activities. This finding suggests that although parasocial relationships are similar to real-world relationships, viewers more frequently replace them with other media exposure' (Lather and Moyer-Guse 2011, 211).

For other respondents, the links formed were broader and reached beyond connections to the texts or creators. For example, one respondent who was a fan of a range of Nordic Noir television including *Borgen* and *The Bridge* noted, '[I] have become interested in other forms of Scandinavian TV. Extremely curious about the modes of broadcasting which led to *Forbrydelsen* and am constantly seeking past works from the careers of the creative personnel'. For this fan, interest continues not only from looking at the previous work of the creators but from studying the context that produced these shows. Fan links can also encompass forms of media beyond new television series. As discussed in Chapter 8, stories that originate on television are often now continued in other media including cinema, novelizations and comic books. Links to aspects of a fan object can also be continued via other media forms as two respondents who identified as fans of *Twin Peaks* briefly commented by noting 'No [I haven't followed the writers or actors]. I do love movies by Lynch, though' and 'I always follow Lynch's cinema'. Fandom links can be varied and, as the range of replies discussed here attests, they demonstrate the breadth of 'individuals' "textual fields"' and how they 'select from the myriad texts around them, [and] what common patterns [there are] in what they select' (Couldry 2000b, 73).

The responses discussed in this chapter highlight the links between fan objects and shed light on how fans discover new fan objects and move between objects. They also suggest that ontological security and self-identity are, for many fans, not solely dependent upon one particular fan object. For such fans a sense of self and trust are instead renegotiated in relation to a range of different texts and objects across the mediated landscape and their '"textual field" of multiple fan interests' (Couldry 2000b, 73). Fans who take up the opportunity to follow certain aspects of an object onto new texts demonstrate that ontological security and identity may be dependent on certain elements of a fandom, such as specific actors or producers and writers. As long as this element continues to work and produce new television shows or other forms of media, then these fans can continue to derive ontological security and a sense of self-narrative from the new fan objects that are produced. Here, ontological security is not threatened by the cessation of one show since attachments to elements of that programme can be carried on via new programmes. As Georgiou explains, 'ontological security provides a dialogical system of management of the self within social systems; it represents an attempt to explain how individuals are not constantly anxious, even when risks are all around them' (2013, 306). In the case of the fans discussed here, the sense of ontological security derived from the continuation of aspects of a fandom means that these fans often fail to display an overt sense of anxiety about the ending of a show. Instead, their broader trust in the ability of the media to produce alternative objects that they will discover and utilize allows such anxiety to be dealt with and warded off.

Conclusion

Television 'contributes to ordering everyday life, especially in its embeddedness in routines and rituals' (Georgiou 2013, 307). Many of the fans discussed in this chapter are aware of the ongoing economic and artistic drives of the television landscape – a landscape that continually produces new shows and which, in many cases, draws on familiar actors, writers, producers and creators. The fans examined here may experience ruptures in their sense of fan connection with certain objects, but, rather than a sense of ontological security being linked solely to one specific text, their trust both in television as a source of security and in their own identity as a fan allows them to move on to new programmes and begin new fandoms from scratch or, in many cases, follow pre-existing elements of interest. Furthermore, television's routines and rituals mean that every new television 'season' offers a plethora of new programmes to become involved with, while new modes of delivery such as the creation of online content such as *House of Cards* and *Arrested Development* via platforms such as Netflix expand the range of potential fan objects even further. In contrast to the more extreme reactions of fans who either reject a show or reiterate their fandom to maintain their emotional attachments, the fans explored here occupy a middle ground in order to negotiate the possibility of threat to their sense of self-identity or ontological security. The 'sense of the reliability of persons and things' that Giddens argues is 'so central to the notion of trust, is basic to feelings of ontological security' (Giddens 1990, 92) can be continued for fans who rely not on singular television shows to provide such security but, rather, have a broader sense of trust in the television landscape as a whole. Knowing that actors or showrunners and writers will move on to produce new objects of interest and fandom allows fans to demonstrate that they trust these figures. Such reactions also back up the assertion that 'One of the limitations of fandom research has been the tendency to assume that fans are "one hundred percenters" dedicated to singular objects' (Duffett 2013, 280) when, in fact, 'It is common for fans to move nomadically between different interests – a process sometimes called "serial fandom" – or to engage with multiple objects at the same time' (Duffett 2013, 280). Furthermore, such responses indicate that fan ontological security can be complex, offering varied layers of trust in different elements of a series and security that may result both from an affection for, and fandom of, a particular narrative universe as a whole but also from more specific fandom of certain actors, writers or directors.

This chapter concludes the section on fan discourses and reactions at the moments before and as a favourite television show ends. The final section of the book moves on and examines what happens in the years after a series ceases production in more depth. First, the use of new media such as DVDs, downloads and streaming services such as Netflix are examined to consider how new fans come to discover texts in a period of post-object fandom. Second, both official and fan user-generated endings and continuations will be explored to consider how fanfiction, videos and other forms of fan creativity are used to keep a series alive after its official cancellation. In focusing more specifically on the 'afterlife' (Levine and Parks 2007) of television series and the periods of what Bertha Chin (2013) refers to as 'post-series fandom' the final two empirical chapters explore how connections to characters, narrative worlds and fellow fans are continued through both official and unofficial channels.

7

'Living in DVD-Land': Post-Object Fandom, Re-Watching and Digital Media

The next two chapters move away from fan reactions before and as television series air their final episodes. Instead, the final section of the book considers how fans continue to engage with these shows after the cessation of their original 'lives' on television, examining how fan practices allow individuals to maintain and develop their connections with fan objects and fellow fans. In the contemporary landscape of television viewing that encompasses traditional scheduling and broadcast patterns, DVD and Blu-ray, downloads, streaming services such as Amazon Prime (formerly LoveFilm Instant) and Netflix and the opportunities to watch television 'on the go' via mobile technology, the ways in which fans now view their fan objects must be considered. Indeed, 'new ways of watching television are providing different ways of viewing that require more thinking about what their consequences may be for meaning making and the cultural role of television. Empirical examinations and evidence gathering that takes such thinking into the world of viewers ... are needed' (Lotz 2006, online). This chapter is primarily concerned with how fans re-watch series and how their discussions of this allow continued involvement with a series and its narrative world. It focuses largely on how fans use DVD and Blu-ray box sets to re-view programmes, since this was the form of re-watching that was most often discussed both on online forums and in the survey conducted with fans of cancelled shows in 2013. Respondents to that survey indicated a range of ways in which their fandom had continued, but the majority of these involved re-watching shows and maintaining engagement with the narrative world itself. Almost all of the respondents stated that they re-watched specific (presumably favourite) episodes (53 of the 66 fans), while 47 engaged in reviewing whole series and the majority (47 fans) had purchased box sets of a favourite series.

Thus, the chapter adds to the work already undertaken by critics such as Matt Hills (2007a), Derek Kompare (2006) and Inger-Lise Kalviknes Bore (2010) which has considered how DVDs impact upon audience relationships with televisual texts. However, perhaps surprisingly, many fans also highlight their enjoyment of watching reruns or repeats of their favourite shows in the years after they have ended. While DVDs have been seen to 'dislocate our experience of watching television from the ontology of flow and live-ness that has marked understanding of television' (Bennett and Brown 2008, 7), reruns continue to be important to the television industry since 'older platforms such as DVD, cable, and even broadcasting still remain viable, but online distribution continues to grow and develop as a more varied and participatory means through which people use, rather than only view, rerun television' (Kompare 2010, 80). This chapter explores how and why reruns might have been viewed as an addition, or alternative, to watching episodes on DVD. It argues that, contrary to the argument that new forms of access to programmes such as downloads, DVDs and time-shifting have rendered the notions of televisual flow and scheduling outdated, for some fans the ability to view shows as they were originally broadcast provides a source of enjoyment and reassurance. Through both a specific case study of *The West Wing* and the broader comments of survey respondents, the chapter considers how fans choose to re-view dormant texts in the post-object period, seeking to complicate arguments about the provenance of new technologies and the pleasures they afford fans. It also explores the different forms of 'ontological security' (Giddens 1984) that routinized television schedules or DVD viewing can provide.

'Not with a bang but a whimper': DVDs, commodification and fan disappointment

While DVDs were once considered to be at the cutting edge of 'new' media, they have already begun to be replaced by the superior technology of the Blu-ray disc as well as the availability of legal and illegal downloads or internet streaming of television shows. The latter can be extremely attractive for fans who seek to view favourite shows as soon as possible. For instance, in relation to *Lost*, Will Brooker notes that fans embraced downloading since 'by the time a show like *Lost* reaches DVD, the season is complete, a finished text. The case is closed, the detection is over. Watching on download, by contrast, combines the ability to study each shot in close detail with the intensity and immediacy of live TV' (2009, 52). Although such sentiments may be true while fans are engaging with an ongoing television series, my focus here is on examining how fans of a cancelled show use DVDs (rather than downloads or internet viewing) in a period of 'post-object fandom'. This section considers fan responses to the release of *The West Wing* on DVD and how fans watch these. This includes their watching of the episodes but it is also concerned with how the box sets function as 'aesthetic objects' (Kompare 2006).

The final season DVD box set of *The West Wing* was released after the show's finale in May 2006. Many fans responded with disappointment to the special features and these reactions were impacted on by the show's status as 'dormant'. When fans express disappointment with DVDs they are also articulating an obligation owed to them by the show's producers. Their comments therefore belie some of their intensely affective connections to the fan object itself. Derek Kompare argues that the television box set 'functions as an intriguing aesthetic object in its own right. It culminates the decades-long relationship between television and its viewers, completing the circle through the material purchase—rather than only the ephemeral viewing—of broadcast texts' (2006, 338). Specifically discussing *The West Wing*, Janet McCabe suggests that the DVD releases of the series meant that 'investing time now translated into investing quite literally in buying the series, first on video and later DVD. *The West Wing*, repackaged in these ways, finds income-rich, time-poor viewers able to run their own "appointment-to-view" diaries' (McCabe 2013, 26). Indeed, fans often anticipate the release of DVD box sets since they offer the opportunity to re-view the episodes, allow access to behind-the-scenes features and offer the chance to accrue fan knowledge and 'subcultural capital' (Thornton 1995). Some *West Wing* fans discussed the DVDs in the post-series thread *The West Wing* at Television Without Pity and expressed interest in watching these features and commentaries, noting for example that 'I am a very happy camper – I just received my Season 1 dvds! Of course now I have to order a few more seasons. Right now, I am watching the "extras" on the fourth disc, I find the "behind the scenes" stuff fascinating' (Post #344, July 2006, 'The West Wing') and 'I'm up to the S5 commentaries, egg & special features now. I've really enjoyed all of the extras, now that I've actually seen more than I hadn't before' (Post #7,510, July 2008, 'The West Wing'). However, in some discussions that occurred after the show finished broadcast, fans treated news about the release of the final season and a complete series box set with disappointment, expressing contempt towards Warner Brothers, who were responsible for producing the DVDs. Many appeared to have been expecting the final DVD releases to be 'special' and hoped that Warner Brothers would reward them with a range of extra features and insider knowledge. However, when the DVD features were revealed many fans found these lacking, especially since they focused on an unpopular episode 'The Debate'. Online posters commented that 'choosing to focus on the debate as the "extra" to entice DVD buyers simply reflects that [the producers and writers] of the last three seasons never had a clue what made viewers tune in' (Post #322, July 2006, 'The West Wing') and 'it sounds like the bonus material on the Season 7 set is very much focused toward the debate episode, which I'd just as soon have deleted from the discs ... so the disc release is "not with a bang but a whimper" for me' (Post #317, July 2006, 'The West Wing'). Such posters expressed that fans were often let down by producers: 'Based on past experience I think we can only assume that we'll be promised things that won't be delivered' (Post #356, July 2006, 'The West Wing'). Prior work on DVDs has tended to assume that 'extra-texts' such as commentaries, documentaries and deleted scenes (Kompare 2006, 349) perform crucial functions in terms of adding to the original episode, positioning the DVD as a 'superior' version of the television text since 'extras add filters of meaning to the original episodes and function as significant texts on their own' (Brookey and Westerfelhaus 2005, 349). However, in the case of *The West Wing* DVDs these 'filters of meaning' are not present since the DVD features are deemed to be deficient by some fans. Indeed, rather than allowing creators of shows to 'assert authority and maintain the role of author' (Gray 2010, 110) via extra-texts, some posters at Television Without Pity rejected the notion of privileged insight and instead dismissed the commentaries as self-serving and dull. They post 'While I am pissed off at the lack of extras, I don't think that I will miss the lousy commentary (*Isn't he good here? Let's just watch this scene*). The conversations here are much more insightful and interesting' (Post #368, July 2006, 'The West Wing') and 'I thought all the commentary on the DVDs was awful. Long pauses, punctuated with "Oh, he/she was so good in this scene" and an occasional lecture from [director] Tommy Schlamme ... about what lens he used' (Post #666, August 2006, 'The West Wing'). These quotes indicate disappointment with the content of the commentaries but also that the commentaries and features cannot tell the fans anything new, since their own knowledge of the show is so detailed: 'I wonder if the general consensus here, that the commentaries are generally boring and self-congratulatory, is partly informed by the fact that as obsessed [fans] we all probably knew a lot of the nuggets and anecdotes that the commentaries do touch on, just from reading and watching whatever *West Wing*-related stuff we could find over the years' (Post #666, August 2006, 'The West Wing').

While fans may dislike extras for 'spoiling' certain aspects of texts such as reducing the 'mystique of special effects' (Kerr et al. 2006, 77), such explicit condemnation of DVD extras as being patronizing, dull or entirely lacking is less common. Why, then, were fans so incensed by the apparently disappointing DVD releases, especially since the show had ceased broadcast? I suggest that the box sets, which were often perceived as a way to maintain links with both the text itself and one's fandom of it, failed to provide fans with the opportunity to maintain and relive their fandom as fully as they would have liked. In relation to movies on DVD, Skopal notes 'how important memories are for both the marketing of the DVD and the process of watching its extras as a means of an imaginary journey into the viewer's past experiences. As the film-makers are overwhelmed by the incomparable memories of the film-making process, the viewers are invited to let the memories of the incomparable filmic experience come back' (2007, 190). If DVD releases fail to adequately provide special features, interviews or commentaries that would convey 'the memories of the incomparable filmic [or television] experience', fans cannot fully experience the return of memory or engage in the imaginary journey that Skopal suggests. Given the links between DVD re-viewing and ontological security discussed in the next section, we can view these fans' disappointment within the context of *The West Wing* as a dormant text which functions differently as a fan object from when it was an ongoing television series.

'Living forever in DVD-land': Watching and using DVDs

In addition to treating DVD box sets as valuable objects and as a key part of their fandom, fans also discuss how they choose to watch the episodes contained in those box sets. Indeed, 'DVD box sets can enable fans to set their own pace of consumption, "bingeing" on a series by watching multiple episodes at any one time if the narrative pull is sufficient ... and so redefining the way in which "textual" interpretation may work across periods of time' (Hills 2007a, 58). As discussed, the work of Moores (2005) and Silverstone (1994) on ontological security and television has been crucial to understanding the links between the media, self and security. However, since this work focused on scheduling and has been closely tied to the traditional broadcast model of television it cannot account for the opportunities afforded by DVD and reruns. The following discussion challenges ideas about ontological security, suggesting that the experiences of watching television on DVD and through repeats offer different forms of security for fans.

The West Wing fans at Television Without Pity discussed their viewing of the DVDs in a range of ways. For one poster DVDs offer a place to momentarily forget the ending of the show and the poster's statement that 'I. Must. Get. Past. The. West. Wing.'s Cancellation. Or live forever in DVDland' (Post #294, July 2006, 'The West Wing') invokes the imaginative consolation of the fictional world. However, while some fans were re-watching the show for comfort and escapism, others were doing so for the first time, often with the encouragement of established posters. For example, one long-term poster responds to another, 'A new convert!? How do you like the show so far? What do you think about the characters? It's quite refreshing to see someone who's just watching the show, coming from me whose seen a lot these episodes over and over again' (Post #3,711, May 2007, 'The West Wing'). There is, thus, a sense of vicarious pleasure for long-term fans who can re-experience their own first impressions of the programme. Much like the fans who preferred to view reruns discussed below, for the posters who engaged with new viewers there is an opportunity to re-experience first viewing and the pleasures associated with the 'discovery' of the fan object. Another poster indicates the value of a new cohort of fans who are encountering the show on DVD, reassuring a new viewer that their interpretations are sanctioned by the fan community: 'In the post Sorkin years it seemed a little dummied down, then totally left field at times ... But yes, you've got it all correct. We're so proud of a new generation' (Post #8,402, December 2008, 'The West Wing'). Such encouragement fits with existing patterns of how established members of a fan community often educate newcomers. For example, Mark Kermode notes how to be ignorant – a 'know-nothing dilettante' (Kermode 1997, 48) – in horror fandom is to be avoided, while Julian Hoxter's study of *The Exorcist* fans explores how some adopt the pedagogic mantle of a 'sage advisor' (Hoxter 2000, 175) to educate new fans. In the case of *The West Wing* this also functions as a way for posters to maintain links to the fan object via the development of interpretations by newer fans. Furthermore, those who discover programmes in the years after their finales via DVD or, more recently, via streaming services such as Netflix, are likely experiencing a quite different form of fandom since watching via these modes enables viewers to experience 'a more "trustable" or "ontologically secure" re-versioning of broadcast TV' (Hills 2007a, 58). Matt Hills suggests that fans' sense of trust in a programme is undermined when that show is cancelled, whereas DVDs enable fans 'begin watching a series knowing that they will be able to follow it through to its conclusion (or perhaps knowing in advance that it will end at a particular point)' (2007a, 57). This equips them for the cessation of the show and increases the level of 'trust' they have in the text. Hills's work on DVDs as a 'trustable' or 'ontologically secure' alternative to watching broadcast television indicates the threat that fans may feel to their ontological security when beloved fan objects are cancelled.

Fans of cancelled shows often distinguish 'between watching new and unfamiliar episodes, which for [some is] now only a nostalgic memory, and [the] current practice of re-viewing the show on DVD and video, or catching a repeated episode by chance on TV' (Brooker 2007, 160–1). There are clear differences between how fans view shows for the first time and how they re-view episodes. For some, DVDs were less about replicating the experience of the 'new' and were instead related to their provision of familiarity and comfort, functioning as 'reassuring, therapeutic, cheering sessions with familiar guides and confidantes' (Brooker 2007, 161). Re-viewing also helped some fans cope with the fact that they missed the programme. As one noted after *The West Wing*'s finale, 'my Season Six DVDs arrived from Amazon.com this morning. It's comforting' (Post #291, April 2006, 'Tomorrow'), highlighting the emotional consolation that return to a beloved text can provide. Such knowledge and familiarity is engendered by the completeness and ease of the DVD format, since 'having a film [or TV series] on DVD, recording it on a DVR or downloading it onto a computer subjects it to playback's variables, pausing, rewinding, fast-forwarding, repeat viewing and copying … scenes, characters and dialogue may be burned into the viewer's memory, becoming signature aspects of meaning and pleasure' (Klinger 2010, 3–4).

For some fans who responded to the 2013 survey and who discussed a range of different television shows, the preference for re-watching via DVDs was expressed clearly in relation to cost and convenience. They responded, variously, that this was the preferred method because of 'high availability and low cost', 'convenience' and 'because a DVD is right there'. Related to this were issues of control and the opportunity that DVDs offer for fans to choose which episodes to watch; one respondent noted that 'It allows me to watch the episodes on my schedule' and another commented that 'I can control when I consume DVDs. Mine to treasure forever'. The idea of 'treasuring' the DVDs echoes the responses of online fans of *The West Wing* and their discussions over the aesthetic merits of the box sets and the use (or otherwise) of special features. The presence of such features was alluded to by many survey respondents, again indicating the importance of collection and ownership of physical copies of a favourite series for many fans. For example, they responded that: 'The DVDs often provide extras such as behind the scenes interviews, outtakes and commentary which aren't available elsewhere'; 'I prefer to have my favourite shows on DVD/blu-ray, because I always like to watch the behind-the-scenes specials and when I feel like it, re-watching them and my favourite episodes'; and 'I like owning DVD and have a "collection" of box sets + I can "control" my viewing experience (freeze, rewind)'. For some respondents, however, DVD is a necessity rather than a choice. One German survey respondent noted that 'DVDs also have often special features, behind-the-scenes stuff, which is also interesting. Or audio commentaries. Also, for me as a German, watching in English is important. In our TV everything is dubbed, but I want the original voices of the actors. DVDs also offer subtitles'. One UK-based fan of *Twin Peaks* offered a different take on the need for DVDs, given the lack of broadcasting of that series in the United Kingdom: '*Twin Peaks* isn't repeated on UK TV so [DVD] is the only chance I have. I'll always buy the new edition of the DVDs, however, so long as there's extra material added or notable improvements. If the rumours re: *Twin Peaks* on BluRay are true, I'll buy it to have the improved sound and picture quality'. While the presence of DVDs, and in the US the addition of the series to Netflix, has meant that 'more people are being turned onto [*Twin Peaks's*] unapologetically wacky world' (Clark 2013, 14), for this fan DVDs offer the only avenue of connection and re-watching of the show. While the discourse of aesthetics is present here in the sense that re-issues of the series, especially on Blu-ray, would offer greater quality and improvement, the limited access to the show in the UK is also a key concern, again demonstrating that fans' choice of mode of re-viewing is not always made on an equal footing.

Clearly, not all fans watched DVDs in the same way or for the same reasons. For example, some online discussion about *The West Wing* indicated that the desire or opportunity to watch old episodes was often tied to real-life events and circumstances. For some, the demise of the show had led them to watch DVDs less often: 'I remember thinking that I'd watch [my DVDs] again eventually but I haven't. Not even the real life election has inspired me. I briefly thought about selling them but that made me sad. I think I'd miss knowing they were on my shelf in case I ever needed to quickly confirm a random fact or just watch something brilliant' (Post #6,748, May 2008, *The West Wing*). This comment suggests that a sense of ontological security can be attained from simply knowing that a fan object remains available even if one does not actively use it. This poster's fandom lies dormant but can be returned to when needed. A survey respondent who identified as a fan of *The West Wing* offered similar comments:

> Usually with *The West Wing*, there will be certain political events where I either want to share a relevant clip on Facebook (though there are no official ones and I can't always find the right one) or I purposely watch campaign related episodes before the American campaign season. But I also think some distance is good, to not overdo it, so I enjoy it more when I do.

Here, the show is drawn on when needed, often coinciding with real-life physical events, but the respondent also expresses a fear that 'overdoing' it and re-watching the series too often can lessen her enjoyment. Ontological security here appears to be potentially threatened by over-reliance on the series; familiarity breeds less enjoyment, while more careful and infrequent returns to the show allow the connection and the enjoyment to be sustained. A similar sense of attachment to the DVDs is articulated by a poster who comments:

> I just yesterday loaned my season 1 DVDs to a friend and I feel like I've given away my first born child ... I know she'll take care of them, but she's not a big TV watcher like I am so it will probably be summer before she gets through 22 episodes plus commentary. Don't know if I can stand it. (Post #8,407, December 2008, *The West Wing*)

While this comment is clearly humorous in tone, anxiety regarding the absence of the DVDs is also expressed. In the comments 'Don't know if I can stand it' and the self-reassuring 'I know she'll take care of them' this post exemplifies the complex relationships fans have with texts and their material forms. For other fans, viewing the DVDs functions as a 'special' event; one notes that: '[I] Still watch them. I "save up" my viewings for when TV is crappy ... I treasure them' (Post #6,750, May 2008, *The West Wing*). This notion of 'treasuring' the DVDs' links to the concept of the box set as a commodity, as an object with 'ostensible aesthetic value ... meant for permanent ownership and domestic display' (Kompare 2004, 209–10).

However, the DVD box set as a commodity that can be purchased and viewed long after the cancellation of a show like *The West Wing* may imply that the notion of post-object television fandom is unsustainable – that the very existence of these objects means that fandom can be ongoing. To clarify, while post-object fandom does not mean that people cannot become fans of dormant objects, television's scheduling and presence – its 'liveness' – supports the idea that watching a television show on a DVD box set after its cancellation is very different from watching it while it remains an 'active object'. In their discussion of the end of *Friends* Eyal and Cohen argue that the show's presence in reruns and on DVD may have alleviated some of the sadness that fans felt when the show finished. However, they state that watching 'live' is the superior way of engaging with any programme, suggesting that 'one can conceive of reruns and DVDs for shows that no longer run as similar to looking at photos or home videos of a lost friend or partner. They may help, but it is not really the same. What is lost is the participation in the progression of the story' (Eyal and Cohen 2006, 516–17). This may account for why some fans preferred to watch reruns, as discussed below.

Threats to ontological security can be felt differently when watching a series unfold or when watching via box sets. Ontological security can develop from the constancy of a fan object, although the potential for the sudden cancellation of a series threatens the security that television series can offer. As noted, with DVD 'viewers can begin watching a series knowing that they will be able to follow it through to its conclusion (or perhaps knowing that it will end at a particular point), rather than being subjected to the disruption of a broadcast show's sudden cancellation. DVD, in a sense, therefore offers a more "trustable" or "ontologically secure" re-versioning of broadcast TV' (Hills 2007a, 58). According to Hills the viewing of DVDs contains less risk because the viewer has a sense of the end point before viewing and is reassured, since the prospect of unexpected rupture in the viewing experience is lessened. There are, however, still threats to the ontological security offered by watching television on DVD. One online poster comments that I 'realized that it is not nearly as much fun watching [DVDs] knowing that the show won't be coming back and that the characters are done' (Post #138, July 2006, 'The West Wing'). Here, the pleasure of watching DVDs is not related to the 'newness' of a new episode or to the practice of watching episodes 'live'. Rather, this poster indicates that the knowledge of forthcoming narrative events and the certainty that the characters are 'done' lessens his/her enjoyment of the programme. This fan view seems to contradict Hills's argument regarding the ontological security offered by the watching of television shows on DVD. However, Hills is discussing the security offered to viewers who are watching the shows on DVD for the first time (i.e. they have not watched them on television), whereas the fans of *The West Wing* at Television Without Pity were largely re-watching the show. Here, then, their ontological security is not threatened by unknown narrative events or the potential sudden cancellation of a show. Rather, their responses are linked to attachment to characters or to the different experiential aspects of watching episodes on DVD or on television.

DVDs formed a significant element of the fan discussion and practices surrounding the post-object fandom of *The West Wing* and also for the respondents to the 2013 survey. While some fans were revisiting the text, others were watching for the first time, offering a chance for established fans to vicariously re-experience their own initial encounters with the show. This offered potential ontological security via the opportunity to return to the diegesis of the show and to become reacquainted with a beloved fan object. For other fans, however, this sense of security was threatened by the knowledge of the show as dormant and finite, suggesting that fans negotiate ontological security in a range of different ways. Indeed, as the next section argues, some posters preferred to avoid DVDs entirely or watch them alongside televised reruns of the show. Continuing the discussion of ontological security, the pleasures of reruns will be examined to suggest that, like the efforts of fans to relive their own fan experience via new posters, many fans sought to create the conditions of the first viewing of the show. For some this meant watching it within the flow of the television schedule, a condition that best replicated their original encounter with the series and in common with an imagined audience of fellow (re)-viewers.

Reruns, becoming-a-fan and recreating first viewings

Many contemporary television viewers are 'choosing to consume a show entirely on DVD box set long after its original broadcast and/or in complete segregation from televised repeats' (Hills 2007a, 43–4). However, while the impact of DVDs and Blu-ray, downloads, time-shifting and portable media such as smart phones should not be underestimated, not all fans embrace the changes in access that these media have created. Although some do enjoy re-viewing a show on DVD, others prefer to view via reruns on television channels. This section explores the reasons for this preference, arguing that for many this is an attempt to return to the affective moment of 'becoming-a-fan' (Hills 2002, 6–7) and to recreate the moment of first viewing.

On the Television Without Pity forum, there were a range of online comments related to the distinctions between watching DVDs and reruns of *The West Wing* which, although sharing common ideas, articulated various fan positions. There was some debate over the preference for DVDs or reruns, as the following exchange on the post-series *The West Wing* thread indicates:

> I suppose this [the repeating of episodes on Bravo] is good, but personally, I find it not a problem at all to put my DVD's into the player and have my OWN 'marathon' – commercial free – anytime I want. ;-) (Post #7,440, August 2008, 'The West Wing')

> To me, it's not the same. (Post #7,441, August 2008, 'The West Wing')

> You LIKE having episodes interrupted every few minutes for commercials and promos ... not to mention those annoying graphics at the bottom of the frame promoting whatever else Bravo is showing? OK. to each their own. (Post #7,442, August 2008, 'The West Wing')

Here, reruns are derided for being interrupted by the network in a way that disrupts intensive viewing of the show. The intrusion of commercial breaks is a source of particular contention since they interrupt the narrative and dislocate the fan from their engagement. However, some fans who viewed reruns expressed that the experience of re-viewing failed to live up to the viewing of new episodes. There is a range of complex reasons expressed as to why this may be the case. For example, one poster notes that 'I miss this show beyond belief. There is nothing on that compares and while there are always DVDs and Bravo fixes it just is not the same as a fresh new episode (yes, I will dare say even a Wells' episode)' (Post #65, July 2006, 'The West Wing'). In referring to the common fan dislike of episodes by John Wells (the producer of the last three seasons of the show), the fan invokes subcultural knowledge and the practices of the Television Without Pity fan community to demonstrate the depth of their missing of the show. Here, fan affectivity ('missing the show beyond belief'), fan capital and implicit desire for new episodes of the text are inextricable. However, for other posters watching reruns is seen as a superior viewing experience to DVD sessions. Such discussions are often linked to 'liveness' and the experience of watching episodes with an imagined audience: 'There is something about watching the repeats on Bravo, even if I DVR them, that is better than watching my DVDs' (Post #12,564, May 2010, 'The West Wing'). Here, the act of watching *The West Wing* within the 'flow' of television offers greater pleasure than watching DVDs. This might be since the process of viewing repeated shows more closely echoes the process the fan went through when first viewing new episodes of the show on television. For many fans the moment of becoming-a-fan is a crucial point in their lives and there are many examples of 'fans' accounts of encountering media texts that resonate so powerfully that they transform one's identity, daily activities, and life trajectories' (Harrington and Bielby 2010a, online). This experience can often be hugely influential in the life of the fan and it is likely that some fans seek to recreate the moment of 'becoming' by emulating the conditions of their first encounter with the fan object.

The fan focus here on an experience of re-viewing that most closely replicates the experience of first viewing shares parallels with other fan practices in both television and music fandom. For example, Lucy Bennett has discussed the importance for some fans of the rock group REM in experiencing the authentic 'first listen' of a new album by the band and the ways in which they seek to preserve this experience. She argues that this subset of fans (referred to as Trobes) seek the 'ultimate first listen' (Bennett 2012a, 749) and are 'driven by a nostalgic aim to recapture the experience of buying a new release by a band without any prior knowledge of its contents, other than information which has been officially released' (Bennett 2012a, 749). Such fans thus refrain from acquiring any knowledge of the new album such as lyrics or artwork in order to best experience the '"awe and surprise" of the occasion' of first listening to the new album (Bennett 2012a, 750). A similar parallel between some fans' desires to try to best replicate the experience of first viewing via reruns can be seen in the case of fans and spoilers, defined as 'information about what will happen in an on-going narrative that is provided before the narrative itself gets there' (Gray 2010, 147). This often contributes to power struggles between spoiled and unspoiled fans, with those 'in the know' able to demonstrate their knowledge and discursive power (Jenkins 1995; Cantwell 2004; Williams 2004). Indeed, those who avoid spoilers for favourite television series are also engaging in similar ways by trying to prevent knowledge of anything that might taint the experience of sitting down to watch a new episode of a favourite programme. While many fans do actively seek out spoilers for the knowledge and fan subcultural capital that they can grant (see Williams 2004) or, as Henry Jenkins (2006, 26–31) discusses, to engage in a form of 'collective intelligence' (Lévy 1997), others are more reticent about accruing spoiled knowledge. For instance, in Gray and

Mittell's 2007 survey of *Lost* fans, 'only 16 per cent of [228] respondents indicated that they avoid spoilers as much as possible' since 'spoilers were seen as directly "ruining" the experience of watching *Lost*, and many expressed concerns of being accidentally spoiled by reading improperly labeled material online or coming across revealing entertainment news, like the announcement that an actor is leaving the show'. Spoiler avoiders in this research 'generally seemed mystified and dismissive of the practice and often compared spoiled fans to "kids on Christmas Eve who sneak a look at their presents" or called them "bad sports".' (Gray and Mittell 2007). They also 'suggested that spoiler fans lacked the maturity and patience needed to follow a slowly-evolving show like *Lost* "properly" as designed, regarding their consumption of narrative spoilers as character flaws' (Gray and Mittell 2007). This reflects an earlier study of fans of *Buffy the Vampire Slayer* where the unspoiled fans suggested that 'the spoiled are in some way reprehensible and that the unspoiled are innocent of such "sinful" indulgence and decadence. It therefore assumes a negative stance towards spoilers, devaluing the spoiled fans and simultaneously privileging the unspoiled as stronger and more restrained, while also patronizingly labelling them as naïve and helpless' (Williams 2004, paragraph 40). Those fans who prefer spoilers are here seen as odd, as displaying a child-like impatience, and fans who are able to wait for the 'untarnished' version of the fan object are clearly privileged. For those who do seek out spoilers, however, Gray and Mittell suggest that this may be to 'lessen the experience of suspense throughout an episode, decreasing the emotional unease that most fans of suspense narratives find pleasurable' since 'a few respondents suggested that spoilers helped them enjoy episodes by eliminating feelings of tension and suspense that they found unpleasant' (Gray and Mittell 2007).

In a more recent study, Matt Hills (2012a) has related these fears and tensions more specifically to the concept of ontological security, suggesting that spoilers can offer some protection against potential anxiety about watching events unfold onscreen without prior 'warning'. In relation to *Doctor Who*, Hills argues that the acquisition and knowledge of television spoilers offer one way for fans to control potential anxiety about their fan objects. He argues that 'the knowledge that new official, canonical TV episodes are in production and are forth-coming, coupled with relatively little information about them, can also provide fan anxiety' (2012a, 114) since forthcoming developments may undermine a fan's interest and trust in the show. This, he argues, means that: 'The idealized fan object is potentially threatened (in a way in which tie-ins, spin-offs and unofficial material cannot pose a threat) – what if the new episodes are no good?

What if unwanted story developments occur? Or much loved-characters leave?' (2012a, 114). For spoiled fans, knowing what is going to happen in advance is a way to ward off anxiety about possible changes to their beloved fan objects and to protect the sense of ontological security that they gain from their fandom. However, for other fans it is the act of avoiding spoilers that may offer a greater sense of ontological security. Thus, unspoiled fans appear to have a stronger sense of trust in the text itself, are able to place their trust in potential narrative events and are secure in the knowledge that they will be able to tolerate and adapt to any changes in the show. Spoiled fans appear to have less trust in being able to tolerate future developments/events without knowing in advance what these will be via reading spoilers. Thus, their fan–object relationships are less able to withstand stress and instability and these fans instead desire trust in the knowledge of future events, rather than in the text itself. This is not to suggest that either type of fan is 'better' than the other, or that they have a 'stronger' investment in their chosen object. Rather, for these fans trust in the text itself not to disappoint is greater than the potential anxiety caused by not knowing what will happen, suggesting again that ontological security is negotiated by different fans in a range of ways across fan practices. Such fans, like the music fans who 'resisted the temptation of hearing leaked material ... as a way to nostalgically evoke the thrill of virginal listening' (Duffett 2013, 75), or those who display a preference for re-viewing televised reruns over DVDs or downloads, seek an 'untainted' form of engagement with a fan object, attempting to ensure both a 'pure' first encounter with a new episode or album and pursuing a recapturing of this first experience in their subsequent post-object fan practices.

'Others are watching with me': Reruns, imagined others and fan community

In addition to the attempt to re-watch in the same mode as the first encounter with the text, there are other pleasures to be gained from watching reruns. Indeed, in contrast with arguments that the 'television of "sharedness" ... is no longer with us' (Katz 2009, 6), the communal experience of knowing other fans are watching offers pleasures that DVD viewing cannot:

> I've watched the entire series through several times, as well as random episodes countless times, but there is still something about watching the show on

broadcast/cable TV. I guess it's something about the shared experience, knowing there are other [*The West Wing* fans] watching right along with me. (Post #7,443, August 2008, *The West Wing*)

I get happy when Bravo airs a marathon, even when I can't watch it. There's what you said about the 'shared experience'. (Post #7,445, August 2008, 'The West Wing')

I can exist in rerun heaven ... I actually own the DVDs but find myself watching the reruns anyway. Something about knowing others are watching with me. (Post #12,078, March 2010, 'The West Wing')

Thus, in addition to the ontological security provided by a comforting attempt to return imaginatively to the early period of fandom, such security can also be gained from the imagined community of fellow viewers. In discussion of DVD 'binges' (watching several, or sometimes all, episodes of a box set in succession) Newman argues that 'Watching this way, we lose our connection to the larger viewing audience as community and to the temporality of broadcasting that unites a program with the moment of its airing' (2009, online). It is this connection to the viewing community that fans often invoke when they discuss their preference for reruns rather than DVDs, since they express enjoyment in relation to watching the show 'as it was meant to be seen' and following the narratives and characters in a linear fashion. One poster comments that 'Although I can watch the DVDs anytime I like, it's still nice to be able to watch on TV each week. I'm hoping they'll show all seven seasons from start to finish. I love watching the eps in the right order so that all the plot and character development can be followed in all its glory' (Post #1,131, June 2006, 'The West Wing'). US-based fans display a similar desire for viewing in the 'right order' when Bravo, the network showing reruns in the US, skips over some episodes and shows them out of sequence:

I was also highly annoyed with Bravo today when I got home and went to watch my DVR'd eps and realized they skipped from Josh going to Santos in Texas to get him to run, to the ep[isode] where they're in NH campaigning. (Post #10,099, June 2009, 'The West Wing')

Part of the fun, for me, is watching all the eps in order/as close to in order as I can get them on TV--I know I can do it with the DVDs though. (Post #94,210, June 2010, 'The West Wing')

This idea of the 'right order' suggests that not all fans engage in sporadic binge viewing of favourite episodes. It also highlights again the desire to as closely as possible recreate the experience of first viewing.

I have argued above that the re-creation of 'becoming a fan' can offer familiarity, comfort and ontological security. However, there are also threats to the show's broadcast on reruns and fans' trust in the text can be threatened. For those fans who prefer scheduled repeats the potential for the cessation of broadcast must be protected against. While some fans view reruns even though they own DVD sets, for others (often those with limited financial means) this offers the only chance to re-watch episodes. The threat of *The West Wing* disappearing from the schedule completely is acute for such fans who comment, for example, on the possibility that '[rerun channel] Bravo is getting ready to send the show to live on the nice farm that parents send the stray cats and dogs their children bring home' (Post #12,597, May 2010, 'The West Wing'). Finally, it is worth noting that some fans engaged in accidental viewing of reruns and did not (or could not) plan these in the same way as others. For example, one UK-based fan in *The West Wing* thread comments after the series finale 'Ah, well then. It's back to the DVDs and the relative serendipity of whatever More4 are showing on a Sunday evening' (Post #398, July 2006, 'The West Wing'). Owing to the somewhat arbitrary nature of how the show is scheduled in the UK context, some fans' viewing of the show remains dependent upon the scheduling choices of broadcasters. Those who choose to watch reruns may be able to better recreate the original experience of viewing and a greater sense of communal viewing that those who view on DVD but they can only watch whatever episodes happen to be aired. They must tolerate sudden changes in scheduling and unwelcome interference with the text: 'While on Europe over break I just got really annoyed at how More4 butchers *The West Wing*'s commercial breaks … I could always watch my DVDs, but I'm usually too lazy to decide which episode to watch, I like it when the TV people decide for me ;-)' (Post #3,970, June 2007, 'The West Wing'). The admission that 'I like it when the TV people decide for me' highlights another potential pleasure in viewing reruns, namely a sense of surprise as to what episode will be screened. However, the trade-off for this pleasure is the annoyance at how the UK broadcaster interferes with the show, adding commercial breaks at inappropriate points in the narrative. Again, the enjoyment for fans who view reruns must be negotiated against the potential threat of disruption to the viewing experience via either the unexpected interruption of the show's rerun schedule or intrusions into specific episodes.

Such preference for watching reruns allows us to make sense of a range of issues relevant to the study of new media, television and audiences. In contrast to arguments that the majority of people now watch through new technologies such as DVR time-shifting, download or on online, such modes of viewing suggest that, for the posters discussed here, watching television within televisual flow remains important. While 'the DVD frees us from the program schedule and the flow of content, which in many cases includes commercials, promos, and idents' (Newman 2009), many of the fans studied enjoyed the patterns of scheduling and flow. As argued, for some this offers an increased opportunity to try to recreate the moment of first viewing, which DVDs cannot provide. It is, therefore, viewing of reruns that can best offer fans the re-experience of moments of 'becoming' fans – an opportunity that may provide great pleasure and comfort in a period of post-object fandom.

Streaming a series

While reruns and DVDs were the main topics of conversation after *The West Wing* ended in 2006, respondents to the 2013 survey were more likely to discuss their preference for DVDs or the use of streaming services such as Netflix. On the most basic level, this is linked to the huge increase in use of such streaming sites in the past few years; according to *Newsmax* (2014) as of January 2014, Netflix had 33.1 million Web subscribers in the US alone. However, it also raises different issues in terms of understanding how fans re-watch favourite shows in the post-object fandom era and how this might relate to ontological security derived from such re-viewing. This section considers the impact of streaming series for fans and how factors such as a lack of a physical version of a favourite series, or the unreliability of the continuation of a show's provision may have an impact.

For fans who articulated that they often did re-watch favourite shows via streaming services such as Netflix, the reasons were varied. For example, one respondent claimed that 'I prefer streaming online because then I don't have to try and find the one disc that's inevitably missing from the box set because somebody "borrowed" it without telling me'. For some fans, DVDs and Netflix were used for different reasons: one notes that 'Netflix, its like comfort eating, and very convenient. Dvd, for the extra content commentaries and behind the scenes etc'; while another comments that 'DVDs – [have] special features. Netflix – easy access at home or travelling'. Like the fans discussed above who preferred DVDs owing to their convenience, for these three respondents services like Netflix offer similar accessibility and ease of use. As the first quote illustrates, nobody can 'borrow' from a fan's Netflix library or list without their knowledge, meaning that the disappointment or annoyance that may result from finding that a favourite episode or DVD disc is missing is avoided. The second two respondents indicate that DVDs offer greater information and involvement via the presence of special features but the focus on access when travelling suggests a desire for contemporary fans to have access to episodes on their own terms and through a variety of media; if a fan desires to watch a favourite episode when on public transport, for example, the fan object is ready and waiting via on-demand services. In some senses, a fan object's availability in this way offers a heightened sense of trust or ontological security for these fans since the object can be accessed whenever it is needed and is ever-present, only a few touches of a button and a Wi-Fi connection away.

For other fans, however, relying on on-demand services poses more threats that it assuages. Like the fans opposed to watching via rerun discussed above, the contingent nature of streaming sites can pose a threat to continued access to a favourite series. For example, one fan notes that 'I do sometimes prefer to buy DVDs, because I don't trust Netflix or iTunes (or some other distributor) to carry the show indefinitely'. Here, as in the case of a television series that ends before it is meant to, the sudden loss of an object can cause anxiety and disappointment for fans. For example, in the promotional push for the revived series *24: Live Another Day* the production company removed the earlier seasons from the US version of Netflix (Jeffery 2014). The assumption that a distributor will carry all seasons of a series and that these will remain permanently accessible cannot be made. This is linked to fans' awareness of the operations of the media industry; another fan comments that they prefer DVDs because they 'offer me maximum control over what I want to watch and when. I know my favourite series well enough to make these decisions without relying on who Netflix has what sort of contract with or how good my internet connection is'. The fact that services such as Netflix have deals with certain television networks and not others is clearly recognized by this fan. For example, Netflix currently carries no HBO programming, meaning that loyal fans of series such as *True Blood, Game of Thrones* or *Boardwalk Empire* cannot rely on the service to allow them access to their favourite programmes. Moreover, this respondent articulates a clear sense of 'knowing' their favourite show enough to want to be able to interact with it whenever they choose without being in sway to the economic and industrial conditions of the television production system. The same fan goes on to note that 'While I'm not necessarily opposed to downloading TV, I love these series enough to want them sitting on my shelf and wanting to invest money'. Here, there is an implicit suggestion made about what loyal and loving fans should do and the sense of owning a favourite series is clearly important to this fan. It's not enough to be able to simply access a programme in many cases; instead, the object needs to be possessed and owned, operating both as an aesthetic object of collection and as a stable point of access to re-watching and engaging with the beloved fan series. The need to own a series is also discussed by a fan who watches via DVD, Netflix and reruns but who professes a preference for DVD or Blu-ray. This is because 'there is the "play all" button which means I can have a 4–6 episode marathon without thinking too much about how much time I'm spending (sad, I know) … Lastly, and most shamefully for me, I like the feeling of ownership that I get from collecting a series'. This fan's comment about not knowing how much time is being spent on re-watching also invokes a sense of embarrassment or 'sadness'; there is an implicit sense that this is something that could be seen as a waste of time by others. The fannish invocation of discourses of 'sadness' or 'not having a life' allows fans across fandoms to self-deprecatingly defend against any such accusations (Thomas 2002, 121). In this fan's response, however, there is a sense too that the allusion to 'shame' regarding a sense of ownership has links back to the ongoing tension that many fans experience regarding their status as consumers.

Conclusion

Much contemporary work on television audiences has emphasized the importance of choice afforded by a range of new media such as digital recorders, downloads, live streaming and DVD/Blu-ray technologies. New consumers are perceived to be 'disrupting the notion of a "common culture" constructed by TV schedules' (Brereton and O'Connor 2007, 147) since DVD allows 'people to use their sets to create or access programming on their own terms rather than stay locked to the fare and schedule dictated by the broadcasting industry' (Kompare 2006, 336). In this way, the familiarity of the box set's presence on the shelf offers the chance to ward off threats to fan ontological security, since the narrative world can be revisited and experienced whenever the fan wishes. Ontological security generated by the constancy of the narrative world can, for some fans, be sustained since 'the availability of DVD collections of the episodes, also likely alleviated some of the anxiety associated with [a] show's ending, as viewers knew they could rely on those for continued interactions with [a] show's characters' (Eyal and Cohen 2006, 516–17). For some fans, simply knowing that episodes are available for them to watch on DVD is a source of ongoing ontological security, while the presence of the physical object of the box set embodies the fans' ongoing connection to a series. As McCabe notes, 'Owned, sometimes without necessarily being watched, the collector's box set sits on shelves alongside novels, music and film titles, sending out important messages about what we culturally invest in' (2013, 26).

However, as this chapter has demonstrated, not all fan viewers seek to abandon this enforced 'fare and schedule' and like, or in some cases prefer, to view favourite shows in reruns within the flow of television and experience the 'common culture' this engenders. Indeed, for some fans the 'noise' (Kompare 2006, 352) of television is desired since it best replicates the original experience of viewing a programme such as *The West Wing* that has long since been cancelled. Like music fans who seek the 'ultimate first listen' (Bennett 2012a) of a new album or TV fans who avoid engaging with spoilers owing to issues of trust, control and anxiety (Hills 2012a), viewing reruns can offer the moment of reliving a fan's first viewing of the show and a feeling of community with an imagined audience of fellow fans. The rerun thus offers different pleasures and forms of ontological security than DVD. The decision by many fans to eschew online viewing or DVDs for watching reruns, complete with commercial breaks, logos and idents and with the associated irritations of irregular scheduling, suggests that arguments regarding the irrelevance of televisual flow need to be re-examined.

We must acknowledge that fans are still using a range of options and 'rather than seeing DVDs, online catch-up services and file-sharing as evidence of a "post-broadcast era" television and newer technologies "should not be positioned as competitors but as hugely complementary"' (Mills 2010, 2). It appears, then, that ontological security can be achieved in different ways through different modes of re-viewing. Finally, it is worth noting that analysis of post-object fan practices is possible partially since programmes such as *The West Wing* are accessible on DVD and still repeated (Hills 2007a, 49). How fans of shows that seldom find their way onto DVD, such as reality TV or soap operas, negotiate the relative absence of these texts (which remain part of television's 'ordinary' and ephemeral output) would likely be quite different. Thus,

given ongoing technological convergence, the often intense affective relationships between individuals and a range of cultural objects and the recognition
that fandom helps us negotiate our 'social, political, and cultural realities and
identities' (Gray et al. 2007, 10), the study of how fans respond to 'old' media
texts through 'old' technological forms continues to cast light on audience
practices and uses of the media in contemporary mediated society.

The next chapter continues this focus on fan practices and discussions in the
era after a series has ended. Considering how both official and unofficial texts
allow the narrative world to be continued and how they work to reinforce or
transform fans' modes of engagement and attachment, the chapter examines
fanworks including fanfiction. Drawing primarily on survey responses, the
chapter reconsiders the boundaries of textuality and the very notion of 'post-
ness' when considering fan activity after a primary object of fandom has ended.

8

Continuing the Show: Interim Fandom, Resurrections and Fan-Created Texts

Having examined how fans use new media technologies to watch and engage with a series after its demise, this chapter continues in a similar vein by examining resurrections of television programmes and both official and unofficial continuations of a series. C. Lee Harrington notes that continuation is often desired by media producers and that 'the closure that fans hope for contrasts with the afterlife sought by the industry' (2013, 590). Responses from my 2013 fandom survey indicated that many fans continued their fandom after the final episodes of a television series: 54 per cent of respondents had interacted with official paratexts such as official comics or novelizations; 44 per cent had read fanfiction based on a favourite show; and 41 per cent had viewed fan-created videos based on a series. However, fewer of the respondents created such works themselves: just 10 per cent had created fan art; 4.55 per cent had made their own videos; and 21 per cent wrote fanfiction. While not purporting to speak for all fans of all ended television programmes, these findings appear to indicate a preference among respondents for official continuations of a programme universe over fan-created works and a tendency towards fanfiction as the most likely form of fan productivity. Conscious of the findings of this survey and broader work on both fanworks and official paratexts, this chapter explores how fans continue engaging with these fan objects, bearing in mind that 'from an industry perspective, the only bad ending is that which ends fandom' (Harrington 2013, 590–1).

The chapter considers the continuation of programmes in the period of post-object fandom by examining the ways in which textual resurrections can breathe new life into dormant programmes, either via televisual resurgences or in other media. Discussing examples such as *Firefly*, *24* and *The X-Files* alongside data from the fan survey, the chapter first considers how the transmediality of contemporary media texts allows cancelled shows to continue their afterlives and, in some cases, return to life. Post-series outings on the cinema screen remain relatively infrequent, although there have been examples including David Lynch's *Twin Peaks* prequel *Fire Walk With Me*, two big-screen outings for HBO series *Sex and the City* and the ongoing series of *Star Trek* films. More recently the television series *Veronica Mars* found a new lease of life in a film released in 2014 that was funded largely by fan donations via a Kickstarter crowd-funding campaign (Abbott 2014). Clearly, the promise of being able to tell stories outside of the narrative structures of the television series remains alluring. For example, the long-running series *The X-Files* enjoyed a post-series appearance on the cinema screen in 2008's *I Want To Believe*. Meanwhile, fan campaigns for a third *X-Files* movie continue unabated, with apparent support from production personnel Chris Carter and Frank Spotnitz as well as stars David Duchovny (who played FBI Agent Fox Mulder) and Gillian Anderson (who starred as Dana Scully). *The X-Files* also maintains a loyal fan base, whose modes of discussion have moved onto new platforms since the show's final televised episodes in 2002 (Chin 2013; Jones 2014) but who still actively support the show, those involved with it and a range of social activist campaigns (Jones 2012) via their fandom. Similarly, the prematurely cancelled series *Firefly* was continued post-cancellation on the big screen in the movie *Serenity* and continues to have a dedicated and creative fan base who produce a broad range of fanworks. As Mittell summarizes, 'Some programs are resurrected after being cut short through cancellation after stoppages or wrap-ups, as with *Firefly* being reborn as the feature film *Serenity* … the motivation seems to be driven by having more stories left to tell, and the freedom to tell them differently in another medium' (Mittell 2013, paragraph 7). *Firefly*'s original cancellation after just fourteen episodes fits into Mittell's notion of the 'stoppage', which he describes as:

> … an abrupt, unplanned end to a series when the network pulls the plug midseason (usually in its first season). A stoppage is always extra-textually motivated, when a network loses faith in a series's ratings or potential for growth, or a personnel issue with a creator or cast member creates a crisis, resulting a premature cessation of a series with no narratively motivated closure or finality. (Mittell 2013, paragraph 3)

As Stacey Abbott summarizes, 'Canceled by the Fox network after fourteen episodes were filmed, the [*Firefly*] concept was picked up by Universal Studios following the persistent lobbying for the series by its creator Joss Whedon, a protest campaign by devoted fans, and the series' successful DVD sales' (2008, 228). *Firefly*'s return to the screen was seen as a triumph for these fans, who perceived themselves as being in a 'David and Goliath' type battle with the network and company that had cancelled the series (see Cochran 2008, 243). While future cinematic outings for the *Firefly* universe appear unlikely, the world lives on in comic book format with three series taking place between the end of the television show and the movie and the 2014 comic book series *Serenity: Leaves on the Wind* taking place after the events of the film.

Alternatively, some television shows have returned to the small screen. In his comprehensive outlining of different forms of televisual ending, Jason Mittell discusses the concept of resurrection where 'an already concluded series returns, either on television or in another medium' (2013, paragraph 7). Recent examples of a return to television for concluded programmes include *24*, which ran on FOX between 2001 and 2010, and *Heroes* (NBC 2006–10). Once *24* had ended, rumours of a feature film circulated for several years until the announcement in May 2013 of a televisual resurrection (*Sky News* 2013) for the show in *24: Live Another Day* (FOX 2014). Similarly NBC's *Heroes* was cancelled in 2010 due to falling ratings but resurrected for a thirteen-episode season entitled *Heroes: Reborn*, which is due to air on NBC in 2015 (Denham 2014). Fox's animated series *Family Guy* was similarly cancelled in 2003, before returning in 2005 following strong sales on DVD. However, while *24*'s original ending had been planned, *Family Guy* was seen by many to have been prematurely laid to rest, leading to the decision to return it to screens in 2005. While *Family Guy*, *24* and *Heroes* were brought back to life on their original networks, a different trajectory can be seen in the case of television comedy *Arrested Development*, which aired on Fox between 2003 and 2006, before being brought back to life in 2013 by the streaming subscription company Netflix. More recently, the BBC series *Ripper Street* (which was cancelled after its second series in January 2014) was revived after a deal between the BBC and Amazon Studios was agreed to stream the series online first via Amazon Prime, before later being screened on BBC1 (Berliner 2014). Here, unlike the example of *24* or *Heroes*, these series were not resurrected by their original producers and saw their televisual returns facilitated by the newer forms of production and broadcast that on-demand services such as Netflix or Amazon Prime Instant Video can offer. There are, however, clear differences in how we can theorize and understand different forms of resurrection. How do we understand fans of 'returning' shows when this is via a different medium such as film or novelizations or comics?

The chapter examines fan discussion of user-generated endings and continuations for dormant television series, considering how fans themselves can keep a narrative universe and characters 'alive' in the post-object era. It explores fan-created ways of maintaining and extending a programme universe after a series' official instalments cease. It examines fanfiction as a way of dealing with an unsatisfactory ending and also as a form of continuation of a beloved narrative world, allowing exploration of the questions 'What happens when fans of a cancelled series want more of it? How does the ending of a series influence the subsequent creative writing about that series?' (Musiani 2010, paragraph 1.2). Continuing to produce or read fanfiction, whether the source text was prematurely ended or had a long lifespan, offers a way for fans to maintain their fandom and links to the series itself and to fellow fans. The communality of fanfiction allows fans to work together to create and protect the memory of a beloved show, also functioning to enable fans to ward off any anxiety or rupture to their fan ontological security. For fans who are interested in fanfiction, the narrative world can continue, albeit unofficially, and threats regarding the cessation of the fandom itself can also be warded off since the fanfiction offers an avenue for continued discussion and connection.

Finally, the chapter considers the case of science-fiction/fantasy series *Torchwood* as an example of a 'zombie' or 'undead' text that has no firm plans to return as a television series but which, equally, has not been officially cancelled. It explores how fans of a series in this position negotiate this lack of clarity or certainty and how this might affect their sense of fan self-narrative and identity. It posits that ontological security is negotiated differently by fans in the period of such interim fandom where fans assume that their fan object is dormant but when it becomes active again. These case studies pose challenges to our understandings of texts and textual boundaries and also allow consideration of fan responses (both positive and negative) to the continuation of an assumed dormant textual world. Indeed, as Harrington notes, fans can often be cautious about the 're-booting' or resurrection of texts:

> … fans are hesitant about industry vs. creative imperatives regarding narrative endings. A textual death that leaves open the possibility of an afterlife or re-boot can be 'good' from a fan perspective insofar as that possibility is realized and well-handled, but otherwise we are left with a missing person scenario (*24* feature film, anyone?) and/or corpse defilement (*Charlie's Angels* [ABC] round two, anyone?). (2013, 590–1)

In exploring fans' reactions to textual returns, the chapter explores how these resurrections can allow fans to maintain or renegotiate their fandom and their often complex responses to the revival or continuation of a fan object.

Key to this are the concepts of paratexts and transmediality. Drawing on the work of Gerard Genette (1997), Jonathan Gray defines paratexts as material that is 'both "distinct from" and alike – or ... intrinsically part of – the text' (2010, 6). This can include physical objects such as 'posters, videogames, podcasts, reviews, or merchandise' along with more 'intangible entities' such as the notion of genre or the concept of spoilers (Gray 2010, 6). Thus, Gray cautions against considering a 'film or program [as] the entire text' and suggests instead that 'a film or program is but one part of the text, the text always being a contingent entity, either in the process of forming and transforming or vulnerable to further formation or transformation' (2010, 6–7). These ideas are clearly significant to understanding post-object fandom, given that it involves texts being supplanted or inflected by paratexts that move outside television and into a range of other media such as comics, novelizations or films. Furthermore, moving away from viewing television series as a complete 'text' and instead treating them as part of a broader web of textual meaning allows examination of how fandom operates across different media objects. Such objects can be interrelated and allow us to better understand fans' ongoing relationships with favourite series in a period of post-object fandom. Drawing on Gray's ideas about textuality allows us to widen the scope of how we understand fan objects and to begin to view them as less discrete bounded entities and, instead, as part of a broader web of textuality and meaning for fans. Related to this is the concept of transmedia storytelling which refers to a story that 'unfolds across multiple media platforms, with each new text making a distinctive and valuable contribution to the whole' (Jenkins 2006, 95–6). According to Jenkins, in the perfect example of such transmedia storytelling, 'each medium does what it does best – so that a story might be introduced in a film and then expanded through television, novels, and comics; its world might be explored through game play or experienced as an amusement park attraction' (Jenkins 2006, 96). In addition, however, audiences and fans can also contribute to transmedia storytelling and 'audience engagement across platforms intended and unintended could also constitute transmedia. A looser definition of transmedia would suggest that audiences as well as official authors coconstruct transmedia narratives, storyworlds and frames for engagement' (Stein and Busse 2012, 14). For example, Jeff Thompson discusses the ongoing fandom around the ABC supernatural soap opera *Dark Shadows* which, as he notes, 'never really went away' (2014, 27) and lived on via syndication, live fan events such as conventions, VHS sales, a 1991 reboot of the series on NBC, comic-book series, Big Finish audio dramas and the Tim Burton film version of the series in 2012 (Thompson 2014, 26–35). This chapter thus explores the transmediality and paratexts of television shows in the period of post-object fandom, moving the focus of analysis beyond the boundaries of the series themselves to encompass the presence and fan discussion of novels, comics and fan-created texts such as fanfiction.

Textual resurrections: Cinema

In survey responses, the five most common film versions of television series that were discussed were *The X-Files*, the *Sex and the City* sequels, *Star Trek*, *Serenity* and the 2014 *Veronica Mars* movie. In most cases, the latter three were held up as examples where movie continuations of television shows were successful, whereas there were more negative comments levelled at *Sex and the City* and *The X-Files*. Indeed, *Serenity* had by far the most positive comments (of the sixteen respondents who cited this as an example, only one mention was negative) and this was often explicitly compared to the two other cases (of thirteen mentions of *The X-Files*, four were positive and nine negative, while of six mentions of *Sex and the City*, just one was positive).

For some respondents cinema resurrections offered a way to provide a sense of finality to programmes that may have ended abruptly, especially those whose cancellation was seen as premature. One fan notes that 'Done right, a movie can help bring closure to a cancelled TV series', while another suggests that 'A movie can be a good way to achieve closure, if this was not done in a series finale, or it can give a series a fresh start. The *Star Trek* movies are great examples'. This was often implicit in responses that discussed *Firefly*, with a dominant sense that the movie *Serenity* had succeeded because it offered narrative closure and had remained 'true' to elements of the original series. Two fans noted that, while the film offered such closure it had not eroded their desire for further continuation of the *Firefly* narrative universe; one notes that '*Firefly* needed a way to say goodbye. But ... I still want the show to come back', while another comments that '*Serenity* made me crave more of the world, and there was nothing to fill the hunger with'. For others, revisiting a revived series allows reconnection with beloved characters; one respondent noted that 'it's also nice, as a fan, to get to visit with old friends for a bit'. Another offers a longer discussion of this sense of familiarity, commenting that 'it's a great way to revisit the universes every few years, like meeting old friends after not having seen them in ages. I think as long as there are stories that remain to be told, it's always good to catch up with these characters every now and then'.

Respondents also displayed clear criteria for successful resurrections of television series on the big screen, including aesthetics, storylines and retaining the 'essence' of the original series. The distinctions that these fans make about 'good' resurrections share clear overlaps with the elements they deemed most important in a series finale. Much like the majority of respondents who indicated that the most important element of a finale was that it 'be true to the series' (nearly 85 per cent of respondents), resurrections are seen by many fans to need to honour a series and to 'do it justice'. Respondents note that:

If the films are *loyal to their fans and the series*, I'm in favour of resurrections.

If written well, with good storylines and arcs, *keep true to the characters* with development, some television series can resurrect as movies with success.

I think if the demand is there … then it could potentially work. However, that's only if they *make it in keeping with what made the original series popular with fans* and usually only if it's the original creative team who've been mulling over the 'shoulda woulda coulda' type decisions for their characters for years.

A great way to keep the fan base alive and to start a new generation of fans, provided it is well done and *stays true to the series* (emphasis added).

The desire for character continuity, loyalty to long-term fans and the involvement of the original creative teams suggests that what fans fear more than a complete lack of continuation of a narrative is that the narrative will be revived but that it will disappoint. While a resuscitated fan object can provide a new focus for fan discussion and may prompt changes in fans' self-identities (causing them, for example, to reassert and strengthen their fan identity when a film is released or a series returns), this identity and the ontological security it can provide can also be threatened if the resurrection is badly handled or disappointing. It is here that distinctions between the cases of *Firefly/Serenity* and *The X-Files* or *Sex and the City* were often made. For instance, replies commented that:

If it's well done (*Serenity* was well done, the latest *X-Files* movie was not) I think it's nice to see a film version. Cinema allows the writers/creator to play with ideas that they couldn't necessarily do … on the small screen. It's also nice, as a fan, to get to visit with old friends for a bit. If the film is badly done though, it's a huge letdown when you go see it as a fan.

While this fan applauds the potential for broader narrative or creative scope that cinema offers over television, there are again anxieties expressed about the potential for being 'let down' if a film fails to work. Other replies elaborate on the common discourse that dismisses the second *X-Files* movie as a failure:

Case in point, *Firefly*'s movie *Serenity* worked because it clearly came from passion and a desire to close things off properly. The latest *X-Files* movie didn't because it was trying to be too many things to too many people, and strayed too far away from what made the original series popular.

I haven't seen the second *X-Files* movie but from what I heard it must have been pretty awful. I did not enjoy the first one much either. Some things are just better in the weekly format but if you try to make a two hour movie out of it, you need a great story. Plus a movie needs to appeal to the fans with all the little details, as well as to the ordinary movie goer, which does not know much about the background. That can be difficult and usually one group loses out.

The two key limitations here are the fact that expanding from a forty-minute episode format to a longer movie version will cast light on storytelling deficiencies and also that televisual resurrections in the cinema need to tread the thin line between pleasing established fans and attracting regular cinema-goers to watch. Another respondent echoes this view, again with reference to the second *X-Files* movie *I Want To Believe*: 'the second *X-Files* movie didn't seem to be satisfying for either long-time fans or casual viewers. I think there has to be a reason to continue the story, a movie-sized question that still needs answering, and the movie needs to actually DO that to make it worthwhile'. The perception that *I Want To Believe* had 'failed' as a textual resurrection can perhaps be traced to the circumstances surrounding its initial demise. Unlike the case of *Firefly/Serenity*, the demise of *The X-Files* occurred, not after fourteen episodes, but after nine seasons, making the show's ending more akin to Mittell's 'conclusion, where a program's producers are able craft a final episode knowing that it will be the end' (Mittell 2013, paragraph 5). In the instance of *The X-Files* there was a widespread perception that the latter seasons had declined in quality, particularly seasons eight and nine which featured original star David Duchovny in a vastly reduced role and introduced the character of Agent Doggett (played by Robert Patrick) as a new foil for the character of Dana Scully. Simon Brown summarizes other perceived issues with the latter seasons:

> Further [online fan] posts suggest a different problem: that the writers lost track of the complicated narrative arcs and started either making mistakes or cheating by reinventing the history. This is expressed in many forms in the discussion but most succinctly by [online poster] 'dig-duggler' who claimed the real problem was the fact that 'Chris Carter was just *making this shit up* as he went along'. User 'bargle' takes up this theme, stating that 'the background conspiracy crap just went in circles and became stupider as time went on'. (Brown 2013, 8)

Such comments share overlaps with the critical *Lost* fans discussed in Chapter 5 and again highlight the potential for disappointment when a series poses narrative questions that it fails to answer as well as the threat to fan attachment when trust in a show's creators is undermined. Thus, although creator Chris Carter stated that 'I want to be able to wrap things up for the fans who have been there from the beginning. My determination was to go out with a series of very, very strong episodes that are going to pull a lot of threads together from the last nine years' (Chris Carter, cited in Brown 2013, 7), the series finale was not widely lauded and attracted a relatively small audience. Brown goes on to argue that, in fact, the latter seasons of the show offered some of the most narratively and aesthetically interesting of the series' episodes. Nonetheless, the popular conception that '*The X-Files* shuffled off to a chorus of silence' (Brown 2013, 10) has tended to endure. The assessment that the second movie was unsuccessful, then, may be connected to the wider assumption that the series deserved to end and was past its best, in contrast with *Firefly*, which was widely perceived to have been unfairly treated by its network FOX and to still have stories to tell.

However, it is worth noting that not all respondents were positive about *Serenity*. The only negative response stated that '*Firefly* was a better film [than *Sex and the City*], but I feel that this one was very much "for the fans". I honestly don't know if it makes any sense to viewers who haven't seen the series. It feels like a final episode, not a film. But I guess this address to fans rather than a wider audience makes it a better example of a film follow-up'. This was the only fan response to explicitly state that 'better' film resurrections are those that seek to address fans, rather than the broader cinema-going audience. Such responses suggest differences in the ways that fans reacted to questions over which sections of the audience a television finale should prioritize. In that instance 43 per cent of respondents indicated that finales should 'appeal to fans more than casual viewers' and almost 60 per cent felt that finales should 'reward the viewer', presumably the fan viewer. When it comes to resurrections, however, there is a shift for some fan respondents who appear aware of the wider demands that films face if they are to be deemed successful. While such a balance failed in *The X-Files* film, *Serenity* is largely viewed to have achieved this, fulfilling the fact that 'the producers and studio needed the film to appeal to a larger audience. At the same time, they had to satisfy the fans, whose loyalty was an intrinsic part of the film's genesis' (Abbott 2008, 228).

Other respondents offered detail about why the transition from television to cinema can be fraught with anxiety for fans. One notes that 'I tend to feel that it devalues the series. I'd rather it didn't happen', while another more ambivalently suggests that 'if the fan demand can support it, then I am all for it. HOWEVER some small screen shows can lose their essence when moved to cinema proportions. Changing the medium and delivery method can change the style/ characteristics'. This respondent doesn't offer any examples of series/films where they feel this change in medium has failed, but this response suggests fans' clear awareness of production conditions and medium specificity when resurrecting fan texts:

> I'm not a big fan of this: part of any TV series is how well it handles its own narrative structures and they tend to be products of a specific historical moment. *Sex and the City* was revolutionary as a TV series, it showed female companionship and women talking about sex and the over-identification of women with this sort of representation is hard to re-capture in a post-*Sex and the City* world. I only saw the first film and felt that it did not capture some major elements of the series – mostly because the narrative felt rushed. You can't tell a story it would usually take a whole series to tell in two hours. It felt like a bad adaptation of a book you really love.

Very few respondents explicitly acknowledged the media industry imperative for bringing dormant texts back to life in the cinema. One questionnaire respondent notes that these are 'not usually as good or fulfilling but entertaining none the less. Obvious business sense'. Similarly, only one survey respondent indicates that one aspect of the pleasure to be gained from resurrections is the creation of new goods to purchase. They note, 'I think it's a great idea. It gives fans a chance to see where the characters are now. It continues the fandom, often creating new fans. Also, it's a chance to purchase new merchandise that's been newly made'. Consumption is clearly a huge part of fandom and the acquisition of fan-related merchandise is a key part of fan engagement and attachment (see Geraghty 2014). However, the fact that only one respondent out of sixty-four mentions this as a positive element of new versions of fan texts may indicate fans' ongoing discomfort with being associated with consumption and economic elements of the media industries. As Hills notes, this tension permeates fandom since 'fans are both commodity-completists and … express anti-commercial beliefs or "ideologies"' (2002, 44). While fans may now be viewed as 'media consumers par excellence' (Gwenllian-Jones 2003, 167), they often remain reluctant to unproblematically embrace this label. Such resistance is alluded to in other responses to the issue of resurrections that comment on the commercial imperatives behind such decisions. Two respondents note: 'Not interested in them, they are never as good, just seems like a money making scheme to me'; and 'this comes across more as merchandising opportunity to fans, rather than a continuation of a beloved storyline, I feel'. There are always economic demands for the return of successful television series since 'the industry itself aims for the profit potential of narrative immortality and/ or resurrection (in syndication, in another medium, etc.)' (Harrington 2013, 584) and 'wish[es] for the profitability of immortality (or resurrection/afterlife in syndication or other platforms)' (Harrington 2013, 588). However, some fans remain ambivalent about openly accepting and embracing the commercial value they possess as target audiences/consumers for new imaginings of dormant fan objects, often preferring to reject such new texts as commercial, economically driven and inferior. Such second-rate versions of beloved fan objects can work to undermine fans' self-identities and sense of ontological security since they threaten to dilute and undermine many of the things that the fan was originally attracted to. Inauthentic or inferior copies of a fan object can, therefore, endanger fan attachments both by highlighting the commercial nature of fandom, as well as threatening to 'betray' the original characters and narrative worlds.

Textual resurrections: Small-screen revivals

When asked about resurrections as television series, survey respondents overwhelmingly mentioned the case of *Doctor Who*, with over half of the respondents highlighting it as an example of a resurrection that had been successful. *Arrested Development* was mentioned by two respondents as a strong example of a revived text, while there were also single mentions of the new versions of *Hawaii 5-0*, *Beauty and the Beast* and *Dark Shadows*. In contrast, negative comments were made about *Family Guy*'s resurrection by one respondent, while two people each mentioned that *24* and *Dallas* had failed or were likely to fail as resurrected TV shows. When asked specifically about the return of their own favourite show, respondents were largely in favour (twenty-seven out of sixty-two respondents) or ambivalent, offering caveats about what they would want to see in a revived show before they welcomed it (twenty-four of sixty-two replies). Eleven respondents declared an outright opposition to this, for reasons discussed below.

There were overlaps between the arguments that fans made regarding the return of television series in cinematic and televisual form. Many fans were overwhelmingly positive about this possibility, offering responses such as 'Thumbs up … do it!', '[I would be] Grateful', 'Would love this!', 'I would be over the moon' and 'EXCITED'. While such responses tended to be brief and to the point, one elaborates that '[I'd feel] **Like its Christmas and my birthday, and a Halloween, and a … well happy'. Several reasons to be positive about a revival are put forward by different respondents, who were also clear that reboots were a way to both reward original fans and attract new ones. They note, for instance:

> I started watching *Dr Who* last year and started at the beginning of the current run of the show. Resurrecting a show often brings new fans into the fold, who sometimes will watch the older version as well. It can also serve to appeal to the original fans who have been left wanting for more.

> As a fan of the original *Doctor Who*, I remember wondering what was going to happen with a series reboot. I think science fiction and fantasy fandoms are more open to the idea of a return or reboot than they would be in other types of genre … I think in the end it worked well because it was well written and was re-imagined without throwing away the past that fans were nostalgic about.

> It's certainly a great treat for loyal fans, and I think it's a perfect opportunity to introduce new fans to the shows this way.

Such discussions have echoes of the debates over original fans versus broader cinema-goers that adaptations to film generated. There is less sense, however, in the comments about televisual resurrections that a broader audience needs to be satisfied. Rather, there is an expectation that fan service will be performed and new dedicated viewers might be introduced, but relatively little concern about the need to attract a broad viewership. Only one respondent touches on the ambivalence around this, noting that in some cases, 'This can be good, but often fan nostalgia means that the "resurrected" version of the show alienates the original "first wave" fans'.

For one fan television revivals offer a chance to 'check in' on characters and be reunited with favourite fictional figures. They note that 'I think it's a great idea to bring a beloved show back, provided the creative team is up to the task. So many fans wonder what might happen to their favourite characters years or decades later and this is a great chance to give them what they wish for or maybe to provoke a heated discussion, which is also good'. Another fan comments on the ways in which reboots or resurrections can lead fans back to the original text, allowing them access to a narrative that they might otherwise not have discovered: 'I love *Arrested Development* and *Doctor Who*, so I'm complete okay with it. I came to *Dark Shadows* only after it ran in the late 80s or early 90s. If it hadn't returned, it would have taken much, much longer for me to discover the original run. The same is True of *Doctor Who*'. As with the fans discussed in the chapter on negotiation and 'moving on', this statement offers some insight into how fans discover new objects of fandom. While the respondents discussed in Chapter 6 related this to specific actors or writers and producers, this fan suggests that new incarnations of television series can engender fandom of the original text as well; indeed, many *Doctor Who* fans speak of discovering the 'classic' series after becoming fans of the post-2005 version. Finally, one respondent alludes to the importance of a revived TV series providing closure, echoing comments about the possibilities for resolution that a cinematic version could offer. They note that '[it] would depend on the programme. Yes, if it did not get a proper ending'. Much like the comments below that centre on issues of originality and innovation, this fan opines that a show that deserves a satisfactory resolution would be welcomed. By implication, however, a revival that adds nothing new to the narrative would be disliked by this particular fan respondent.

Other respondents assumed a position of cautious optimism, stating that they would be pleased but would want to be assured of certain things before getting their hopes up. For several, the involvement of key original cast and crew was paramount:

> Only if the main actors, creator were attached but would be cautious … not to want to be drawn in again.

Only if everyone involved in the original production would be back. I'm not particular keen on reboots for recently cancelled shows (something like [*Battlestar Galactica*] for instance, is an anomaly) …

It depends on whether the original talent and creative team would return.

I would be excited and apprehensive at the same time … I would very much want to know who was involved in resurrection before getting my hopes up.

This is clearly linked to a sense, as in the discussion of cinematic resurrections, that any new version must 'do justice' to the original series and retain its tone and 'essence':

I think resurrections have to be very carefully done and be true to the spirit of the series. Often, they don't work. I think *Doctor Who* became a better series. *24* was a good series, but I think it time was done. I don't watch *Arrested Development*.

As long as the shows are faithful to the originals, I'm all for it.

If it stays true to the narrative, then it works. Otherwise, don't ruin the brand.

For many respondents, the involvement of original cast and crew goes some way to promising that this may be the case, and works to protect fans against potential disappointment and threats to their sense of fan self-identity and ontological security. Indeed, the sense that a return of a fan object may be disappointing or lead to negative emotions was often alluded to. One respondent notes that 'I was worried when it was first announce[d] that they were going to resurrect *Doctor Who* – not because I didn't want to see it come back but because I didn't want to see it fail. Fortunately, I needn't have worried. If a series can be resurrected as successfully as this, then I'm all for it'. The threat to fan identity that may be caused by the failure of a resurrection can be a source of anxiety for many fans. If the return of a beloved object undermines the original attachment and sense of pleasure that is gained from being a fan, then there is a strong desire to ward off this threat and to avoid being disappointed or, even, embarrassed by its failure. The fans above who emphasized the necessity of the presence of original producers or auteur figures draw on this as a potential reassurance against such anxiety, discursively suggesting that such figures work as a 'guarantee of quality'. Matt Hills discusses how an auteur figure 'acts as a point of coherence and continuity in relation to the world of the media cult' (2002, 132) and that 'fans continue to recuperate trusted auteur figures' (2002,

133). In the era of post-object fandom and when the possibility of resurrection looms, it is unsurprising that such figures come to stand in again as points of 'coherence and continuity' and that they are the people in whom fans place their trust. Their previous involvement, their presumed knowledge of and their love for a text suggests that the revived series is in good hands, allowing fans to attempt to avoid any anxiety or threats to fan ontological security that may be caused by news of a resurrection. Some fans are more specific about the necessity for the original cast members to be involved; one notes that any resurrections must be done 'with the original actors', while a *Twin Peaks* fan suggests that they would be 'cautious. I'd like to see a *Twin Peaks* twenty years on but it'd have to be done right' and that they 'would be open to it if original cast was involved'.

While the presence of producers can ward off anxiety or threats via the assumption that such figures have the requisite levels of knowledge and respect to revive a show, the need for original actors perhaps offers different forms of security. The return of the actors provides a parallel return for the characters who fans are attached to, functioning as literal reminders-in-the-present of the narrative world. Indeed, some respondents actively stated that the changes in the actors would be one reason to avoid reboots or resurrections: 'It's unlikely my favourite characters would be literally resurrected, unless it was done in flashback. Realistically, the actors would be older, unless the storyline kept up. Sometimes mini-series with a limited story arc work better for this sort of thing'. Similarly, two *Firefly* fans comment that:

> If *Firefly* returned now, I don't think it would be the same series. I cannot help but think of the *Buffy* episode in which Dawn, Buffy's sister, attempts with magic to resurrect Joyce, their mother. Something comes back, but it isn't Joyce. So I think for some series, resurrection would be more painful than the original loss of the series. Actors would look different, they would bring with them the 'baggage' of other work they've done in between – I mean, there is no guarantee that an original cast could be secured. And casting is really important to my investment in a narrative.

> Mixed, honestly. It's been so long since they've done *Firefly* that they'd have to make a show either about their a lot older, or same universe different characters. And I'm not sure if I'd really enjoy that.

Both of these responses indicate fan anxiety about the fact that the actors would look older or different and, in the first example, a sense that the other characters they have gone on to play in the meantime might colour their characters or the ways that fans viewed them. If some fans resist the return of the embodiment of a character because they would not look 'the same', we need to consider why this may be the case. As an 'embodied presence' (Garner 2013, 203), the physical appearance of actors can often provide a sense of continuity or ontological security via the notion of co-presence. As Garner notes in his discussion of the death of *Doctor Who* actress Elisabeth Sladen, if embodied presence works to provide ontological security via familiarity and a sense of reassurance, 'it is unsurprising that the shocking loss of a favoured actor/character would generate feelings of grief among fans' (2013, 203). However, the fact that actors can provide 'co-temporality' by functioning as 'age cohorts' (Turnock 2000, 48) may also be relevant when they return to play particular roles. Changes in the physical appearance of a favourite character (or actor) may, like the death of an actor, threaten fans' sense of ontological security, highlighting both their own co-presence with aging characters and threatening to undermine their original views of what characters look like. Equally, in other cases, it may actually work by reiterating the sense that a narrative universe, and the characters within it, have continued in the period that a world has been off-screen and that the 'hyperdiegesis' (Hills 2002, 137) of a series has endured. Indeed, the emotional impact of failure is clear for some of the respondents. One replies that '[I would be] conflicted. I would be thrilled and hopeful, but also terrified that it would be cancelled again. It's hard enough to go through that the first time. You don't really want to go through that twice'. Another notes that they would have 'mixed feelings. It all depends on the quality. I don't want to look forward to it and then be disappointed'.

Despite the desire for involvement of original cast and crew expressed by many respondents, there was more emphasis on innovation and doing something new with a series than in the discussions around cinematic revivals. A resurrected series should, according to these fans, have something new to say and should avoid re-treading old and familiar ground. One respondent notes that such revivals are 'nice, if they provide/have innovated. It should not be a rerun of the old days', while another suggests that:

> As long as shows are still showing us something new and developing interesting new characters and stories, then rebooting or bringing back series is good. If the new is just a tired pale imitation than it is less good. Example: *Family Guy* came back (may still be on the air now), but is not as good as the original

seasons (in my opinion), relies too heavily on stereotypes and running gags, is not innovating or telling me new stories.

However, fans were realistic about the chances of favourite shows being revived and some also outlined appropriate time frames for a successful reboot or reinvention to occur. One *Firefly* fan notes that, 'I think there's the potential for a show like *Firefly* to come back. However, the continuation of storylines through the comics etc. is probably the best that'll happen as with all due respect I think it may be too late after 10yrs. Plus, Whedon killed my favourite in *Serenity* ☹'. Another fan, who identified as a fan of *Star Trek: Deep Space 9*, suggested that 'For *DS9*, I would probably not want to see it – it's been too long now and I already have a lot of my own ideas for what happened next. For a show like *Warehouse 13* that has only just been cancelled, I'd love it'. There is a strong sense of a finite period in which a show can be realistically reborn and provide an interesting return to a narrative world. Fans' realistic expectations are informed by their knowledge of the workings of the television industry and they are aware that actors will move on to new shows once their current one is cancelled and that the longer a show is off air the less likely its return becomes. More so than in the discussion of cinematic returns, respondents' discussions of television revivals acknowledge the relevant economic imperatives. While one fan comments that 'if it's good enough, do it. When it done for money, that's when fans get upset', echoing the discomfort with commodification of the fan experience discussed above, another welcomes the chance to purchase and collect new merchandise. This *Doctor Who* fan explains that '[I'm a] huge fan of *Doctor Who* and as it was done so well believe it was a great idea. New generations of fans which has created huge influx of toys, dvds, shirts, collective figurines ... the marketing is enormous and endless. It has also created a huge tourist boom which is fantastic for the Welsh economy'. Again, the sense of a 'new generation' of fans is seen as a positive aspect of returning or rebooting a show, while, along with the possibilities for new products, other benefits are highlighted – in this case the possibility of tourism in South Wales, where *Doctor Who* is produced and often filmed (see Hills 2006).

For other fans, the difficulties of resurrecting a series are related to the specific historical and sociocultural period in which the programme was created. As Levine and Parks note, TV shows 'take on new manifestations and new meanings as they are repositioned in different cultural contexts and historical periods' (2007, 4). According to several respondents, textual resurrections can fail because they take place outside of specific cultural contexts and can therefore find it hard to recapture the sociocultural backgrounds against which they first emerged. One fan of *The Shield* and *Six Feet Under* noted, 'I think TV is very much linked to a specific historical moment, so in many cases I'm not sure a resurrection would have the same effect as the original does'. Another notes that 'situations like this allow for new fan bases and a reconsideration of the show for a new time and changed culture. If a show doesn't take these considerations into account then it is pure fan service and likely to feel false and out of touch'. There is a clear sense that to succeed, a revived series needs to move with the times and adapt to the contemporary era in which it is being made. A failure to do so will lead to a sense of being 'out of touch' and inability to connect with new viewers. When this is done well, as in the case of *Doctor Who*, the reboot succeeds. Various fans of *Doctor Who* commented on the show's ability to deal with twenty-first century concerns in its 'Nu Who' (*Doctor Who* post-2005) (Hills 2010b) incarnation:

> I think for a show like *Doctor Who*, [revival] worked brilliantly because it already had an inbuilt storyline to continue with the same characters years later due to The Doctor's regenerations. I think it also had a wit and slight anarchy in its early years that was slightly ahead of its time and could be easily updated or rebooted for a modern audience. With others, if too much time passes, it usually ends up as a reboot or a kind of spin-off and that can just be a recipe for disaster.

> *Doctor Who* = best resurrection ever! Actually, once again, if it's well done … I think resurrecting shows is awesome! I especially like the idea of bringing a show back years later, or doing an updated version of an old show, because you get to play around with a whole new set of norms and culture that weren't present, or maybe acceptable, the first time around.

> As we can see with *Doctor Who*, this whole resurrection thing can work out nicely; in my opinion this depends strongly on the concept of the show. The pickup of *Dallas* for example was awful to watch because it just didn't fit into our time and way of life anymore and the actors had grown old and grumpy or were paralyzed by one shot of Botox too many.

Such arguments threaten to echo a form of 'zeitgeist fallacy' (Moretti 1988, 25) where one makes 'sweeping generalisations about the era in which a work was produced, and thus about the work itself' (Williamson 2005, 5). Such an argument does not hold when applied to television series that have been resurrected and reworked in quite different historical periods. For example, the science-fiction series *Battlestar Galactica* originally aired in 1978 and 1980 and was subsequently re-imagined for the post-9/11 audience in a new series that ran on the SciFi network between 2004 and 2009 (Ott 2008). However, the fact that some fan respondents articulate potential disjunction between a series' original context and the revived text suggests further fan anxiety about the failure of the reappearance of a beloved fan object.

As discussed above, the overwhelming majority of survey respondents focused their discussion of resurrections on cases where cancelled television series had been resurrected or continued in films. Despite the relatively high number of respondents who indicated that they continued their fandom through reading official novels or comics (54.55 per cent of respondents), only one fan explicitly discussed this in their qualitative response. They commented that '[I] have a large collection of spin off titles for cancelled series and submitted a terrible proposal for Virgin's *Doctor Who New Adventures* range. Spin off novels can give the fandom a new focus and also greatly expand the parameters of a specific franchise'. Despite the focus on television and cinema revivals and continuations in the survey data, it is worth drawing attention to the impact of print media in continuing narrative worlds. For example, Nicholas Pillai has analysed how *The X-Files* universe has been continued officially in a series of licensed comics. He notes how 'The licensed comic's formal properties *recon-ceive* the televisual world of Mulder and Scully, perpetuating these characters' cultural identity and providing some guarantee of their survival in the mass consciousness' (2013, 105) but that they offer new possibilities for creativity and allow a transmedia resurrection of *The X-Files* in a new mode and to a potential new audience. The comics thus maintain a careful balance between 'the source medium, respecting and enriching the meta-text, without contradicting other components' (Pillai 2013, 106). What a post-series presence in another form of media offers, however, is the freedom to set the narrative in whatever time frame the author desires, allowing differences from the source text to be highlighted. As Pillai points out, 'it is no accident that later DC/Wildstorm comics, still depicting the younger Scully and Mulder, set their stories in 2009. Fitting into the spaces between episodes is no longer necessary' (Pillai 2013, 115). As he also notes, however, the continuation of televised narrative worlds in other forms of media in a post-series environment means that many fans may encounter *The X-Files* as a comic first. For some fans, post-object fandom means engaging with the resurrections and continuations of a beloved programme in whatever media form it is presented. For those who discover texts in a post-object period, however, the relationship is different. Ultimately, Pillai points out that, pending a return to the cinema screen or the even more unlikely prospect of a televisual resurrection, 'at the present moment, *The X-Files* is a comic, not a television programme' (Pillai 2013, 116). Indeed, the same could be said in relation to both *Firefly* and *Torchwood*, which are currently a series of comics and an intermittent series of novels, respectively, rather than television shows.

Post-object fandom and fanworks

For series that are resurrected across transmedia and those that are not, fans often seek to continue the narrative worlds they have become attached to. This can take the form of creating fan artworks, videos or fanfiction which can allow fans of shows that have ended to respond to the cancellation and to negotiate their feelings of loss and discontinuity. There is no shortage of scholarly work on fanfiction: for instance Anne Jamison's (2013) volume *Fic: Why Fanfiction is Taking Over the World*, Rebecca Black's (2008) *Adolescents and Online Fan Fiction* and Karen Hellekson and Kristina Busse's *Fan Fiction and Fan Communities in the Age of the Internet* (2006) and *Fan Fiction Studies Reader* (2014) offer comprehensive overviews and analysis. Academic studies have focused on fandoms including *Buffy the Vampire Slayer* (Saxey 2001; Busse 2002), *Enterprise* (Lee 2003), *Star Trek* (Bacon-Smith 1992; Penley 1997), *The X-Files* (Scodari and Felder 2000; Silbergleid 2003), the book and film series *Harry Potter* (Tresca 2014), *Star Wars* (Brooker 2002; Handley 2012), *True Blood* (de Zwart 2011), *Twilight* (Parrish 2010) and a range of other media including *Warhammer* (Walliss 2012), vampire subcultures (Williamson 2005) and celebrities through 'real-person fic' (Busse 2006). The discussion here does not offer in-depth analysis of specific stories or fandoms and the reader would be best placed to read such work in the original studies. Rather, my interest lies in offering an overview of how fanfiction and other fanworks can offer avenues for negotiation of ontological security and self-identity for fans and to consider how the fans who responded to my research survey discussed fanfiction and why they engaged with it or, in some cases, did not.

Indeed, while much fanfiction works to fill in the gaps between episodes – to describe and imagine events that are not seen onscreen or, in the case of slash fiction, to imagine sexual relationships between characters who are not canonically linked – post-series fiction performs slightly different roles. While stories may continue to imagine certain relationships or add stories and scenes between existing episodes, fanfiction produced after the final episodes of a series can also provide avenues for continuation of the narrative world. Discussing fanfiction for the British science-fiction series *Blake's 7*, Sheenagh Pugh notes that 'sequel stories, [are] known in this fandom as PGP (post-Gauda Prime)' (Pugh 2005, 50), which refers to stories written after the final episode, which takes place on Gauda Prime. She argues that such sequels 'leave more scope for the fic writer than stories set within the time-line of canon, because the characters and relationships can quite plausibly develop beyond anything that happened in canon' (Pugh 2005, 52). She points out that 'Whenever a canon closes, someone somewhere will mourn it enough to reopen it … Even though we may feel that the canonical ending is "right" artistically, if we liked the story we may still not be ready for it to end' (Pugh 2005, 47). This can be especially crucial for fans when the ending of a series is not expected or desired. In discussion of *Earth 2* fanfiction Musiani argues that:

> […] in the case of canceled series, the story is not only unsatisfactory or lacking; it is abruptly cut off and left incomplete. Writing fanfiction is then no longer about creating variations of or alternatives to an existing story. Instead, it is about filling in gaps, writing an ending for characters whose destinies were left uncertain, detailing the lives of characters that were left in the background, and developing relationships that had started to blossom. Beyond their immediate result—a corpus of works establishing and cementing a community—these gap-filling activities shed light on the ways in which the cancellation of a series is countered with a re-creation—in short, on how official closure is dealt with through fanfiction. (Musiani 2010, paragraph 1.3)

Similarly, in the era after the movie *Serenity*, fan productivity and dedication around *Firefly* has continued. In addition to fanfiction some fans have produced a fan film entitled *Browncoats: Redemption* (see Barton 2014a), while others make a range of fan crafts, including replicas of an iconic hat worn by the character Jayne Cobb. Furthermore, despite the alleged 'decline' in the series' final few seasons (see Brown 2013), *The X-Files* has maintained a loyal fanbase in the years following its televisual cessation. For example, in her discussion of post-series fandom of the show, Bertha Chin notes the ongoing presence of fans at *X-Files News* (*XFN*), exploring the ongoing fan/producer relationships and asking 'What sort of fan–media producer collaborations can a post-series fandom have with its media producers, many of whom have moved on to other things?' (2013, 92). She concludes that:

> In the absence of new materials to be discussed, analysed and expanded on creatively, a new type of website has become popular among certain groups of X-Philes in recent years, which highlights fan–producer collaborations. Sites like *XFilesNews.com* (*XFN*) offer exclusive and original interviews with the cast and crew as those involved with the show move on to new projects. The site also acts as a grassroots promotional vehicle for them as fans are kept updated with the latest news, including the ongoing campaign for a third *X-Files* film, which the producers support. (Chin 2013, 88)

In fact, Chin argues, some fans continue to work closely with producers, although the distinctions and hierarchies that demarcated the fandom when the show was ongoing have not been eroded. She notes that:

> […] boundaries are drawn between fans who have taken an 'activist' role – such as the *XFN* contributors who view themselves as fans who are preserving the fandom for future generations, and who support the cast and crew beyond their work on *The X-Files* – and those who, according to these fan activists, prefer to embrace the identity of the 'fangirl' concerned with gossip and the aesthetic pleasures of the show and its actors. (Chin 2013, 88–9)

It is the development of social media that has largely contributed to the ongoing presence of fans of the series. As Bethan Jones notes, it is useful to examine 'how post-series fandoms adopt and use social media' since 'fans' adoption of social media sites such as Facebook and Twitter has led to a resurgence of online activity' (Jones 2014, 92–3). Thus the ending of the television series has clearly not eroded *The X-Files* fandom. In many cases, it has caused it to thrive, especially with regard to fanfiction. Fanfiction written about *The X-Files* has been often explored (see Scodari and Felder 2000; Wakefield 2001; Wills 2013; Jamison 2013; Kaplan 2006) and there is much to be said about the ways in which this fiction represents concerns about gender, sexuality and the body among other important topics. As Wills notes:

> *The X-Files* has a long and storied history of fannish production; the major fandom-specific archive, Gossamer, holds over 35,000 individual stories, and thousands more are on other archives, in authors' journals, and on personal Web sites. When scholars of fandom want to analyze how certain types of fic

work or how their authors approach a subject, any stories that fit our needs are relevant. (2013, paragraph 2.7)

For instance, an overview of *The X-Files* category at FanFiction.net in January 2014 reveals a total of 9,700 stories, archived across a range of categories organized by time frame, character, or theme. Many of these take place in the post-series period; for example a series of four stories entitled 'Transmission', 'Transference', 'Transcendence' and 'Transformation' form a sequence of sequels that focus on Mulder and Scully's quest to find their son. However, in addition to such post-series stories, much of the fanfiction being written continues to be set during the series itself and, as with works written while series remain on air, attempts to fill in missing scenes, explain plot points, or seek insight into characters' motivations and feelings.

While almost half of the respondents to my 2013 survey indicated that they had read fanfiction in the post-object period of fandom, very few explicitly discussed the impact of a series' cancellation on the content of that fanfiction. Indeed, most who mentioned fanfiction drew on established ideas about the possibility that fanfiction provides to expand a programme universe or to fill in the blanks. These are pleasures that fanfiction also provides for fans of ongoing series. For instance, one *Firefly* fan notes that ' … the show was FANTASTIC. And I really enjoy being able to play with the characters Joss created by writing/reading the fiction', while a *Star Trek: Enterprise* fan commented, 'I was a Trekker before *Enterprise* aired and the show just added to my level of fandom. I enjoy writing fanfiction, as it allows me to place my own spin on the *Star Trek* universe. Sometimes I will rewatch the show for inspiration, or simply out of enjoyment'. Another fan, a *Babylon 5* viewer, makes a similar point that: 'For fan fiction, it is a chance to re-tell the stories with more depth than what was allowed for within the episode itself. Or to fill in the blanks between episodes to explain the change in relationships that weren't overly shown'. There is thus little sense among these respondents that the cessation of new episodes of a programme has impacted upon the type of fanfiction that is being written. Indeed, no respondents explicitly stated that reading or writing fanfiction offered an avenue for them to re-write unsatisfactory endings to a series or to overtly continue a narrative or characters beyond the final frames of the series. While this is undoubtedly part of the 'filling in the blanks' or 'placing a spin' on a universe that the fans above allude to, it is interesting that the post-series aspects of fanfiction were not discussed in more depth. This is especially pertinent given

Musiani's study of fanfiction written about the series *Earth 2* and her conclusion that, in such cases 'the story is not only unsatisfactory or lacking potential; it is abruptly cut off and then disappears. In the face of this absence, fans use their disappointment at the cancellation to find inspiration for re-creation' (2010, paragraph 4.4).

When the existence of fanfiction in a period of post-object fandom was mentioned this was often in relation to resistance to the studio's or network's decision to cancel a series. However, rather than focusing on reworking content, this is instead expressed via notions of resistance against the economically-driven media industry, which tends to ignore what fans want because of financial factors. Two respondents note that they continue with fandom and fan creative works 'because I love that show and the characters. If the companies won't give us what we want, then we'll make it ourselves' and 'it's an incredible community full of like-minded, ridiculous creative people who share a passion that refused to end just because idiotic, penny pincher studio execs decided it should'. Here, it is the long-held idea of fans as 'modern-day Robin Hoods, folk heroes busily snatching back "our" popular cultural texts from the greedy global conglom-erates' (Gwenllian-Jones 2003, 163), is drawn upon. Fanfiction can offer a broad way to avoid accepting the commercially driven demise of a favourite series by allowing many fans to continue what they did while a series was on-air, namely borrowing and reworking elements of a series to create their own works.

Not all respondents, however, indicated that they were writers or readers of fanfiction. As noted above, while 44 per cent had read fanfiction based on a favourite show, only 21 per cent wrote fanfiction themselves. One *Torchwood* fan noted a preference only for certain types of fiction: 'I enjoy the fanfiction, as most of it is based on series 1 and 2 of the show, when it was at its strongest. If the fanfiction had moved into encompass series 3 and 4 I would probably have stopped reading'. This indicates a fan partiality for fanfiction set in the earlier series of *Torchwood*, also implying that this fan is unconcerned, not only with fiction set during the third series *Torchwood: Children of Earth* or the fourth season *Torchwood: Miracle Day*, but with fiction that takes place in the aftermath of *Miracle Day*. Indeed, fan predilection for fiction set in specific periods of a series may go some way to explaining the lack of overt discussion of post-series fanfiction in the survey. If a fan's interest has waned towards the end of a series and his/her preference is for earlier seasons, it stands to reason that they would seek out fanworks set in this preferred period. For these fans, ontological security gained from the fandom is provided by revisiting the earlier favourite periods of the show's narrative universe, rather than from attempts to rewrite and reclaim any unwelcome elements of the later seasons and the actual finale. Another fan indicates a move away from fanfiction, not owing to favourite periods of a series, but because of the time-consuming nature of the practice. This *X-Files* fan notes that 'I wrote *X-Files* fanfiction for many years and continued to be a part of that briefly after the show [went] off the air. But after a while, I let go of that simply because it felt more burdensome than fun any longer'. For another two fans who replied, this avoidance of fanfiction was linked to a preference for re-watching the show itself and, in one case, a preference for the visual medium over the written word. One notes that 'I'm more keen on reliving the show through watching it again than some of the more overt fan activities. As a whole I'm not too keen on fanfiction of TV shows – reading a story doesn't feel the same as watching it for me', while another respondent argues that 'one of my favourite actors is in there, so it's always good to re-watch stuff he's in. And since I don't read fanfic of the show, re-watching is the best way to relive the things I enjoy about it'. The responses discussed here suggest that many fans revisit and continue narrative worlds through the creation of fanworks such as fanfiction. As Musiani points out, such writers may view themselves as 'the natural heirs to the authorship of [a] series, empowered to keep it alive' (2010, paragraph 6.7). In her case study of *Earth 2* fans she concluded that 'writing *E2* FF allowed the show to continue even though it had been cancelled. It allowed [fans] to fill in gaps and continue the story past the cancellation' (Musiani 2010, paragraph 6.7). Such continuations can be seen in the responses of many of the fans discussed here. However, we must be cautious about assuming that all fans create or read fanfiction in an era of post-object fandom. As some of the responses above indicate, some fans actively avoid fanfiction, preferring to review older episodes of a series and returning to the official narrative universe instead. Fanfiction has been much discussed in academic studies of fan cultures and, while it is undoubtedly a vibrant and fascinating aspect of fandom, it is important not to allow it to become a synonym for fan culture as a whole and to remain open to the experiences of those who participate in post-object fandom through a range of diverse practices.

Falling through the rift: *Torchwood* and interim fandom

This final section continues to focus on the instability of endings and the constant process of negotiation that fans face regarding their ontological security, fan identity and self-narrative. It examines periods where fan texts are neither officially cancelled nor assured of a return (a textual version of Whiteman and Metivier's (2013) 'zombie' fan community) and fan reactions to the official returns or continuations of texts to suggest the notion of 'interim fandom' through the example of science-fiction/fantasy series *Torchwood*. This show has followed a complex trajectory from its beginnings on the niche BBC3 channel, through its promotion to BBC2 and to 'event television' on BBC1 and beyond to its most recent incarnation as a cross-production between the BBC and the US network Starz on the *Miracle Day* series, which aired in 2011. Over three years on from *Miracle Day*s finale, however, and *Torchwood*'s ambivalent status as neither cancelled nor currently on air or in production offers little resolution for fans. While most of the shows explored in this volume are definitively cancelled and the viewer or fan is relatively certain that it is not returning, the case of *Torchwood* complicates this. Although there are currently no plans for a new series, both stars such as John Barrowman and creator Russell T. Davies have discussed the possible future of the show. In late 2012 Davies claimed that the 'series hasn't been cancelled' but was, rather, 'in a nice limbo' (Davies cited in Rowley 2012). Barrowman, who plays lead character Captain Jack Harkness, reiterated this point, similarly referring to the show as being 'in limbo at the moment and beyond my control' (cited in Jeffery 2011b), while Executive Producer Julie Gardner has been equally tentative (Gardner cited in Jeffery 2011a). In the Spring of 2013, star Eve Myles was still teasing the possibility of a return (Caron 2013), but at the time of writing this in early 2014 there is still no clarity on *Torchwood*'s status. The reason for the limbo – as opposed to making a clear statement on the show's future or lack thereof – can be attributed to a number of possible reasons. The fourth series *Miracle Day* failed to attract the audience or the critical acclaim of the third five-part series *Children of Earth*, while creator Russell T. Davies has been busy with other projects such as the children's series *Wizards vs. Aliens* and the Channel 4 drama *Cucumber*. What the unusual state of *Torchwood* forces those who are interested in televisual endings (in all their forms) and fans who continue their interest after these endings to do is to consider the anomalous examples: the shows that don't quite fit. In the move towards calling for TV studies to take advantage of the opportunities that looking back at concluded series offers in terms of understanding narrative arcs, production contexts, or audience and fan responses, what threatens to fall through the cracks is the status of a programme like *Torchwood* which is neither 'alive' or in its clearly defined 'afterlife'. Rather, it is dormant, with the potential for a return but without any sense of quite when, or even if, this will happen. What happens to audiences of a series in this period? How do fans endure in their fandom in a period of uncertainty over a show's future? I suggest that we can view such periods as 'interim fandom' when fans assume that their fan object is dormant and must readjust or negotiate this when the object becomes active again. These examples pose challenges to our understandings of texts and textual boundaries and also allow consideration of fan responses (both positive and negative) to the continuation of an assumed dormant textual world.

In his work on television endings, Mittell discusses the concepts of cessation, 'which is a stoppage or wrap-up without a definite finality that it will be the end of the series. It's fairly common for a series to go on hiatus midseason, leaving its narrative future in limbo until it either returns to the air or disappears from next year's schedule' (2013, paragraph 6). In these cases, the future of a show remains uncertain and fans are often left to speculate on whether it will return. Although the fourth series of *Torchwood* ended as it was planned to, it arguably still fits into the idea of the cessation since 'cessation is lodged at the crosshairs intersecting creativity and commerce, as storytelling progress is held in check by the bottom line of profitability, leaving the narrative world in a state of perpetual limbo awaiting a possible return' (Mittell 2013, paragraph 6). However, while fans await the possible return to television of the series, there are both official and unofficial ways for them to continue the narrative universe. Several survey respondents mentioned *Torchwood*'s ambivalent status as neither cancelled nor returning. One fan comments specifically on the limbo that this status forces fans into, noting that 'it hasn't yet been cancelled officially, so I still have hope. But, we (the fans) hate the waiting'. Here there is a sense of collective waiting for a decision to be made, expressed through the use of 'we' as 'the fans', rather than the singular 'I', indicating a wider fandom who are waiting for a final decision to be made. The lack of certainty surrounding *Torchwood*'s fate places such fans in an unusual position: not entirely sure about whether to grieve or mourn the passing of a favourite series or to keep their hope for a return alive. Another *Torchwood* fan noted that at the end of *Miracle Day* they were 'sad because it was one of the greatest British TV series and it hasn't a real end. So there has to be more ... ' In this case, it is the presumed lack of closure that causes some anxiety and sadness, echoing the large percentage of survey respondents who indicated that a satisfactory ending to a series was a desired element of a successful finale. For this fan respondent, the absence of a 'real end' is used to defend the view that the show should continue – 'there has to be more ... ' – in order to provide more coherent resolution to the characters and their stories for the fans. The ending of *Miracle Day* offers opportunities for continuation with the lead characters of Jack Harkness, Gwen and Rhys Williams and new character Rex Matheson seemingly able to continue as a *Torchwood* team. The show also offers an enigma regarding Matheson's new apparent immortality as a result of narrative events in the series which seem to suggest possibilities for new storylines. For many fans, the series has the potential to continue or, at least, to be concluded in a more finite manner.

For two other respondents, however, the show was noted to have continued albeit outside of the televisual medium. They note:

> We don't actually know yet about *Torchwood*. It isn't exactly cancelled but not in production at the moment either. It might come back after a few years though, there are still books and audio books made, so there is hope.

> [*Torchwood's*] not technically cancelled but there are no plans to keep it produced, so it's as good as cancelled. When the latest series was over, I felt sad but also hopeful that id see the story go on in books or other media. Another TV series would make me happiest though.

Both fans here acknowledge that the show isn't 'exactly' or 'technically' cancelled but that it is, nonetheless, a dormant television series. While both replies offer a sense that the show may return and that this would be welcomed, they also mention the show's continuation in other media such as tie-in novels. The apparent desire of these fans for a resurrection of the televisual *Torchwood* suggests that fans' feelings about revivals are different when texts are perceived to be in some sort of limbo or liminal space between 'alive' and 'dead'. While fans of decisively cancelled series are often reticent about reviving a narrative universe for reasons discussed above, fans of texts that are in an indeterminate state, and who find themselves in periods of interim fandom, are often more enthusiastic about a return. This can be to allow closure for a narrative that has ended abruptly or to simply continue stories and characters that fans love. While this promise is maintained and a show is not officially cancelled, fans' negotiation of ontological security and self-identity can be complicated. Although many respondents to the survey continued to strongly identify as *Torchwood* fans, there is also a sense of suspension of ontological security. In the absence of an ongoing television narrative, ontological security cannot be gained from the regular routines and rhythms of transmission, but, since the series has not been officially 'killed off', fans cannot either entirely work to deal with the threats to ontological security that are often engendered by a cancellation. Since the 'loveshock' (Giddens 1992) that can be caused by this is not entirely experienced, such fans cannot always unproblematically embrace the discourses used by fans faced with definitive cessation of a programme. Instead, they continue to negotiate both their desire to see the series return and the acceptance that, in all likelihood, it will not.

As the above comments about *Torchwood*'s tie-in novels and audio books indicate, however, the series has continued outside of television. Like the examples of *Firefly* and *The X-Files*, *Torchwood* has a clear transmedia presence in '17 novels, a collection of short stories – comprising 5 different titles – 7 radio plays, and 10 original audio books' (Hills 2012b, 409; see also Hills 2013b). *Torchwood*'s tie-ins released before the fourth series *Miracle Day* allowed 'established characters [to be] frequently rewritten, reworked and reinvented' (Hills 2013b, 77) and offered '"more of the same" in some cases, yet challenging, critiquing and expanding the show's narrative universe in others' (Hills 2013b, 80). The production of transmedia texts has continued in *Torchwood*'s post-*Miracle Day* period – the space where fans can be considered to be involved in a form of interim fandom – with the publication of the novel *Exodus Code* in September 2012, which was co-written by star John Barrowman and his sister Carol E. Barrowman. Four exclusive audio books were released throughout 2012, along with the audio book version of *Exodus Code*. Initially, as Matt Hills points out, this allowed *Torchwood*'s continuation post-series:

> *Torchwood*'s fan factions can re-connect with the brand through audios such as *Army of One*, *Fallout*, *Red Skies* and *Mr. Invincible*. As such, it was perhaps no accident that the *Miracle Day* sequels were released approximately one year after the premiere of series four, making them part of a lived cycle of *Torchwood* consumption for fans, and filling in what would otherwise be a gap year with no new TV series on the horizon. Where the prequels attempted to fill in the hyperdiegesis of *Torchwood*'s series history, the sequels attempt to fill in (fans') time, recognising rhythms of media production, e.g. annually broadcast series. (Hills 2012b, 424)

Hills argues that these sequels function as 'transmedia paratexts [to] maintain a brand presence; they offer a sort of looped continuation, keeping *Torchwood* ticking over and cycling through its hyperdiegetic back catalogue' (Hills 2012b, 424). They partially work to reinstate the 'original' *Torchwood* for some fans, refusing to 'make any significant contribution to building on [*Miracle Day's*] diegetic consequences' and leading to a 'narrative "holding pattern" where *Torchwood's* future feels cyclical rather than linear or directional' (Hills 2012b, 423). However, as *Miracle Day* becomes more distant, there are fewer paratexts produced around *Torchwood*; there were no transmedia releases in 2013 and neither the comics nor the radio plays have continued in the post-*Miracle Day* period. Thus, while fans await confirmation of either *Torchwood's* resurrection or its permanent demise, there are actually few official transmedia tie-ins through which they can continue engaging with the narrative and characters. Instead fan engagement with *Torchwood* has to rely on other ways of maintaining connection with the world of *Torchwood* in a period of interim fandom.

In terms of unofficial fan-created continuations of *Torchwood*, fans are operating in a slightly different zone from those in a post-series era of *Firefly* or *The X-Files*. While *Firefly* fans have an almost endless narrative to expand upon and flesh out the prematurely aborted narrative world and *The X-Files* fans have nine years' worth of televised material to draw on, *Torchwood* fans are more ambiguously placed. While fans of prematurely cancelled series may create fanfiction as a result of 'the disappointment, anger, or sense of emptiness felt at the cancellation of the series and the inability of the official writers to tell any story at all' (Musiani 2010, paragraph 6.6), *Torchwood's* liminal status offers a different set of opportunities for writers to 'scribble in the margins' (Jenkins 1992, 155). Given the fan issues with *Torchwood's* numerous reinventions including the move from a Cardiff-focus towards greater internationalization and the contested death of Ianto (see Cubbison 2012), fanfiction both while the series was airing and in the current dormant period allows fans to 'identify continuity errors before "retconning" them away, for example via fanfiction fixes that rework the canonical text so that contradictions are retroactively ironed out' (Hills 2012b, 412). While official transmedia content offers 'a refuge from disliked transformations within the TV text' (Hills 2012b, 416) fanfiction perhaps allows even greater opportunities for returning to the periods of *Torchwood's* 'golden ages' (Tulloch and Jenkins 1995) and for fans to continue to both fill in the gaps and create new stories while they wait for final confirmation of *Torchwood's* televisual fate.

Conclusion

Fandom does not end once a television series ceases to produce and air new episodes. Whether fan practices in this period of post-object fandom continue via re-watching the series, as discussed in the prior chapter, or through engagement with official and unofficial fan-created texts, it is clear that strong fan connections remain. As this chapter has argued, exploring how programmes continue after their final episodes and how fans engage across different forms of media allows examination of use of the transmediality of media objects. Texts are often no longer bounded or finite, rather 'integrating multiple texts to create a narrative so large that it cannot be contained within a single medium' (Jenkins 2006, 95). Such transmediality can be both officially created and also generated by audiences and fans, as in the case of *Firefly/Serenity* fan movie *Browncoats: Redemption* or the fanfiction written after the ending of new episodes of shows such as *Earth 2* or *The X-Files*. Periods of post-object fandom can, thus, be periods of strong ongoing connection with series and fellow fans. Rather than abandoning the fandom, fans in this period often have a range of official and fan-created paratexts or transmedia objects to engage with to continue their attachments and to provide ongoing ontological security or a sense of trust in their fandom.

However, it is worth noting that not all post-object fandom is reliant on the presence of new transmedia products. For example, the television series *Twin Peaks* has 'continued to enjoy a high level of cultural penetration several decades after its release ... the loyal fanbase has done more than just maintain the profile of the series, driving a second-hand market in *Twin Peaks*-themed memorabilia' (Howe 2013, 41). Despite numerous calls for new *Twin Peaks* texts, whether a new feature film or a return to television, there has been little in the way of official continuations of the *Twin Peaks* universe. The only materials to emerge in the 25-year period since the show ceased airing have been box sets of the show: first the *Twin Peaks: Definitive Gold Box Edition* (which included both series of the show, both versions of the pilot episode and a comprehensive documentary) and, latterly, a Blu-ray box set containing both series, a range of special features and the accompanying prequel *Fire Walk With Me* (Collura 2014). However, despite this relative lack of continuation, the series' fans continue to engage with the show in a range of ways, including attending annual events such as the US *Twin Peaks* Fest or the *Twin Peaks* UK Festival, discussing the series online or buying merchandise. As Clark notes:

[...] fan fodder abounds. Whether presented through our TV or computer screens, at art exhibits or fan festivals, its tale continues to unfold. By keeping up with its virtual presence and continuing to revel in its existence, fans can hold on to the dream that maybe on some other Lynchian plane, the *Twin Peaks* universe remains very much alive, and its characters are still dreamily jazz-dancing to Angelo Badalementi tunes in the mysteriously quirky small town that forever changed the world. (Clark 2013, 14)

Clark's statement evokes many of the ideas discussed throughout this book, in relation to fans' ongoing and often deeply affective connections to television's narrative worlds. While these fans do not believe literally that *Twin Peaks* 'exists', the ongoing aspects of post-object fandom that they can engage with and experience makes possible a constant source of ontological security from the connection they can maintain with the fan object. As discussed, while transmedia continuations of favourite characters and narrative worlds can encourage fan attachment, it is also worth paying attention to fandoms where such texts are not forthcoming and where fans instead rely on the limited materials they can access to sustain their connections to the fan object in the period of post-object fandom.

9

Conclusion: Immortal Fandom

Understanding the relatively under-theorized area of endings of fan objects and the subsequent period of 'post-object fandom' is crucial since 'observation of the way we react to the expiration of a television show offers us another chance to understand the complexities involved in the institution of television as a portion of our social fabric' (Anderson 2005). Paying attention to fans' reactions to changes, transitions and endings offers one route for understanding how fandom is related to self-narrative, identity and a sense of ontological security. The work of sociologist Anthony Giddens offers one theoretical avenue for exploration of this aspect of fandom and his notion of 'loveshock', allows understanding of how fan–object and fan–fan pure relationships provide ontological security and an avenue for identity work and to witness what happens when such relationships end. Examining how fans embrace periods of mourning and remembrance or, in other cases, express relief and joy at favourite programmes being 'euthanized' is of interest to scholars researching not only fans themselves but also how texts end, or have 'endings', more broadly.

Fan responses are far from uniform. Some react in terms of grief and sadness and respond by reiterating their attachment to their fandom, offering lengthy rationales for their interest in favoured shows and vowing to continue their involvement. Others concede that while programmes such as *Lost* or *The West Wing* once had an important place in their lives, this will necessarily change as new episodes of a show cease to be produced. Finally, many fans reject favourite shows, expressing relief at their demise and critically evaluating their final episodes. These discourses enable fans to re-establish their identity as a fan (in the reiteration discourse), rework this identity (the renegotiation discourse) or distance themselves from a show that they perceived no longer to be 'worthwhile' (the rejection discourse). Furthermore, all three responses relate to issues of capital and distinction in fan discussions of the 'quality' of particular programmes or their battles over whether the narrative will satisfy their interpretations of the show before a series finale. For some, the ending of a series leads to a sense of loss and mourning, echoing Anderson's discussion of how 'friends and acquaintances acted, as if they, too, had lost a significant proportion of their lives' (Anderson 2005) when *Six Feet Under* ended. For others, however, a 'bad' finale highlights some of the more negative aspects of television fandom, including distrust in production staff and networks, disappointment in narrative resolutions or a sense of being misled by an unfolding text. In addition, discussion of what practices fans actually undertake in the period of post-object fandom underlines the diverse range of discourses and activities present in the years after a series ends. For every fan who desires a resurrection or a reboot of a favourite series there is one who feels that this would be a disaster; for every fan who seeks to continue a story via fanfiction there is another who prefers to revisit the official narrative world; for every fan who prefers the convenience and comfort of re-watching a show on DVD or Blu-ray there is someone else who desires the sense of imagined community engendered by viewing reruns on broadcast television. Post-object fandom is a broad and varied period which cannot be easily categorized.

As television shows end it is clearly important for some fans to re-narrate their self-identities by reiterating the importance of the show to their own lives and intertwining characters or narrative events with events in their 'real lives'. If we accept the argument that the media provides ontological security, examination of how audiences cope when this is threatened allows understanding of how they adjust to the fact that their interactions with fan objects and communities will change once the object becomes 'dormant'. As the often divergent or contradictory views expressed by fans indicate, however, fans do not respond in a homogeneous way to the endings of TV series nor do they all continue the same practices in the period of post-object fandom. As the opposed responses of rejection, reiteration and the more 'moderate' response of renegotiation indicate, fans can deal with threats to their sense of ontological security or ruptures in their self-narratives and identity in a range of ways. This can be linked to an existing critique of Anthony Giddens' use of ontological security – namely that he too neatly demarcates between possessing it and not possessing it. Instead, individuals oscillate throughout their lives and have more security at some times than at others. Such 'ontological security is not something that is simply there or not there, it is always a matter of feeling more or less secure so that everyone … may be affected by some feelings of insecurity in this sense' (Layder 1997, 68). Ontological security varies within social and cultural contexts and some people may place more trust in fan objects, thus gaining greater ontological security from these than from other aspects of their lives. For example, it could be argued that those fans who responded within the 'reiteration discourse' may require a greater level of ontological security from their fan objects than those who critically distanced themselves, although such a view is not intended to pathologize fans or suggest that they are caught up in a 'fantasy' world (Jenson 1992). Fans may dislike some aspects of their fan objects, loathing unwelcome narrative plotlines in a television show or a disappointing album by a band. However, these fans do not suddenly lose all trust in the object. Rather they negotiate their feelings and rework their self-narratives to account for disappointing elements of their fan objects. Furthermore, other fans often declare themselves fans of more than one object at a time and may find that their trust in various fan objects changes over time and according to the situation. For example, a fan of several different television series may feel disappointed by a poor run of episodes or a disappointing series and find their trust in one programme is threatened, whereas their trust in the others remains strong. It is not, then, the case that fans simply possess ontological security as a result of the routine and familiarity of their fan object, which then vanishes when the object challenges their trust in it. Rather, ontological security, as Craib (1992), Layder (1997) and Moores (2005) argue, is experienced along a continuum and one's sense of trust can fluctuate over time and in various contexts: 'our internal worlds also contain fear, self-questioning, doubt and agonies which at times enhance the banality of our commonsense world. We are regularly thrown by external processes over which we have no control, processes that result in wars, unemployment, poverty' (Craib 1998, 72).

It has been argued that use of Giddensian theories of self-identity over-emphasizes the 'presence' of the self, failing to account for 'the texture of fan experience … in favour of citable, quotable bits of fans' linguistic self-accounts' (Hills 2007b, 152). To assume that fans can coherently trace links between their fan objects and their own lived experiences and sense of identity presumes a stable, fixed 'self' and may be accused of ignoring fans' more 'dimly sensed half-graspings of their self-identities' (Hills 2007b, 152). Giddens himself notes that post-structuralist accounts of culture have led to the view of 'the self in modern society [as] frail, brittle, fractured, fragmented' (Giddens 1991, 169) and the very notion of reflexive self-narratives accounts for the readjustment and re-narration of the self. Furthermore, the self may 'evolve over a lifetime; and [is] subject to injury' (Levin 1992, 209) and contemporary theorists have argued that the self is now 'diffused' though a 'multiplicity of [mediated] experiences and forms' (Longhurst 2007, 118). The suggestion that we view fans' declarations about their self-identities and experiences as performative displays of their fandom that cannot be treated as transparent or 'true' acknowledges that any sense of the fan self can only ever be partial or nominal. What is key here are the choices that fans make when they select which aspects of their identities to present to fellow fans (in online postings) and a researcher (in their questionnaires). Indeed, fans' intertwining of their real-life experiences with fan objects to form self-narratives or their use of these to work through issues and emotions in their lives is highly performative (see Hills 2005c, ix–xiii). Therefore, it is futile trying to access some 'true' fan self which may never be fully known by fans themselves or, therefore, by a researcher. Researchers must instead attempt to treat fans' comments as 'texts', which must be read 'symptomatically … for what is behind the explicitly written' (Ang 1982, 11). Furthermore, we must continue to highlight moments of instability and rupture in fans' self-identities and ontological security, to demonstrate an acknowledgement that any understanding of fans' 'selves' must account for the constant processes of renegotiation of identity and self-narrative that fans engage in. Indeed, the presence of such moments of insecurity and renegotiation highlights that potential threats to fans' ontological security were navigated by fans in each of the case studies discussed here. Although these, variously, result from violation of the perceived rules or ideologies of a show or from the permanent cessation of a programme, fan attempts to cope with these threats and to assimilate them into their coherent self-narrative or identity are homologous across each fan community. It can be suggested, then, that the demonstration of fans' negotiation of self-identity and ontological security substantiates the theoretical proposition that fandom be viewed as forms of 'pure relationship' that engender such rewards.

However, textual endings and their potential resurrections do not happen solely *for* fans or *because of* fans. The media industry possesses a clear economic imperative surrounding the production of television series and the promotion of finales that are planned for and allow celebration of a show is intended to attract high audience figures and appease advertisers. As Todd notes in relation to the *Friends* finale, 'when seemingly disparate media surrounding the show were experienced en masse, the last episode of *Friends* became an intertextual media event, which contributes to our understanding of television's production of cultural meaning. The series finale offers a glimpse at the infiltration of television broadcasts into other aspects of mediated life' (Todd 2011, 856). In many cases it is a lack of viewing figures and issues around financing that lead to the ending of series in the first place and decisions over whether or not to resurrect a programme are also fundamentally a question of the bottom line. When money can still be made, series are more likely to be resurrected as the high DVD sales of shows such as *Family Guy* and *Firefly* attest. When support from major producers is not forthcoming more niche shows can also return, but they must, as in the case of *Veronica Mars*, rely on crowdfunding by the fans who support the series. As in many other aspects of fandom, fans' status as potential consumers should not be overlooked; nor should fans' own ambiguity regarding this position. Fans who are less inclined to welcome resurrections of their beloved series often reject attempts to capitalize on the fandom, dismissing such efforts as blatant attempts to make more money or to sell more merchandise. While the fan duality of being 'both commodity-completists and ... express[ing] anti-commercial beliefs or "ideologies"' (Hills 2002, 44) continues, we must ensure that the economics of endings, transitions and resurrections are explored, even as we develop our understanding of fans' more affective and personal responses.

It is also worth bearing in mind that if researchers do seek to explore fandoms surrounding older media texts and objects, access to fan spaces and communities can be more difficult. The closure of the Television Without Pity message boards in the spring of 2014 means that those fan archives are almost entirely lost to researchers and that the wealth of debate and discussion around a broad range of television shows across many years is now inaccessible. This has obvious implications for the fan discussions drawn on here in terms of accountability, since the words of posters at that site can no longer be traced and verified via the archives of Television Without Pity. More pressingly, however, the changes in online spaces pose broader questions about how we conduct research into fandoms; as Whiteman and Metivier (2013) and Gatson and Zweerink (2004) have discussed, fan sites and forums often do close and fans then move on to other spaces, both online and off. Fan scholars must consider how we might continue to access and research fans from spaces that no longer exist – in many ways a form of 'post-object fandom' in its own right. As the shows that fans love get older and become less 'valuable' to researchers, so too do the spaces that surround them. It is perhaps unsurprising that as texts 'end' and 'die', so too do many of the places where fans discuss them.

The fans examined here are those who had an enunciative presence online and fans who were not involved in online fandom have not been considered. This is not to undermine the importance of such individual or lone fans but is rather an issue of availability since access to fans who do not engage in any cohesive fan community is difficult owing to their lack of participation. As Booth and Kelly point out, 'many fans choose not to go online, and many integrate digital technology into their offline practices in ways that may not be immediately visible to online fan researchers' (2013, 57). As digital media fandom continues to shift and develop and the lines between what it means to be 'online' or 'offline' blur further, exploration of post-object fandom across these contexts would be instructive. Indeed, lone fans may have very different reactions in the post-object period and consideration of how they continue to interact with fan objects in individual contexts would prove an interesting extension of the work begun here. Equally, another element of post-object fandom for future research is the importance of live events and offline fan spaces in periods of post-object fandom. These are not meaningfully discussed here owing to the lack of mentions of such events (such as conventions, theme park experiences, meet-and-greets or signings with stars) either in the online message boards or in the survey responses. Only eight survey respondents indicated that they had continued their fandom by attending relevant fan events and very few elaborated on this in any depth in their qualitative replies. Despite this, there is clear potential in researching fan attendance at such events after favourite series air their final episodes. There have been several *Firefly* fan conventions since the series was cancelled, and the in-limbo *Torchwood* similarly offers fans a chance to meet the stars and writers of the series. *Twin Peaks* fans can attend the UK-based *Twin Peaks* Festival or an all-night screening of all thirty-one hours of the series and its prequel movie *Fire Walk With Me*. Both official and unofficial live events allow fans to retain their connection with favourite texts and with fellow fans, maintaining both their sense of fan self-narrative and identity. For instance, Jermyn points out the importance of the *Sex and the City* 'Sex and the Hot Spots' New York bus tour in terms of working to 'keep the show "alive" for old viewers lamenting its loss or seeking connection with other fans and to support HBO's continuing commercial interests in the show by attracting new viewers only now discovering it, be that through taking the tour or watching it on DVD or network syndication' (2009, 93).

There is also merit in considering how endings operate in different television genres such as soap opera, which often features a long-running episodic narrative that runs over several years or decades (for instance, the British soap *Coronation Street* has been on air for over fifty years). In such genres, departures are clearly more likely and, although seen as inevitable, fans may still respond emotionally to the loss of favoured characters. Examination of the differences between 'finite (mortal) vs. infinite (immortal) serial texts' (Harrington 2013, 590) offers interesting new avenues for research beyond the televisual dramas explored here and presents scope for understanding of fan reactions to other genres such as soap opera, reality television and beyond. The analysis presented here has focused entirely on television (and when TV shows have been returned to life in other media) and it is worth noting that television has a different temporal structure from other media. For example, it would be useful to consider how post-object fandom can be understood in cinema fandom, where the majority of texts (excluding trilogies, sequels or prequels) are often singular and fans may not respond in the same way as when a long-running television series ends. For instance, given the links made between post-object fandom, pure relationships and ontological security, we might consider whether the 'event' status of cinema, in comparison with the everyday-ness of television, might be responded to differently by fans. Similarly, music fandom could be considered to examine how fans of bands who have split up (e.g. The Beatles), reunited (such as Take That) or deceased acts (e.g. Michael Jackson) respond and how their fandom is renegotiated in the absence of the original fan object but where re-issues, compilations or newly found recordings or footage might continue to be released.

C. Lee Harrington notes how the language of death has littered academic analysis of both textual endings and how fans react to them and how this 'literature employs a *discourse* of death and dying in its consideration of textual mourning, legacy, resurrection, afterlife, the narrative undead and so forth' (2013, 580). Similarly, in their discussion about the 'afterlife' of *Buffy the Vampire Slayer*, Levine and Parks note that:

> If American dramatic television had a cemetery, it would be overflowing with coffins by now; since nearly six decades' worth of series have ended. Yet one of the most distinctive features of commercial television series is that they rarely disappear. Television series, like vampires, are made to return from the dead. Indeed, the American commercial television economy is predicated upon such revivals, re-emergences, and re-appearances. (2007, 4)

The discussion here of resurrections of television shows in other media forms such as cinema, comics or novelizations, or sometimes returns to the small screen, back up Levine and Parks' suggestion that 'the notion of a "final episode", an "end" to a series, is ultimately somewhat misleading, for it suggests the ending of something that doesn't really end' (2007, 4). However, it remains of interest to interrogate how fans themselves view periods of ending and transition; although a series such as *Lost* or *Buffy* may return in the future, fans usually treat the airing of final episodes as meaningful and as providing an ending of sorts. If fans themselves continue to draw on a discourse of death and dying, it behoves those of us researching fans to explore the reasons for this as well as bearing in mind the possibility of a media text's reboot, resurrection or revival. My work here continues to draw on such language since this is a discourse that fans themselves use, articulating notions of grief, mourning, resurrection and loss to negotiate their responses to changes to or the ending of favourite programmes and, in some cases, their eventual returns. From the metaphors of turning off life support or euthanasia employed by *West Wing* and *Lost* fans who adopted more critical positions of rejection, to the overt expressions of bereavement and loss displayed by those mourning dead characters or actors such as Cordelia Chase, John Spencer or Leo McGarry through to the invocation of resurrection or the zombie-like 'coming back wrong' of revived texts such as *Firefly*, *Veronica Mars*, *The X-Files* or *Sex and the City*, fans themselves invoke the spectre of a discourse of death. The 'afterlives' of television series continue to demand our attention. What the ongoing fan discussion of, and devotion to, specific series shows is that some fan objects appear to be able to withstand different forms of change or endings, whether reboots, total cancellations or the revival of a long-dead series. Fandoms such as those surrounding *Twin Peaks*, *Firefly*/*Serenity*, *The X-Files*, *The West Wing* and *Lost* suggest, perhaps, that some fan objects are immortal, able to continue an almost eternal life through either transmedia resurrections or via continued discussion and endorsement by the surrounding fan communities. Paying attention to a range of endings and fan reactions to them is key to understanding fan responses to periods of transition, change and cessation. There is much to be done in the future for those of us interested in studying the changes, transitions and endings that occur within fandom. As Harrington points out:

> In a TV studies context, death occurs both *within* texts (death of a character or plotline) and *to* texts (the end of a season, a series, a genre), *within* technologies (shift from analog to digital) and *to* technologies (byebye Betamax), *within* formats (stillbirth of the 'real' in reality television) and *to* formats (demise and resurrection of the primetime game show). (2013, 581–2)

Given the differences between objects, fans of other media may respond quite differently or have specificities in their negotiation of the absence of fan objects which could be subject to exploration. The ideas around post-object fandom and fan pure relationships outlined here are not intended to offer an all-encompassing theory of these fan practices but, rather, to provoke future inquiry and to make more visible how fans respond to the absence, rather than the presence, of fan objects.

Bibliography

Abbott, S. (2005), ' "We'll follow *Angel* to hell … or another network": Fan response to the end of *Angel*', in S. Abbott (ed.), *Reading Angel: The TV Spin-Off with a Soul*. London: I. B. Tauris, 230–3.

—(2008), 'Can't stop the signal: The resurrection/regeneration of *Serenity*', in R. V. Wilcox and T. R. Cochran (eds), *Investigating Firefly and Serenity: Science Fiction on the Frontier*. London: I. B. Tauris, 227–38.

—(2009), 'How *Lost* found its audience: The making of a cult blockbuster', in R. Pearson (ed.), *Reading Lost*. London: I. B. Tauris, 9–26.

—(2014), 'A long time ago we used to be friends, but … ', *CST Online*. http://cstonline.tv/long-time-ago [accessed 21 April 2014].

Allington, D. (2007), ' "How come most people don't see it?": Slashing *The Lord of The Rings*', *Social Semiotics*, 17 (1): 43–62.

Anderson, T. (2005), 'Television and the work of mourning', *Flow.TV*. http://flowtv.org/2005/11/television-and-the-work-of-mourning/ [accessed 21 January 2014].

Andrejevic, M. (2008), 'Watching Television Without Pity: The productivity of online fans', *Television and New Media*, 9 (1): 24–46.

Ang, I. (1982), *Watching Dallas: Soap Opera and the Melodramatic Imagination*. London: Routledge.

Armstrong, G. and H. Hognestad (2003), ' "We're not from Norway": Football and civic pride in Bergen, Norway', *Identities: Global Studies in Culture and Power*, 10 (4): 451–75.

Askwith, I. (2009), ' "Do you even know where this is going?": *Lost*'s viewers and narrative premeditation', in R. Pearson (ed.), *Reading Lost*. London: I. B. Tauris, 159–80.

Associated Press (2007), '*Sopranos*' ratings beat most network shows', *Today Television*. http://www.today.com/id/19194093/ns/today-today_entertainment/t/sopranos-ratings-beat-most-network-shows/#.UdbLIzs3t15 [accessed 12 January 2014].

Athkar, I. (2013), 'A study of post object fandom: Frustrated fans grieve over the axing of *Merlin*', paper presented at the International Association for Media and Communication Research 2013 Annual Meeting, Dublin, 25–29 June 2013.

Avins, M. (2006), '*West Wing*'s Scarlett and Rhett finally do the deed', *LA Times*, 10 May 2006.

Bacon-Smith, C. (1992), *Enterprising Women: Television Fandom and the Creation of Popular Myth*. Philadelphia: University of Pennsylvania Press.

Bailey, S. (2005), *Media Audiences and Identity: Self-construction in the Fan Experience*. New York: Palgrave Macmillan.

Barton, K. M. (2014a), 'Can't stop the sequel: How the *Serenity*-inspired *Browncoats: Redemption* is changing the future of fan films', in K. M. Barton and J. M. Lampley (eds), *Fan Culture: Essays on Participatory Fandom in the 21ˢᵗ Century*. Jefferson, NC: McFarland, 9–22.

—(2014b), '*Chuck* versus the advertiser: How fan activism and footlong subway sandwiches saved a television series', in K. M. Barton and J. M. Lampley (eds), *Fan Culture: Essays on Participatory Fandom in the 21ˢᵗ Century*. Jefferson, NC: McFarland, 159–72.

Bateman, A. and J. Holmes (1995), *Introduction to Psychoanalysis: Contemporary Theory and Practice*. Hove and New York: Brunner-Routledge.

Baym, N. (2000), *Tune In, Log on: Soaps, Fandom and Online Communities*. London: Sage.

Bennett, A. (2006), 'Punk's not dead: The continuing significance of punk rock for an older generation of fans', *Sociology*, 40 (2): 219–35.

Bennett, J. and T. Brown (2008), 'Introduction: Past the boundaries of "new" and "old" media: Film and television *after* DVD', in J. Bennett and T. Brown (eds), *Film and Television After DVD*. London: Routledge, 1–18.

Bennett, L. (2012a), 'Music fandom online: REM fans in search of the ultimate first listen', *New Media & Society*, 14 (5): 748–63.

—(2012b), 'Patterns of listening through social media: Online fan engagement with the live music experience', *Social Semiotics*, 22 (5): 545–57.

—(2013), 'Discourses of order and rationality: Drooling REM fans as "matter out of place"', *Continuum: Journal of Media and Cultural Studies*, 27 (2): 214–27.

Berliner, M. (2014), 'Why Amazon revived BBC's *Ripper Street*', *The Guardian Online*. http://www.theguardian.com/media-network/media-network-blog/2014/mar/05/amazon-netflix-bbc-ripper-street [accessed 29 March 2014].

Bird, S. E. (2003), *The Audience in Everyday Life: Living in a Media World*. London: Routledge.

Black, R. (2008), *Adolescents and Online Fan Fiction*. New York: Peter Lang.

Bode, L. (2010), 'No longer themselves? Framing digitally enabled posthumous "performance"', *Cinema Journal*, 49 (4): 46–70.

Booth, P. (2008), 'Rereading fandom: Myspace character personas and narrative identification', *Critical Studies in Media Communication*, 25 (5): 514–36.

Booth, P. and P. Kelly (2013), 'The changing faces of *Doctor Who* fandom: New fans, new technologies, old practices?', *Participations*, 10 (1): 56–72. http://participations.org/Volume%2010/Issue%201/5%20Booth%20&%20Kelly%2010.1.pdf [accessed 12 October 2013].

Bore, I.-L. K. (2010), 'TV comedy audiences and media technology: A comparative study of Britain and Norway'. *Convergence*, 16 (2): 185–200.

Bore, I.-L. K. and J. Hickman (2013), 'Continuing *The West Wing* in 140 characters or less: Improvised simulation on Twitter', *Journal of Fandom Studies*, 1 (2): 219–38.

Bore, I.-L. K. and R. Williams (2010), 'Transnational twilighters: A *Twilight* fan community in Norway', in M. Click, J. Stevens Aubrey and L. Behm-Morawitz (eds), *Bitten by Twilight: Youth Culture, Media, and the Vampire Franchise*. New York: Peter Lang, 189–205.

Bourdieu, P. (1984), *Distinction: A Social Critique of the Judgement of Taste*. London: Routledge.

Brereton, P. and B. O'Connor (2007), 'Pleasure and pedagogy: The consumption of DVD add-ons among Irish teenagers', *Convergence*, 13 (2): 143–55.

Brooker, W. (2002), *Using the Force: Creativity, Community and Star Wars Fans*. New York and London: Continuum.

—(2007), 'A sort of homecoming: Fan viewing and symbolic pilgrimage', in J. Gray, C. Sandvoss and C. L. Harrington (eds), *Fandom: Identities and Communities in a Mediated World*. New York: New York University Press, 149–64.

—(2009), 'Television out of time: Watching cult shows on download', in R. Pearson (ed.), *Reading Lost: Perspectives on a Hit Television Show*. London: I. B. Tauris, 51–72.

Brookey, R. A. and R. Westerfelhaus (2002), 'Hiding eroticism in plain view: *The Fight Club* DVD as digital closet', *Critical Studies in Media Communication*, 19 (1): 21–43.

—(2005), 'The digital auteur: Branding identity on the *Monsters, Inc.* DVD', *Western Journal of Communication*, 69 (2): 109–28.

Brower, S. (1992), 'Fans as tastemakers: Viewers for quality television', in L. Lewis (ed.), *The Adoring Audience: Fan Culture and Popular Media*. London: Routledge, 163–84.

Brown, J. A. (1997), 'Comic book fandom and cultural capital', *Journal of Popular Culture*, 30 (4): 13–31.

Brown, M. E. (1994), *Soap Opera and Women's Talk: The Pleasure of Resistance*. London: Sage.

Brown, S. (2013), 'Memento mori: The slow death of *The X-Files*', *Science Fiction Film and Television*, 6 (1): 7–22.

Bury, R. (2005), *Cyberspaces of Their Own: Female Fandoms Online*. New York: Peter Lang.

Bury, R., R. Deller, A. Greenwood and B. Jones (2013), 'From Usenet to Tumblr: The changing role of social media', *Participations*, 10 (1): 299–318. http://participations. org/Volume%2010/Issue%201/14%20Bury%20et%20al%2010.1.pdf [accessed 14 March 2014].

Busse, K. (2002), 'Crossing the final taboo: Family, sexuality and incest in *Buffy*verse fan fiction', in R. Wilcox and D. Lavery (eds), *Fighting the Forces: What's at Stake in Buffy the Vampire Slayer*. Maryland: Rowman and Littlefield, 207–17.

—(2006), 'My life is a WIP on my LJ: Slashing the slasher and the reality of celebrity and internet performances', in K. Hellekson and K. Busse (eds), *Fan Fiction and Fan Communities in the Age of the Internet*. Jefferson, NC: McFarland, 207–24.

—(2013), 'Geek hierarchies, boundary policing, and the gendering of the good fan', *Participations*, 10 (1): 73–91. http://www.participations.org/Volume%2010/Issue%20 1/6%20Busse%2010.1.pdf [accessed 14 March 2014].

Busse, K. and K. Hellekson (eds) (2006), *Fan Fiction and Fan Communities in the Age of the Internet.* Jefferson, NC: McFarland.

—(2012), 'Identity, ethics, and fan privacy' in K. Larsen and L. Zubernis (eds), *Fan Culture: Theory/Practice.* Cambridge: Cambridge Scholars Publishing, 38–56.

Cantwell, M. (2004), 'Collapsing the extra/textual: Passions and intensities of knowledge in *Buffy the Vampire Slayer* online fan communities', *Refractory: A Journal of Entertainment Media* 5. http://www.refractory.unimelb.edu.au/ journalissues/vol5/cantwell.htm [accessed 12 October 2014].

Caron, N. (2013), 'Eve Myles teases future *Torchwood*, says it's "still bubbling away"', *Blastr.com.* http://www.blastr.com/2013-4-25/eve-myles-teases-future-torchwood-says-its-%E2%80%9Cstill-bubbling-away%E2%80%9D [accessed 12 January 2014].

Cavanagh, A. (1999), 'Behaviour in public? Ethics in online ethnography', *Cybersociology*, 6. http://www.socio.demon.co.uk/magazine/6/cavanagh.html [accessed 19 September 2013].

Cavicchi, D. (1998), *Tramps Like Us: Music and Meaning among Springsteen Fans.* New York and Oxford: Oxford University Press.

Cherry, B. (2013), 'Oh no, that won't do at all – it's ridiculous! Observations on the *Doctor Who* audience', in A. O'Day (ed.), *Doctor Who: The Eleventh Hour.* London: I. B. Tauris, 204–27.

Chin, B. (2013), 'The fan–media producer collaboration: How fan relationships are managed in a post-series *X-Files* fandom', *Science Fiction Film and Television*, 6 (1): 87–99.

Clark, J. E. (2005), 'The Bartlet Administration and contemporary populism in NBC's *The West Wing*', in M. Hammond and L. Mazdon (eds), *The Contemporary Television Series.* Edinburgh: Edinburgh University Press, 224–43.

Clark, L. S. (1998), 'Dating on the net: Teens and the rise of "pure relationships"', in S. Jones (ed.), *Cybersociety 2.0.* Thousand Oaks, CA: Sage, 159–83.

Clark, S. L. (2013), 'Peaks and pop culture', in M. C. Hayes and F. Boulegue (eds), *Fan Phenomena: Twin Peaks.* Bristol: Intellect, 9–15.

Clerc, S. (1996), 'DDEB, GATB and Ratboy: *The X-Files* media fandom, online and off', in D. Lavery, A. Hague and M. Cartwright (eds), *Deny All Knowledge: Reading The X-Files.* London: Faber and Faber, 36–51.

Cochran, T. R. (2008), 'The Browncoats are coming! *Firefly*, *Serenity* and fan activism', in R. V. Wilcox and T. R. Cochran (eds), *Investigating Firefly and Serenity: Science Fiction on the Frontier.* London: I. B. Tauris, 239–49.

Cohen, J. (2003), 'Parasocial breakups: Measuring individual differences in responses to the dissolution of parasocial relationships', *Mass Communication and Society*, 6: 191–202.

Collura, S. (2014), 'David Lynch shoots down *Twin Peaks* revival rumours', *IGN*. http://uk.ign.com/articles/2014/01/22/david-lynch-shoots-down-twin-peaks-revival-rumors [accessed 21 January 2014].

Corrigan, J. M. and M. Corrigan (2012), 'Disrupting flow: *Seinfeld, Sopranos* series finale and the aesthetic of anxiety', *Television & New Media*, 13 (2): 91–102.

Costello, V. and B. Moore (2007), 'Cultural outlaws: An examination of audience activity and online television fandom', *Television and New Media*, 8 (2): 124–43.

Couldry, N. (2000a), *The Place of Media Power: Pilgrims and Witnesses of the Media Age*. London: Routledge.

—(2000b), *Inside Culture: Re-Imagining the Method of Cultural Studies*. London: Sage.

—(2002), *Media Rituals: A Critical Approach*. London: Routledge.

Craib, I. (1992), *Anthony Giddens*. London: Routledge.

—(1997), 'The Problem with People', in C. G. A. Bryant and D. Jary (eds), *Anthony Giddens: Critical Assessments: Volume II*. London: Routledge, 349–58.

—(1998), *Experiencing Identity*. London: Sage.

Crawford, G. (2003), 'The career of the sport supporter: The case of the Manchester storm', *Sociology*, 37(2): 219–37.

—(2004), *Consuming Sport: Fans, Sport and Culture*. London: Routledge.

Crawley, M. (2006), *Mr. Sorkin Goes to Washington: Shaping the President on Television's The West Wing*. Jefferson, NC: McFarland.

Cubbison, L. (2012), 'Russell T. Davies, "Nine Hysterical Women", and the death of Ianto Jones', in B. Williams and A. A. Zenger (eds), *New Media Literacies and Participatory Popular Culture Across Borders*. London: Routledge, 135–50.

Daniels, C. (2013), '*Glee* to air Cory Monteith tribute before "long hiatus"', *Digital Spy*. http://www.digitalspy.co.uk/ustv/s57/glee/news/a499974/glee-to-air-cory-monteith-tribute-before-long-hiatus.html [accessed 23 July 2013].

Day-Preston, B. (2013), '*Dexter* finale: A betrayal of the characters we knew', *Guardian TV and Radio blog*. Theguardian.com/tv-and-radio/tvandradioblog/2013/sep/30/dexter-finale-betrayal-characters [accessed 12 February 2014].

De Certeau, M. (1984), *The Practice of Everyday Life*. London: University of California Press.

Deller, R. (2011), 'Twittering on: Audience research and participation using Twitter', *Participations*, 8 (1) 217–45. http://www.participations.org/Volume%208/Issue%201/deller.htm [accessed 12 March 2014].

Denham, J. (2014), '*Heroes* reborn: Sci-fi series set to return in 2015', *The Independent*. http://www.independent.co.uk/arts-entertainment/tv/news/heroes-reborn-scifi-tv-show-set-to-return-in-2015-9148800.html [accessed 24 February 2014].

De Vaus, D. A. (1996), *Surveys in Social Research: Fourth Edition*. Australia: Allen and Unwin.

De Zwart, M. (2011), 'Anyone for a vampwich? *True Blood*, online identity and copyright', in G. Schott and K. Moffat (eds), *Fanpires: Audience Consumption of the Modern Vampire*. Washington, DC: New Academia Publishing, 205–22.

Dobson, N. (2006) 'Wasn't that show cancelled? The increasing DVD phenomenon', *Flow*, 4 (12). http://jot.communication.utexas.edu/flow/?jot5view&id51963 [accessed 12 March 2014].

Donaghy, J. (2007), 'Help me save Television Without Pity', *The Guardian Online*. http://www.theguardian.com/culture/tvandradioblog/2007/apr/04/ helpmesavetelevisionwithou [accessed 21 November 2013].

Duffett, M. (2013), *Understanding Fandom: An Introduction to the Study of Media Fan Culture*. London and New York: Continuum.

Ess, C. (2002), 'Introduction', *Ethics and Information Technology*, 4 (3): 177–88.

Eyal, K. and J. Cohen (2006), 'When good *Friends* say goodbye: A parasocial breakup study', *Journal of Broadcasting & Electronic Media*, 50 (3): 502–23.

Feuer, J. (2005), 'The lack of influence of *Thirtysomething*', in M. Hammond and L. Mazdon (eds), *The Contemporary Television Series*. Edinburgh: Edinburgh University Press, 28–36.

—(2007), 'HBO and the concept of quality TV', in J. McCabe and K. Akass (eds), *Quality TV: Contemporary American Television and Beyond*. London: I. B. Tauris, 145–57.

Frankel M. and S. Siang (1999), 'Ethical and legal aspects of human subjects research on the internet: A report of a workshop', *American Association for the Advancement of Science*, Washington, DC. http://www.aaas.org/spp/dspp/sfrl/projects/inters/ main.htm [accessed 18 February 2014].

French, D. (2009), '*Ashes To Ashes* finale draws 6.5 million', *Digital Spy*. http://www. digitalspy.co.uk/tv/s49/ashes-to-ashes/news/a159005/ashes-to-ashes-finale-draws- 65-million.html [accessed 24 June 2013].

Freund, K. and D. Fielding (2013), 'Research ethics in fan studies', *Participations*, 10 (1): 329–34. http://www.participations.org/Volume%2010/Issue%201/16%20 Freund%20Fielding%2010.1.pdf [accessed 28 November 2013].

Gajjala, R. (2002), 'An interrupted postcolonial/feminist cyberethnography: Complicity and resistance in the "Cyberfield"', *Feminist Media Studies*, 2 (2): 177–94.

Gallifrey Base (2011), 'David Tennant's leaving the show! Matt Smith announced as Eleven!' http://gallifreybase.com/forum/showthread.php?t=99493 [accessed 13 May 2014].

—(2011), 'So are you over David Tennant yet?' http://gallifreybase.com/forum/ showthread.php?t=125203 [accessed 13 May 2014].

—(2013), 'Matt Smith and practical reasons for leaving'. http://gallifreybase.com/ forum/showthread.php?t=170973 [accessed 13 May 2014].

Garde-Hansen, J. (2011), Media and Memory, Edinburgh University Press: Edinburgh.

Garner, R. P. (2013), 'Remembering Sarah Jane: Intradiegetic allusions, embodied presence/absence and nostalgia', in M. Hills (ed.), *New Dimensions of Doctor Who: Exploring Space, Time and Television*. London: I. B. Tauris, 192–215.

Gatson, S. N. and A. Zweerink (2004), *Interpersonal Culture on the Internet: Television, the Internet and the Making of a Community*. Lampeter: Edwin Mellen Press.

Genette, G. (1997), *Paratexts: Thresholds of Interpretation*, trans. Jane E. Lewin. Cambridge: Cambridge University Press.

Georgiou, M. (2013), 'Seeking ontological security beyond the nation: The role of transnational television', *Television and New Media*, 14 (4): 304–21.

Geraghty, L. (2014), *Cult Collectors: Nostalgia, Fandom and Collecting Popular Culture*. London: Routledge.

Gibson, M. (2007), 'Some thoughts on celebrity deaths: Steve Irwin and the issue of public mourning', *Mortality*, 12 (1): 1–3.

Giddens, A. (1981), *A Contemporary Critique of Historical Materialism, Volume 1*. Berkeley, CA: University of California Press.

—(1984), *The Constitution of Society: Outline of the Theory of Structuration*. Cambridge: Polity Press.

—(1990), *The Consequences of Modernity*. Cambridge: Polity Press.

—(1991), *Modernity and Self-Identity: Self and Society in the Late Modern Age*. Cambridge: Polity Press.

—(1992), *The Transformation of Intimacy: Sexuality, Love, and Eroticism in Modern Societies*. Stanford: Stanford University Press.

Glaser, B. G. and A. L. Strauss (1971), *Status Passage*. London: Routledge.

Goh, D. H. Lian and C. S. Lee (2011), 'An analysis of tweets in response to the death of Michael Jackson', *Aslib Proceedings: New Information Perspectives*, 63 (5): 432–44.

Goletz, S. W. (2012), 'The Giddyshame Paradox: Why *Twilight*'s anti-fans cannot stop reading a series they (love to) hate', in A. Morey (ed.), *Genre, Reception, and Adaptation in the Twilight Series*. Farnham, Surrey: Ashgate, 147–62.

Gray, J. (2003), 'New audiences, new textualities: Anti-fans and non-fans', *International Journal of Cultural Studies*, 6 (1): 64–81.

—(2005), 'Anti fandom and the moral text: Television Without Pity and textual dislike', *American Behavioral Scientist*, 48 (7): 840–58.

—(2008), 'Television pre-views and the meaning of hype', *International Journal of Cultural Studies*, 11(1): 33–49.

—(2010), *Show Sold Separately: Promos, Spoilers and other Media Paratexts*. New York: New York University Press.

Gray, J. and J. Mittell (2007), 'Speculation on spoilers: *Lost* fandom, narrative consumption and rethinking textuality', *Participations*, 4 (1). http://www.participations.org/Volume%204/Issue%201/4_01_graymittell.htm [accessed 24 March 2014].

Gray, J., C. Sandvoss and C. L. Harrington (2007), 'Introduction: Why study fans?', in J. Gray, C. Sandvoss and C. L. Harrington (eds), *Fandom: Identities and Communities in a Mediated World*. New York and London: New York University Press, 1–16.

Green, S. (2011), 'Dexter Morgan's monstrous origins', *Critical Studies in Television*, 6 (1): 22–35.

Grossberg, L. (1992), 'The affective sensibility of fandom', in L. A. Lewis (ed.), *The Adoring Audience: Fan Culture and Popular Media*. London: Routledge, 50–65.

Gruzd, A., B. Wellman and Y. Takhteyev (2011), 'Imagining Twitter as an imagined community', *American Behavioral Scientist*, 55 (10): 1294–318.

Gwenllian-Jones, S. (2000), 'Starring Lucy Lawless', *Continuum: Journal of Media and Cultural Studies*, 14 (1): 9–22.

—(2003), 'Web wars: Resistance, online fandom and studio censorship', in M. Jancovich and J. Lyons (eds), *Quality Popular Television*. London: BFI, 163–80.

Hadas, L. (2013), 'Resisting the romance: "Shipping" and the discourse of genre uniqueness in *Doctor Who* fandom', *European Journal of Cultural Studies*, 16 (3): 329–43.

Handley, C. (2012), ' "Distressing damsels": Narrative critique and reinterpretation in *Star Wars* fanfiction', in K. Larsen and L. Zubernis (eds), *Fan Culture: Theory/ Practice*. Cambridge: Cambridge Scholars Publishing, 97–118.

Harding, J. and D. Pribam (2004), 'Losing our cool? Following Williams and Grossberg on emotions', *Cultural Studies*, 18 (6): 863–83.

Harman, S. and B. Jones (2013), 'Fifty shades of ghey: Snark fandom and the figure of the anti-fan', *Sexualities*, 16 (8): 951–68.

Harrington, C. L. (2013), 'The *Ars Moriendi* of US serial television: Towards a good textual death', *International Journal of Cultural Studies*, 16 (6): 579–95.

Harrington, C. L. and D. B. Bielby (1995), *Soap Fans: Pursuing Pleasure and Making Meaning in Everyday Life*. Philadelphia: Temple University Press.

—(2010a) 'Autobiographical reasoning in long-term fandom', *Transformative Works and Cultures* 5 http://journal.transformativeworks.org/index.php/twc/article/view/209 [accessed 14 June 2013].

—(2010b), 'A life course perspective on fandom', *International Journal of Cultural Studies*, 13 (5): 429–50.

—(2013), 'Pleasure and adult development: Extending Winnicott into late(r) life', in A. Kuhn (ed.), *Little Madnesses: Winnicottian Film Studies*. London and New York: I. B. Tauris, 87–102.

Harrington, C. L., D. B. Bielby and A. R. Bardo (2011), 'Life course transitions and the future of fandom', *International Journal of Cultural Studies*,14(6): 567–90.

Harris, J. (2014), '*Lost* showrunners explain ending: "They were not dead the whole time" ', *Digital Spy*. http://www.digitalspy.co.uk/ustv/s10/lost/news/a557960/lost-showrunners-explain-ending-they-were-not-dead-the-whole-time.html#ixzz2wVqUpmKz [accessed 14 March 2014].

Hastie, A. (2007), 'The epistemological stakes of *Buffy the Vampire Slayer*: Television criticism and marketing demands', in E. Levine and L. Parks (eds), *Undead TV: Essays on Buffy the Vampire Slayer*. Durham and London: Duke University Press, 74–95.

Hellekson, K. and K. Busse (eds) (2006), *Fan Fiction and Fan Communities in the Age of the Internet*. Jefferson, NC: McFarland, 207–24.

—(2014), *The Fan Fiction Studies Reader*. Iowa: University of Iowa Press.

Henderson, S. and M. Gilding (2004), ' "I've never clicked this much with anyone in my life": Trust and hyperpersonal communication in online friendships', *New Media & Society*, 6 (4): 487–506.

Hermes, J. (2005), *Re-reading Popular Culture*. London: Blackwell.

Hills, M. (2002), *Fan Cultures*. London: Routledge.

—(2003), 'Putting away childish things: Jar Jar Binks as an object of fan loathing', in T. Austin and M. Barker (eds), *Contemporary Hollywood Stardom*. London: Arnold, 74–89.

—(2004), '*Dawson's Creek*: Quality teen TV and mainstream cult', in G. Davis and K. Dickenson (eds), *Teen TV*. London: BFI, 54–67.

—(2005a), 'Patterns of surprise: The "Aleatory Object" in psychoanalytic ethnography and cyclical fandom', *American Behavioral Scientist*, 48 (7): 801–21.

—(2005b), 'Ringing the changes: Cult distinctions and cultural differences in US fans' readings of Japanese horror cinema', in J. McRoy (ed.), *Japanese Horror Cinema*. Edinburgh: Edinburgh University Press, 161–74.

—(2005c), *The Pleasures of Horror*. London: Continuum.

—(2006), '*Doctor Who* discovers … Cardiff: Investigating trans-generational audiences and trans-national fans of the BBC Wales production', *Cyfrwng: Media Wales Journal*, 3: 56–74.

—(2007a), 'From the box in the corner to the box set on the shelf', *New Review of Film and Television*, 5 (1): 41–60.

—(2007b), 'A review of *Fans: The Mirror of Consumption*, by Cornel Sandvoss, and *Media Audiences and Identity: Self-construction and the Fan Experience*, by Steve Bailey', *Popular Communication*, 5 (2): 149–54.

—(2010a), 'When television doesn't overflow "beyond the box": The invisibility of "momentary" fandom', *Critical Studies in Television*, 5 (1): 97–110.

—(2010b), *Triumph of a Time Lord: Regenerating Doctor Who in the Twenty-first Century*. London: I. B. Tauris.

—(2010c), 'Making sense of M. Night Shyamalan: Signs of a popular auteur in the "Field of Horror" ', in J. A. Weinstock (ed.), *Critical Approaches to the Films of M. Night Shyamalan*. New York: Palgrave Macmillan, 103–18.

—(2012a), 'Psychoanalysis and digital fandom: Theorizing spoilers and fans' self-narratives', in R. A. Lind (ed.), *Produsing Theory in a Digital World: The Intersection of Audiences and Production in Contemporary Theory*. New York: Peter Lang, 105–22.

—(2012b), '*Torchwood's* trans-transmedia: Media tie-ins and brand "fanagement"', *Participations*, 9 (2). http://www.participations.org/Volume%209/Issue%202/23%20 Hills.pdf [accessed 14 June 2013].

—(2013a), 'Media users: An introduction', in A. Kuhn (ed.), *Little Madnesses: Winnicottian Film Studies*. London and New York: I. B. Tauris, 79–86.

—(2013b), 'Transmedia *Torchwood*: Investigating a television spin-off's tie-in novels and audio adventures', in R. Williams (ed.), *Torchwood Declassified: Investigating Mainstream Cult Television*. London: I. B. Tauris, 65–83.

Hills, M. and R. Williams (2005), '"It's all my interpretation": Reading Spike through the "subcultural celebrity" of James Marsters', *European Journal of Cultural Studies*, 8 (3): 345–65.

Hine, C. (2000), *Virtual Ethnography*. London: Sage Publications.

Hodkinson, P. (2011), 'Ageing in a spectacular "youth culture": Continuity, change and community amongst older Goths', *The British Journal of Sociology*, 62 (2): 262–82.

Horton D. and R. R. Wohl (1956), 'Mass communication and para-social interaction: Observations on intimacy at a distance', *Psychiatry*, 19: 215–29.

Howe, A. (2013), 'The owls are not what they seem: Cultural artefacts of *Twin Peaks*', in M. C. Hayes and F. Boulegue (eds), *Fan Phenomena: Twin Peaks*. Bristol: Intellect, 40–9.

Hoxter, J. (2000), 'Taking possession: Cult learning in *The Exorcist*', in X. Mendik and G. Harper (eds), *Unruly Pleasures: The Cult Film and its Critics*. Surrey: FAB Press, 172–85.

Jamieson, L. (1999), 'Intimacy transformed? A critical look at the "pure relationship"', *Sociology*, 33 (3): 477–94.

Jamison, A. (2013), *Fic: Why Fanfiction is Taking Over the World*. Dallas, TX: Smart Pop.

Jancovich, M. (2000), 'A real shocker': Authenticity, genre and the struggle for distinction', *Continuum: Journal of Media and Cultural Studies*, 14 (1): 23–36.

Jefferies, M. (2013), 'Steven Moffat is rewriting *Doctor Who* folklore to produce a Christmas cracker', *Radio Times* online. http://www.radiotimes.com/ news/2013-11-25/steven-moffat-is-rewriting-doctor-who-folklore-to-produce-a-christmas-cracker [accessed 02 September 2014]

Jeffery, M. (2011a), '*Torchwood* exec: "I don't know if there will be more"', *Digital Spy*. http://www.digitalspy.co.uk/ustv/s8/torchwood/news/a348037/torchwood-exec-i-dont-know-if-there-will-be-more.html#ixzz2tUmCO87T [accessed 28 October 2013].

—(2011b), 'John Barrowman: *Torchwood* is in limbo', *Digital Spy*. http://www.digitalspy. co.uk/tv/s8/torchwood/news/a350447/john-barrowman-torchwood-is-in-limbo. html [accessed 28 October 2013].

—(2014), '*24* pulled by Netflix US from April, will remain on Netflix UK', *Digital Spy*. http://www.digitalspy.co.uk/ustv/s9/24/news/a560232/24-pulled-by-netflix-us-from-april-will-remain-on-netflix-uk.html#~oAaRejlDnlMuIE [accessed 28 March 2014].

Jenkins, H. (1992), *Textual Poachers*. London: Routledge.

—(1995), 'Do you enjoy making the rest of us feel stupid? Alt.tv.twinpeaks, the trickster author and viewer mastery', in D. Lavery (ed.), *Full of Secrets: Critical Approaches to* Twin Peaks. Detroit: Wayne State University Press, 51–69.

—(2002), 'Interactive audiences', in Dan Harries (ed.), *The New Media Book*. London: BFI, 157–70.

—(2006), *Convergence Culture: Where Old and New Media Collide*. New York: New York University Press.

—(2007), 'Afterword: The future of fandom', in J. Gray, C. Sandvoss and C. L. Harington (eds), *Fandom: Identities and Communities in a Mediated World*. New York and London: New York University Press, 357–64.

Jenson, J. (1992), 'Fandom as pathology: The consequences of characterization', in L. A. Lewis (ed.), *The Adoring Audience: Fan Culture and Popular Media*. London: Routledge, 9–29.

Jermyn, D. (2009), *Sex and the City*. Detroit, MI: Wayne State University Press.

Jermyn, D. and S. Holmes (2006), 'The audience is dead: Long live the audience! Interactivity, "telephilia" and the contemporary television audience', *Critical Studies in Television*, 1 (1): 49–57.

Johnson, D. (2007a), 'Fan-tagonism: Factions, institutions, and constitutive hegemonies of fandom', in J. Gray, C. Sandvoss and C. L. Harington (eds), *Fandom: Identities and Communities in a Mediated World*. New York and London: New York University Press, 285–300.

—(2007b), 'Inviting audiences in', *New Review of Film and Television Studies*, 5 (1): 61–80.

Jones, B. (2012), 'Being of service: *X-Files* fans and social engagement', *Transformative Works and Cultures*, 10. http://journal.transformativeworks.com/index.php/twc/article/view/309/275 [accessed 14 March 2014].

—(2014), 'The fandom is out there: Social media and *The X-Files* online', in K. M. Barton and J. M. Lampley (eds), *Fan Culture: Essays on Participatory Fandom in the 21st Century*. Jefferson, NC: McFarland, 92–105.

Jones, S. and J. Jensen (eds) (2005), *Afterlife as Afterimage: Understanding Posthumous Fame*. New York: Peter Lang.

Kantor, J. (2001), 'Livia let die: Let her rest in one piece', *Slate*. http://www.slate.com/id/101783/ [accessed 14 October 2013].

Kaplan, D. (2006), 'Construction of fan fiction character through narrative', in K. Hellekson and K. Busse (eds), *Fan Fiction and Fan Communities in the Age of the Internet*. Jefferson, NC: McFarland, 134–52.

Kaspersen, L. B. (2000), *Anthony Giddens: An Introduction to a Social Theorist*. London: Blackwell.

Kastenbaum, R. J. (2004), *On Our Way: The Final Passage through Life and Death.* Berkeley, CA: University of California Press.

Katz, E. (2009), 'The end of television?', *Annals of the American Academy of Political and Social Science*, 625 (6): 6–18.

Kaye, P. (2007), 'Writing music for quality TV: An interview with W. G. "Snuffy" Walden', in J. McCabe and K. Akass (eds), *Quality TV: Contemporary American Television and Beyond*. London: I. B. Tauris, 222–7.

Kermode, M. (1997), 'I was a Teenage Horror Fan', in M. Barker and J. Petley (eds), *Ill Effects: The Media/Violence Debate*. London: Routledge, 48–55.

Kerr, A., J. Kucklich and P. Brereton (2006), 'New media – new pleasures?', *International Journal of Cultural Studies*, 9 (1): 63–82.

Kinnvall, C. (2004), 'Globalization and religious nationalism: Self, identity, and the search for ontological security', *Political Psychology*, 25 (5): 741–67.

Kirby-Diaz, M. (2009), *Buffy and Angel Conquer The Internet: Essays on Online Fandom*. Jefferson, NC: McFarland.

Klein, M. (1952), 'Some theoretical conclusions regarding the emotional life of the infant', in J. Riviere (ed.), *Developments in Psychoanalysis*. London: Hogarth Press, 198–236.

Klinger, B. (2010), 'Becoming cult: *The Big Lebowski*, replay culture and male fans', *Screen*, 51 (1): 1–50.

Knaggs, A. (2011), '*Prison Break* general gabbery: Extra-hyperdiegetic spaces, power, and identity in *Prison Break*', *Television and New Media*, 12 (5): 395–411.

Kompare, D. (2004), *Rerun Nation: How Repeats Invented American Television*. London: Routledge.

—(2006), 'Publishing flow: DVD box sets and the reconception of television', *Television and New Media*, 7 (4): 335–60.

—(2010), 'Reruns 2.0: Revising repetition for multi-platform television distribution', *Journal of Popular Film and Television*, 38 (2): 79–83.

Kuhn, A. (2002), *An Everyday Magic: Cinema and Cultural Memory*. London: I. B. Tauris.

Laing, R. D. (1960), *The Divided Self: An Existential Study in Sanity and Madness*. Harmondsworth: Penguin.

Lane, C. (2003), 'The White House culture of gender and race in *The West Wing*: Insights from the margins', in P. C. Rollins and J. E. O'Connor (eds), *The West Wing: The American Presidency as Television Drama*. Syracuse: Syracuse University Press, 32–41.

Lather, J. and E. Moyer-Guse (2011), 'How do we react when our favourite characters are taken away? An examination of a temporary parasocial breakup', *Mass Communication and Society*, 14 (2): 196–215.

Lawson, M. (2005), 'Foreword: Reading *Six Feet Under*', in K. Akass and J. McCabe (eds), *Reading Six Feet Under: TV To Die For*. London: I. B. Tauris, xvii–xxii.

Layder, D. (1997), *Modern Social Theory: Key Debates and New Directions*. London: Routledge.

Lee, C. S. and D. H. L Goh (2013), ' "Gone too soon": Did Twitter grieve for Michael Jackson?', *Online Information Review*, 37 (3): 462–78.

Lee, K. (2003), 'Confronting *Enterprise* slash fan fiction', *Extrapolation*, 44 (1): 69–82.

Lembo, R. and K. H. Tucker Jr (1990), 'Culture, television, and opposition: Rethinking cultural studies', *Critical Studies in Mass Communications*, 7: 97–116.

Levin, J. D. (1992), *Theories of the Self*. Washington: Taylor and Francis.

Levine, E. and Parks, L (2007), 'Introduction', in E. Levine and L. Parks (eds), *Undead TV: Essays on Buffy the Vampire Slayer*. Durham and London: Duke University Press, 1–15.

Lévy, P. (1997), *Collective Intelligence: Mankind's Emerging World in Cyberspace*. New York: Plenum Trade.

Lindelof, D. (2013), 'Damon Lindelof on why *Breaking Bad*'s finale let him say goodbye to *Lost*', (Guest Column) *The Hollywood Reporter*. http://www.hollywoodreporter. com/news/damon-lindelof-breaking-bad-finale-639484 [accessed 14 January 2014].

Longhurst, B. (2007), *Cultural Change and Ordinary Life*. Berkshire: Open University Press.

Lotz, A. D. (2006), 'Rethinking meaning making: Watching serial TV on DVD', *Flow* 4 (12). http://flowtv.org/2006/09/rethinking-meaning-making-watching-serial-tv-on-dvd/ [accessed 31 May 2014].

MacDonald, A. (1998), 'Uncertain Utopia: Science fiction media fandom and computer mediated communication', in C. Harris and A. Alexander (eds), *Theorizing Fandom: Fans, Subculture and Identity*. New Jersey: Hampton Press, 131–52.

McCabe, J. (2005), 'Creating "quality" audiences for *ER* on Channel Four', in M. Hammond and L. Mazdon (eds), *The Contemporary Television Series*. Edinburgh: Edinburgh University Press, 207–23.

—(2013), *The West Wing*. Detroit, MI: Wayne State University Press.

McKinley, E. G. (1997), *Beverly Hills, 90210: Television, Gender and Identity*. Philadelphia: University of Pennsylvania Press.

Mellor, P. A. and C. Shilling (1993), 'Modernity, self-identity and the sequestration of death', *Sociology*, 27 (3): 411–31.

Menon, S. (2007), 'A participation observation analysis of the "Once & Again" internet message bulletin boards', *Television and New Media*, 8 (4): 341–74.

Mills, B. (2010), 'Invisible television: The programmes no-one talks about even though lots of people watch them', *Critical Studies in Television*, 5 (1): 1–16.

Mittell, J. (2004), *Genre and Television: From Cop Shows to Cartoons in American Culture*. London: Routledge.

—(2013), *Complex TV: The poetics of contemporary television storytelling*. http:// mediacommons.futureofthebook.org/mcpress/complextelevision/ends/ [accessed 14 October 2013].

Moores, S. (2005), *Media/Theory*. London: Routledge.

Morreale, J. (2003), 'Sitcoms say good-bye: The cultural spectacle of *Seinfeld*'s last episode', in J. Morreale (ed.), *Critiquing the Sitcom: A Reader*. Syracuse: Syracuse University Press, 274–85.

—(2010), '*Lost*, *The Prisoner*, and the end of the story', *Journal of Popular Film and Television*, 38 (4): 176–85.

Moretti, F. (1988), *Signs Taken For Wonders: Essays in the Sociology of Literary Form*. London: Verso.

Murray, N. (2008), 'Interviews: *Lost*'s Damon Lindelof and Carlton Cuse', *The Onion A.V. Club*. http://www.avclub.com/content/interview/losts_damon_lindelof_and [accessed 14 November 2013].

Musiani, F. (2010), ' "May the journey continue": *Earth 2* fan fiction, or filling in gaps to revive a canceled series', *Transformative Works and Cultures*, 5. http://journal.transformativeworks.org/index.php/twc/article/view/206/168 [accessed 14 March 2014].

Newman, M. Z. (2009), 'TV binge', *Flow* 9 (5). http://flowtv.org/2009/01/tv-binge-michael-z-newman-university-of-wisconsin-milwaukee/ [accessed 19 January 2014].

Newsmax (2014), 'Netflix seen reporting web users grew to 33.1 million', *Newsmax*. http://www.newsmax.com/SciTech/netflix-reporting-web-grown/2014/01/22/id/548377 [accessed 22 January 2014].

Nochimson, M. P. (1995), 'Desire under the Douglas firs: Entering the body of reality in *Twin Peaks*', in D. Lavery (ed.), *Full of Secrets: Critical Approaches to Twin Peaks*. Detroit: Wayne State University Press, 1995, 144–59.

—(1997), *The Passion of David Lynch: Wild at Heart in Hollywood*. Austin, TX: University of Texas Press.

O'Brien, L. (2013), 'Damon Lindelof quits Twitter', *IGN.com*. http://uk.ign.com/articles/2013/10/17/damon-lindelof-quits-twitter [accessed 13 November 2013].

Ott, B. (2008), '(Re)framing fear: Equipment for living in a post 9/11 world', in T. Potter and C. W. Marshall (eds), *Cylons in America: Critical Studies in Battlestar Galactica*. New York and London: Continuum, 13–26.

Paproth, M. (2013), ' "Best. Show. Ever.": Who killed *Veronica Mars*?', *Journal of Popular Television*, 1 (1): 39–52.

Parrish, J. (2010), 'Back to the woods: Narrative revisions in *New Moon* fan fiction at Twilighted', in M. Click, J. S. Aubrey, and L. Behm-Morawitz (eds), *Bitten by Twilight: Youth Culture, Media, and the Vampire Franchise*. New York: Peter Lang, 173–88.

Pearson, R. (2007), '*Lost* in transition: From post-network to post-television', in J. McCabe and K. Akass (eds), *Quality TV: Contemporary American Television and Beyond*. London: I. B. Tauris, 239–56.

—(ed.) (2009), *Reading Lost: Perspectives on a Hit Television Show*. London: I. B. Tauris.

Penley, C. (1997), *NASA/TREK*. London: Verso.

Perry, J. (2002), *Identity, Personal Identity, and The Self*. Indianapolis, IN: Hackett Publishing Company.

Peters, M. (2006), 'Getting a wiggins and being a bitca: How two items of slayer slang survive on the Television Without Pity message boards', *Slayage: The On-Line International Journal of Buffy Studies* 20. http://www.slayageonline.com/essays/slayage20/Peters.htm [accessed 12 March 2013].

Pillai, N. (2013), 'What am I looking at, Mulder?': Licensed comics and the freedoms of transmedia storytelling', *Science Fiction Film and Television*, 6 (1): 101–17.

Porter, L. (2012), *The Doctor Who Franchise: American Influence, Fan Culture and the Spinoffs*. Jefferson, NC: McFarland.

Porter, R. (2004), '*West Wing* romance? Actors aren't in love with it', *Zap2it.com*. http://www.romanticsgarden.com/WW-Articles-page14.htm [accessed 29 April 2014].

Priest, S. H. (1996), *Doing Media Research: An Introduction*. London: Sage Publications.

Pugh, S. (2005), *The Democratic Genre: Fan Fiction in a Literary Context*. Bridgend: Poetry Wales Press.

Puoskari, E. (2004), 'A desire called cultural studies: We gotta get out of this place', *European Journal of Cultural Studies*, 7 (2): 167–76.

Radford, S. K. and P. H. Bloch (2012), 'Grief, commiseration, and consumption following the death of a celebrity', *Journal of Consumer Culture*, 12 (2): 137–55.

Reid, E. M. (1996), 'Informed consent in the study of on-line communities: A reflection on the effects of computer-mediated social research', *Information Society*, 12 (2): 169–74.

Riegert, K. (2007), 'The ideology of *The West Wing*: The television show that wants to be real', in K. Riegert (ed.), *Politicotainment: Television's Take on the Real*. New York: Peter Lang, 213–36.

Ritchie, D. (2003), 'Loss, grief and representation: "Getting on with it"', *Double Dialogues*, 4: 1–3.

Rixon, P. (2007), 'American programmes on British screens: A revaluation', *Critical Studies in Television*, 2 (2): 92–112.

Rodman, G. B. (1996), *Elvis after Elvis: The Posthumous Career of a Living Legend*. London: Routledge.

Ross, S. M. (2008), *Beyond The Box: Television and the Internet*. Oxford: Blackwell.

Rowley, A. (2012), ' "*Torchwood* hasn't been cancelled" says Russell. T. Davies', *Digital Spy*. http://www.digitalspy.co.uk/tv/s8/torchwood/news/a433851/torchwood-hasnt-been-cancelled-says-russell-t-davies.html#~oCPOLHkT3ru4I8 [accessed 29 April 2014].

Sandvoss, C. (2005), *Fans: The Mirror of Consumption*. Cambridge: Polity Press.

Saxey, E. (2001), 'Staking a claim: The series and its slash fan fiction', in R. Kaveney (ed.), *Reading the Vampire Slayer: An Unofficial Critical Companion to Buffy and Angel*. London: I. B. Tauris, 187–210.

Scardaville, M. C. (2005), 'Accidental activists: Fan activism in the soap opera community', *American Behavioral Scientist*, 48: 881–901.

Scodari, C. and J. Felder (2000), 'Creating a pocket universe: "Shippers," fan fiction, and *The X-Files* online', *Communication Studies*, 51 (3): 238–57.

Sheffield, J. and E. Merlo (2010), 'Biting back: *Twilight* anti-fandom and the rhetoric of superiority', in M. A. Click, J. S. Aubrey, and E. Behm-Morawitz (eds), *Bitten by Twilight: Youth Culture, Media and the Vampire Franchise*. New York: Peter Lang, 207–22.

Shefrin, E. (2004), '*Lord of the Rings, Star Wars*, and participatory fandom: Mapping new congruencies between the internet and media entertainment culture', *Critical Studies in Media Communication*, 21 (3): 261–81.

Shuker, R. (1994), *Understanding Popular Music*. London: Routledge.

Silbergleid, R. (2003), '"The truth we both know": Readerly desire and heteronarrative in *The X-Files*', *Studies in Popular Culture*, 25 (3). http://pcasacas.org/SPC/spcissues/25.3/Silbergleid.htm [accessed 14 October 2013].

Silverstone, R. (1994), *Television and Everyday Life*. London: Routledge.

Skopal, P. (2007), '"The adventure continues on DVD": Franchise movies as home video', *Convergence*, 13 (2): 185–98.

Sky News (2013), 'Kiefer Sutherland returning for new *24* Series', *Sky News*, 14 May 2013.

Smithsonian (2013), 'Why it's okay to be so upset over yesterday's *Game of Thrones*', *Smithsonian.com*. http://blogs.smithsonianmag.com/smartnews/2013/06/why-its-okay-to-be-so-upset-over-yesterdays-game-of-thrones/?utm_source=twitter. com&utm_medium=socialmedia&utm_campaign=20130603&utm_content=smartnewsgameofthrones3 [accessed 3 June 2013].

Stake, R. (1994), 'Case studies', in N. Denzin and Y. Lincoln (eds) *Handbook of Qualitative Research*. Thousand Oaks, CA: Sage.

Stein, L. A. and K. Busse (2012), 'Introduction: The literary, televisual and digital adventures of the beloved detective', in L. A. Stein and K. Busse (eds), *Sherlock and Transmedia Fandom: Essays on the BBC Series*. Jefferson, NC: McFarland, 9–24.

Stevenson, N. (2002), *Understanding Media Cultures: Social Theory and Mass Communication*. London: Sage.

—(2009), 'Talking to Bowie fans: Masculinity, ambivalence and cultural citizenship', *European Journal of Cultural Studies*, 12 (1): 79–98.

Subramanian, J. (2011), 'R.I.P. F.N.L.' *Flow TV*. http://www.flowtv.org/2011/02/rip-fnl [accessed 27 October 2013].

Symonds, G. (2003), 'Bollocks! Spike fans and reception of *Buffy the Vampire Slayer*' in *Refractory: A Journal of Entertainment Media*, 2. http://www.sfca.unimelb.edu.au/refractory/journalissues/index.htm [accessed 27 September 2013].

Tabron, J. L. (2004), 'Girl on girl politics: Willow/Tara and new approaches to media fandom', *Slayage: The On-Line International Journal of Buffy Studies*, 13–14. http://www.slayageonline.com/essays/slayage13_14/Tabron.htm [accessed 14 June 2013].

Takeda, A. (2013), 'Cory Monteith's *Glee* character won't die of drug overdose, says Ryan Murphy', *US Weekly*. http://www.usmagazine.com/entertainment/ news/cory-monteiths-glee-character-wont-die-of-drug-overdose-says-ryan-murphy-2013158 [accessed 14 August 2013].

Television Without Pity (2006), '*Lost* – *Lost* is its own monster: "The Bitterness Fiesta"'. http://forums.televisionwithoutpity.com/topic/3120925-lost-is-its-own-monster-the-bitterness-fiesta/page-428#entry [accessed 13 February 2014].

—(2006), '*The West Wing* archives'. http://forums.televisionwithoutpity.com/index. php?showforum=598 [accessed 13 February 2014].

—(2006), '*The West Wing* post-series thread'. http://forums.televisionwithoutpity.com/ index.php?showtopic=3143108 [accessed 13 March 2014].

—(2006), '*The West Wing* – "Requiem"'. http://forums.televisionwithoutpity.com/ topic/3139075-7-18-requiem-20060416/page-1 [accessed 13 March 2014].

—(2006), '*The West Wing* – "Running Mates"'. http://forums.televisionwithoutpity.com/ topic/3134449-7-10-running-mates-20060108/ [accessed 13 February 2014].

—(2006), '*The West Wing* – "The Reflecting Pool: A Look Back at the Show"'. http:// forums.televisionwithoutpity.com/topic/3126187-the-reflecting-pool-a-look-back-at-the-show/ [accessed 13 February 2014].

—(2006), '*The West Wing* – "Tomorrow"'. http://forums.televisionwithoutpity.com/ topic/3140613-7-22-tomorrow-20060514/page-19#entry [accessed 13 February 2014].

—(2006), '*The West Wing* – "*West Wing* to conclude Sunday, May 14"'. http://forums. televisionwithoutpity.com/topic/3134906-its-official-west-wing-to-conclude-sunday-may-14/page-10#entry [accessed 13 February 2014].

—(2010), '*Lost* – "The End"'. http.//forums.televisionwithoutpity.com/topic/3195807-6-17-the-end-20100523 [accessed 13 February 2014].

—(2010), 'The *Lost* archives'. http.//forums.televisionwithoutpity.com/forum/1176-lost/?prune_day=100&sort_by=Z-A&sort_key=last_post&topicfilter=all [accessed 13 February 2014].

Theodoropoulou, V. (2007), 'The anti-fan within the fan: Awe and envy in sport fandom', in J. Gray, C. Sandvoss and C. L. Harrington (eds), *Fandom: Identity and Communities in a Mediated World*. New York: New York University Press, 316–27.

Thomas, L. (2002), *Fans, Feminisms and 'Quality' Media*. London: Routledge.

—(2009), 'The *Archers*: An everyday story of old and new media', *The Radio Journal*, 7 (1): 49–66.

Thompson, J. B. (1995), *The Media and Modernity: A Social Theory of the Media*. Cambridge: Polity Press.

Thompson, J. (2014), '*Dark Shadows* fandom, then and now (1966–2013)', in K. M. Barton and J. M. Lampley (eds), *Fan Culture: Essays on Participatory Fandom in the 21st Century*. Jefferson, NC: McFarland, 23–35.

Thompson, R. J. (1990), *Adventures on Prime Time: The Television Programs of Stephen J. Cannell*. New York: Praeger.

Thornton, S. (1995), *Club Cultures: Music, Media and Subcultural Capital*. Cambridge: Polity Press.

Todd, A. M. (2011), 'Saying goodbye to *Friends*: Fan culture as lived experience', *Journal of Popular Culture*, 44 (4): 854–71.

Tresca, D. (2014), 'Spellbound: An analysis of adult-oriented *Harry Potter* fanfiction', in K. M. Barton and J. M. Lampley (eds), *Fan Culture: Essays on Participatory Fandom in the 21ˢᵗ Century*. Jefferson, NC: McFarland, 36–46.

Tucker, K. (2004), 'Broken wing', *Entertainment Weekly*. http://web.archive.org/web/20040510082604/www.dontsaveourshow.org/eweekly.jpg [accessed 14 May 2013].

Tulloch, J. (1990), *Agency, Audience and Myth*. London: Routledge.

Tulloch, J. and H. Jenkins (1995), *Science-Fiction Audiences: Watching Doctor Who and Star Trek*. London: Routledge.

Turkle, S. (2004), 'Whither psychoanalysis in computer culture?' *Psychoanalytic Psychology*, 21 (1): 16–30.

Turner, V. (1967), *The Forest of Symbols: Aspects of Ndembu Ritual*. Ithaca: Cornell University Press.

Turnock, R. (2000), *Interpreting Diana: Television Audiences and the Death of a Princess*. London: BFI.

Twin Peaks (2014), UK Festival. http://www.twinpeaksukfestival.com/

USA Today (2006), 'NBC cancels *The West Wing* retrospective', *USA Today Online*. http://usatoday30.usatoday.com/life/television/news/2006-05-09-west-wing_x.htm [accessed 14 May 2013].

Van den Bulck, H. and J. Van Gorp (2011), 'Eternal fandom: Elderly fans, the media, and the staged divorce of a Schlager singer', *Popular Communication*, 9 (3), 212–26.

Van Gennep, A. (1908/1960), *Les Rites de Passage* (trans. M. Vizedom and G. Cafee). Chicago: Chicago University Press.

Van Zoonen, L. (2005), *Entertaining the Citizen: When Politics and Popular Culture Converge*. Oxford: Rowman and Littlefield.

Wakefield, S. R. (2001), 'Your sister in St. Scully: An electronic community of female fans of *The X-Files*', *Journal of Popular Film and Television*, 29:3, 130–7.

Walliss, J. (2012), 'Stories by/for boys: Gender, canon and creativity within *Warhammer 40,000* fanfiction', in K. Larsen and L. Zubernis (eds), *Fan Culture: Theory/Practice*. Cambridge: Cambridge Scholars Publishing, 119–33.

Walther, J. (2002), 'Research ethics in internet-enabled research: Human subjects issues and methodological myopia', *Ethics and Information Technology*, 4 (3): 205–16.

Wang, Y. (2007), 'A star is dead: A legend is born: Practicing Leslie Cheung's posthumous fandom', in S. Redmond and S. Holmes (eds), *Stardom and Celebrity: A Reader*. London: Sage, 326–40.

Waskul, D. and M. Douglass (1996), 'Considering the electronic participant: Some polemical observations on the ethics of on-line research', *Information Society*, 12 (2): 129–40.

Whiteman, N. (2009), 'The de/stabilization of identity in online fan communities', *Convergence: The International Journal of Research into New Media Technologies*, 15 (4): 391–410

Whiteman, N. and J. Metivier (2013), 'From post-object to "zombie" fandoms: The "deaths" of online fan communities and what they say about us', *Participations*, 10 (1): 270–98. http://www.participations.org/Volume%2010/Issue%201/13%20 Whiteman%20&%20Metivier%2010.1.pdf [accessed 14 June 2013].

Wilkes, N. (2005), 'More4 launch lineup confirmed', *Digital Spy*. http://www.digitalspy. co.uk/article/ds23931.html [accessed 13 September 2013].

Williams, L. R. (2005), '*Twin Peaks*: David Lynch and the serial-thriller soap', in M. Hammond and L. Mazdon (eds), *The Contemporary Television Series*. Edinburgh: Edinburgh University Press, 37–56.

Williams, R. (2004), ' "It's about power": Spoilers and fan hierarchy in on-line *Buffy* fandom', *Slayage: The In-Line International Journal of Buffy Studies*, 11–12. http:// www.slayageonline.com/essays/slayage11_12/Williams.htm [accessed 12 June 2013].

—(2010), 'Good *Neighbours*? Fan/producer relationships and the broadcasting field', *Continuum: Journal of Media and Cultural Studies*, 24 (2): 179–89.

—(2011a), ' "This is the night TV died": Television post-object fandom and the demise of *The West Wing*', *Popular Communication*, 8 (4): 266–79.

—(2011b), ' "Wandering off into soap land": Gender, genre and "shipping" *The West Wing*', *Participations: International Journal of Audience Research*, 8 (1). http://www. participations.org/Volume%208/Issue%201/williams.htm [accessed 14 October 2013].

—(2011c), 'Desiring the doctor: Identity, gender and genre in online science-fiction fandom', in J. Leggott and T. Hochscherf (eds), *British Science Fiction Film and Television: Critical Essays*. Jefferson, NC: McFarland, 167–77.

—(2013a), ' "Anyone who calls Muse a *Twilight* band will be shot on sight": Music, distinction, and the "interloping fan" in the *Twilight* franchise', *Popular Music and Society*, 36 (3): 327–42.

—(2013b), '*Tonight's the Night* with … Captain Jack! John Barrowman as celebrity/ subcultural celebrity/localebrity', in R. Williams (ed.), *Torchwood Declassified: Investigating Mainstream Cult Television*. London: I. B. Tauris, 154–71.

—(2013c), 'Tweeting the Tardis: Interaction, live-ness and social media in *Doctor Who* fandom', in M. Hills (ed.), *New Dimensions in Doctor Who: Exploring Space, Time and Television*. London: I. B. Tauris, 154–73.

Williamson, M. (2005), *The Lure of the Vampire: Gender, Fiction and Fandom from Bram Stoker to Buffy*. London: Wallflower Press.

Williamson, M. and D. Amy-Chinn (2005), 'The vampire Spike in text and fandom: Unsettling oppositions in *Buffy the Vampire Slayer*', *European Journal of Cultural Studies*, 8 (3): 275–88.

Wills, E. R. (2013), 'Fannish discourse communities and the construction of gender in *The X-Files*', *Transformative Works and Cultures*, 14. http://journal.

transformativeworks.org/index.php/twc/article/view/410/404 [accessed 28 March 2014].

Windolf, J. (2010), 'The *Lost* good-bye', *Vanity Fair*, June 2010. http://www.vanityfair. com/hollywood/features/2010/06/lost-spotlight-201006 [accessed 29 August 2014].

Winnicott, D. W. (2005), *Playing and Reality: Routledge Classics*. London: Routledge.

Wohn, D. Y. and E. K. Na (2011), 'Tweeting about TV: Sharing television viewing experiences via social media message streams', *First Monday* 16 (3). http:// firstmonday.org/htbin/cgiwrap/bin/ojs/index.php/fm/article/viewArticle/3368/2779 [accessed 4 May 2013].

Wood, M. M. and L. Baughman (2012), '*Glee* fandom and Twitter: Something new, or more of the same old thing?', *Communication Studies*, 63 (3): 328–44.

Zaretsky, E. (2002), 'Theorizing 9/11. Trauma and dereification: September 11 and the problem of ontological security', *Constellations*, 9 (1): 98–105.

Zittoun, T. (2006), *Transitions: Development Through Symbolic Resources*. Greenwich, CT: Information Age Publishing.

Zweerink, A. and S. N. Gatson (2002), 'www.buffy.com: Cliques, boundaries and hierarchies in an internet community', in R. Wilcox and D. Lavery (eds), *Fighting the Forces: What's at Stake in Buffy the Vampire Slayer*. Lanham, MD: Rowman and Littlefield, 239–49.

Index